New Thinking for a New Millennium

In this book, Richard Slaughter draws on the relatively new but rapidly developing field of futures studies to illustrate how our thinking must change in order to deal with the challenges presented by the new millennium. In doing so he brings together the latest work from some of the leading international names in futures thinking.

Part One considers the foundations of futures thinking in history, literature and ideas. Part Two explores some of the ways that futures studies have been and are being applied in different educational contexts around the world, from pre-school to postgraduate levels. Part Three takes the crucial step from institutional learning to social learning, and explores how futures provides us with insights which can help guide our society into the new millennium, together with suggestions for the development of the field itself.

This book is essential reading for anyone interested in the perils and promise of the twenty-first century.

Richard A. Slaughter is Director of the Futures Study Centre, Melbourne and has taught futures studies at universities in the United Kingdom and Australia. He is co-author of *Education for the Twenty-First Century* (Routledge 1993). His major interests are changing paradigms of knowledge, the application of futures approaches in education, and the study and implementation of foresight.

D1381688

Futures and Education Series
General Editor: Richard A. Slaughter
Director of the Futures Study Centre, Melbourne, Australia

New Thinking for a New Millennium
Richard A. Slaughter

Educating Beyond Violent Futures
Francis P. Hutchinson

New Thinking for a New Millennium

Edited by Richard A. Slaughter

London and New York

First published 1996
by Routledge
11 New Fetter Lane, London EC4P 4EE

Simultaneously published in the USA and Canada
by Routledge
29 West 35th Street, New York, NY 10001

Typeset in Times by Florencetype Ltd, Stoodleigh, Devon
Printed and bound in Great Britain by
Biddles Ltd, Guildford and King's Lynn

British Library Cataloguing in Publication Data
A catalogue record for this book is available from the British Library

Library of Congress Cataloguing in Publication Data
New thinking for a new millennium/edited by Richard A. Slaughter.
        p.   cm.
    Includes bibliographical references and index.
    1. Forecasting.   2. Twenty-first century.   I. Slaughter, Richard.
CB158.N48   1996
303.49′09′04—dc20   95–31961
                                                                            CIP

ISBN   0–415–12943–5

Contents

Part III Social learning for a new millennium

Illustrations

FIGURES

TABLES

Contributors

Nicholas Albery is a psychotherapist by training, the general secretary of the Council for Posterity and the chairman of the Institute for Social Inventions. He is the author or editor of numerous books, including *The Book of Visions: an Encyclopedia of Social Innovations*, *Re-Inventing Society*, and *How to Save the World: a Fourth World Guide to the Politics of Scale*.

Wendell Bell, Professor of Sociology at Yale University, has been a futurist since about 1960, introducing futures studies courses at Yale beginning in 1967 and co-authoring a book, *The Sociology of the Future* (1971). His book, *The Foundations of Futures Studies: Knowledge, Values and Social Change*, will soon be published.

Kjell Dahle is a political scientist and chief editor of the small press agency Senterpressens Osloredaksjon in Oslo, Norway. He is co-founder of the Ideas Bank and former head of planning for the Alternative Futures Project. He is author of *On Alternative Ways of Studying the Future* (1991).

James Dator is professor and head of the Alternative Futures Option in the Department of Political Science, and director of the Hawaii Research Centre for Futures Studies, in the Social Science Research Centre, University of Hawaii, Manoa. He taught one of the first regularly scheduled futures courses at Virginia Polytechnic from 1967, and has been actively involved in futures studies, research and consultation since then. He has concentrated on governmental – especially judicial – foresight capabilities. He was first secretary-general and then president of the World Futures Studies Federation from 1983 to 1993.

Hazel Henderson is an internationally known futurist, author, lecturer, consultant and analyst on alternative development policy. She is widely respected for her involvement in a range of global issues such as globalization, sustainable development, North–South issues, social innovations and reinventing economics. She is a board member of several of the leading journals of the field, including *Futures*, and *Futures Research*

Quarterly. She is the inventor of an innovative series of Country Futures Indicators. Her latest book is *Paradigms in Progress* (1991).

John C. Hinchcliff is president of Auckland Institute of Technology. He is a graduate of the Institute of Educational Management, Harvard University. His specialism is ethics. He has written nearly 50 papers and edited ten books on this subject, nuclear disarmament, sport, philosophy and religion.

Francis P. Hutchinson is a noted Australian educator with interests in conflict resolution and young people's concerns about the future. His PhD looked at strategies for empowering the young. He teaches in the School of Social Ecology, Faculty of Health, Humanities and Social Ecology, University of Western Sydney.

Lester W. Milbrath is the director of the Research Program in Environment and Society, and Professor Emeritus of Political Science as well as Sociology at the State University of New York at Buffalo. He is the author of many books including *Environmentalists: Vanguard for a New Society* (1984) and his widely praised *Envisioning a Sustainable Society – Learning Our Way Out* (1989).

James Ogilvy is a distinguished writer, lecturer and consultant. With a background in university teaching and advanced research, he is now managing director of the Global Business Network. He has contributed to many classic futures publications including *Changing Images of Man* and *Seven Tomorrows.*

Jane Page is a lecturer in early childhood education at the Department of Early Childhood Studies of the University of Melbourne. She has published a number of articles on the topic of her Master's of Education thesis on the application of futures premises at the early childhood level of education.

Richard A. Slaughter completed a PhD in futures at the University of Lancaster (UK) in 1982. Since then he has explored futures thinking through education, strategic planning, leadership and the identification of a knowledge base for futures studies. He is a consulting editor to *Futures* and co-author of *Education for the 21st Century* (1993*)*. Apart from the present volume, his most recent book is *The Foresight Principle – Cultural Recovery in the 21st Century* (1995). His research interests include: the use of futures concepts and methods in education; the development of critical futures methodologies; and the social implementation of foresight.

Allen Tough is a professor at the University of Toronto. His two major interests are the long-term future and the likelihood of intelligent life elsewhere in our universe. His book *Crucial Questions about the Future* (1991) dealt with both topics. He is now working on a book about future generations.

Introduction

The end of one millennium and the beginning of another is a time of great cultural and symbolic significance. Inevitably there arises the fascinating task of looking back at the last millennium and attempting to come to terms with its long and tangled history. Equally, there is the more demanding task of shifting our view away from what has been toward what may be. It is significant that we are relatively well equipped for the first task, but poorly equipped for the second.

Yet as the twentieth century comes to a close there exists a brief historical opportunity to redress the long-standing temporal bias in Western culture toward the past. I am in no way anti-historical. Yet it strikes me as odd that our universities are equipped with many departments of history and legions of historians who are continually sifting the past, but very, very few futurists. H. G. Wells complained of this in a 1932 BBC address called 'Wanted, Professors of Foresight.'[1] More than sixty years later his comments remain valid. This is a clear failure of social learning and imagination.

It should now be obvious to nearly everyone that, as Lester Milbrath once put it, 'Western culture cannot maintain its trajectory.' So, far from forging into the future with certainty and confidence, we now know that to achieve a viable future means collectively changing course and striking out in a new direction. It is in this sense that *New Thinking for a New Millennium* is needed. It is not that the ideas are all new; some have ancient roots. But if we have learned anything in recent years it is that the pattern, the basic paradigm or 'story' of Western culture no longer works. So the shift to a new millennium, while in one sense merely an artefact of a numbering system and calendar, does provide a genuine opportunity to take stock and rethink, re-imagine, what it is all about. While all too few of our formal educational institutions take this seriously, this book demonstrates that such work is being carried out in them and many other places.

Already a flood of books which attempt to summarise the twentieth century are beginning to appear. Clearly, humans need to make sense of their collective origins. So a century-long perspective tells us much that is useful about our immediate roots and the themes that led to our present. However, people also need to know where they are going. They want to safeguard their children and maintain an expectation of continuity into the future. So the attempt to come to grips with the twentieth century necessarily prefigures the attempt to understand the early twenty-first-century environment.

Now in strict empirical terms this would appear to be a rather problematic enterprise. However, the diminished view of reality suggested by raw empiricism is fortunately not the only one. In direct contrast with prevailing conventional wisdom, the collective view of futurists around the world is that much of value *can* be known about the near-term future. Such knowledge is not factual. It is not the type of knowledge sought by scientists and used by engineers. Rather it belongs to the realm of 'interpretative knowledge'. That is, knowledge that is arrived at by careful thought: analysis, examination of the evidence and argument within an advanced futures discourse – in a word, by scholarship.[2]

While many people still mis-identify futures studies with Nostradamus, crystal balls, prediction and, more recently, the futures market, a new tradition of enquiry has been quietly developing during the latter part of this century. While futures studies were at first taken up and developed by military and commercial interests, these instrumental concerns in no way fulfilled the deeper potential. Since the 1960s, a growing number of scholars, activists and social innovators of many kinds have also looked to the field, drawn on its not inconsiderable resources, and given birth to a new enterprise. Essentially this is about the identification of viable human futures and the pathways toward them.

While most government, business, education and other such entities continue to operate on implicit business-as-usual assumptions, futurists, young people and many others know that this is a sham and a delusion. Futures studies has become an essential discipline in the late twentieth century because the future already presents us with enormous visible challenges and will clearly be very, very different from the past. So where do we go from here? That all depends on how soon we address the future as a central and substantive concern and how quickly we can facilitate the emergence of all that is meant by 'futures thinking' from its present somewhat esoteric origins in universities and research institutes. In the twenty-first century futures thinking needs to be as accepted and commonplace as thinking about the past and present is now. If not, we will surely find out why the hard way.

The present volume is the tip of a much larger iceberg. It is one of a number of publishing initiatives that aim to make futures concepts, ideas and methods much more widely available.[3] The futures literature is certainly a very rich one. Indeed, I would venture to say that lasting solutions to virtually all the major dilemmas we face are, in one way or another, contained in embryo form within it. However, for this volume I have had to rigorously pare down many of the contributions that were submitted. I have tried to select material that provides a number of related snapshots of the best of contemporary futures thinking. Together they represent a broad, deep and fascinating disciplinary perspective.

Part I begins with a very accessible introductory piece by Professor Wendell Bell of Yale University, who is one of the most respected scholars in the field. He looks at the origins of the field, its assumptions, methods and uses. This is followed by a longer piece by James Ogilvy. I am well aware that some will find this chapter challenging. However the perspective it outlines is absolutely central to the further development and application of futures studies. Ogilvy demonstrates with great skill and clarity that the latter should not be 'knocking on the door' seeking academic approval, so much as seen as the fulfilment and culmination of certain key developments across the humanities – and thus a central and vital area of enquiry in its own right. The scope of the subject dictates the length of the piece; however the attentive reader will be richly rewarded. The insights are among the richest available anywhere. It is followed by a very direct and readable introduction to fifty key works in the futures literature by Norwegian futurist Kjell Dahle. For those unfamiliar with futures, this is truly a good place to begin.

Part II makes the connection between futures study and education explicit. It begins with a short piece by James Dator, Professor of Politics at the Manoa campus of the University of Hawaii. This considers the role of futures thinking in the context of higher education. A quite different focus is taken by Nicholas Albery who outlines the work of the London-based Institute for Social Inventions. This organization is both educational and futures-oriented in every sense of the words. Next, Jane Page considers the role of futures in schools. Her chapter suggests that students respond well to such work, but that there are familiar barriers to implementation. This theme is echoed by Richard Slaughter who looks at the way 'critical futures study' has been, and can be, implemented as an educational strategy. Finally, Frank Hutchinson takes a fascinating and more detailed look at one aspect of teaching and learning about futures: the attempt to decode and move beyond images of violence in young people's media. Together these five chapters illustrate some of the ways that futures thinking, methods and approaches have the ability to transform educational thinking and practice.

Part III takes up the theme of social learning for a new millennium. Professor Allen Tough of the University of Toronto suggests some ways in which the knowledge base of futures studies can and should be more thoroughly developed. Lester Milbrath then takes up one of the most central issues facing all cultures and nations: the nature of a transition to sustainability. This fascinating chapter brings great clarity to the question and suggests a range of practicable responses. John C. Hinchcliff's chapter serves to support and amplify the previous one. He looks at the decay of many of our standard 'industrial' assumptions and shows clearly how our ways of thinking and knowing are challenged as never before by the prospects ahead. He sketches in aspects of a renewed worldview which, for some, is the most fundamental concern of all. Finally, Hazel Henderson, one of the most productive and respected futurists in the world, provides a detailed overview of social innovation on a broad, international canvas. As ever, her account gives a sense of qualified optimism and hope, as she reveals how organized, ethical and creative work in many cultures undermines old realities and helps to create new ones. Here the cutting edge of constructive change is revealed and seen to lie in the hands of concerned citizens everywhere.

This, as I suggested above, is only the tip of the iceberg. A careful look through the futures literature, through journals such as *Futures*, bibliographic guides such as *Future Survey*, the *Annotated Futures Bibliography*, or the mail-order catalogue of the World Future Society, will show that there is no shortage of fine, clear and relevant material about the human predicament and the many ways it can be addressed and resolved.[4]

While many more limited and traditional fields continue to play their old games of exclusion and boundary maintenance, futures study and research are among those that are changing the rules and embarking on other enterprises. Only time will tell how successful they will be. However, if this book helps to shift our thinking from a taken-for-granted past and present toward a challenging, but yet to be constructed future, it will have served its purpose.

New thinking is needed not only for the new millennium, but to safeguard future generations and, indeed, the whole human enterprise.

Richard A. Slaughter
Melbourne, Australia
April 1995

NOTES

1 H. G. Wells, 'Wanted: Professors of Foresight', reprinted in *Futures Research Quarterly*, 3, 1, 1987, pp. 89–91.
2 See R. Slaughter, 'The Substantive Knowledge Base of Futures Studies', *Futures*, 25, 3, 1993, pp. 227–233.
3 See, for example, G. Molitor *et al. The Encyclopedia of the Future*, Macmillan, New York (forthcoming). Also R. Slaughter (ed.) *The Knowledge Base of Futures Studies* (series) Volumes 1 – 3, DDM Media/Futures Study Centre, 117 Church Street, Hawthorn 3122, Victoria, Australia, 1995.
4 *Futures* is published ten times a year by Elsevier, the Boulevard, Langford Lane, Kidlington, Oxford, OX5 1GB, UK. *Future Survey* and the WFS

catalogue is available through the World Future Society, 7910 Woodmont Avenue, Suite 450, Bethesda, MD 20814, USA. The *Annotated Futures Bibliography* is available through DDM Media/Futures Studies Centre, Melbourne (address above).

Part I

Foundations of futures studies

Chapter 1

What do we mean by futures studies?*

Wendell Bell

Today, 'Spaceship Earth' has become a compelling and familiar metaphor, conjuring a picture of all the people on earth hurtling through space, dependent for life support on each other and the planet's limited resources. But there is another equally compelling metaphor needed to make the story complete. It is the image of 'Time Machine Earth': the inexorable movement through time from out of the past into the future. Thus, not only are all people on earth space travelers, they are also time travelers. Their tickets through time, however, are good only for a one-way trip. They can travel only forward toward the future.

The future, of course, is still being made. It is what people can shape and design through their purposeful acts. To act intelligently, people need to know the consequences of their own actions, of others' actions and reactions, and of forces beyond their control. These consequences can only occur in the future. Thus, people try to know not only what is happening, but also what might happen, what could happen, or, under particular conditions, what will happen *in the future*. Using such conjectural knowledge, people orientate themselves in the present and, pursuing their projects, navigate through time and physical and social space.

A new field of social inquiry has been created whose purpose is the systematic study of the future. It is sometimes called 'futures studies', 'the futures field', 'futures research', 'futuristics', *'prospective'*, or 'prognostics', and its practitioners are known as 'futurists'. Futurists aim to discover or invent, propose, examine and evaluate possible, probable, and preferable futures. They explore alternative futures in order to assist people in choosing and creating the most desirable future. My purpose in this chapter is to describe some fundamental features of this new field.

HISTORICAL BACKGROUND

The universality of time perspectives

Conceptions of time and the future exist in every known society. They can be seen, for example, in the practice of divination, which is aimed generally at discovering the unknown, sometimes specifically at knowing the future. Such divination has been carried out by a variety of methods, from watching cheese coagulate to observing shoulderblades cracking in a fire to examining the entrails of small animals.

References to the future can be seen, also, in *rites de passage* in which ceremonial activities recognize transitions to future social roles, such as those involved at birth, coming of age, marriage, and death. They can be seen in religious rituals aimed to control the future, such as appeals for plentiful supplies of game, large yields of harvests, or the ample fertility of women of the tribe.

They can be seen, too, in the individual development of each person. The ability to anticipate the future begins soon after birth as children learn that their behavior brings reactions from other people. As children get older, they expand their time horizon, both into the past and into the future. As they learn language, they also learn the time perspectives that are dominant in their culture.

Finally, conceptions of the future can be seen in the history of the development of calendars and clocks. The Gregorian calendar which was constructed in 1582, for example, was a culmination of a long human concern with the movements of astronomical bodies which are themselves a universal measurement of time. It is still in use with an error of only about one-half a minute a year, while, today, advances in the measurement of time have moved to extraordinary precision with the development of the 'atomic clock' based on radiation of the cesium-133 atom and, beyond that, to an even more accurate sapphire-crystal technology that loses only one-100,000 millionths of a second per year.

This is not to say that there are no variations in conceptions of time comparing different societies. There obviously are. The meaning and importance of time and precision in everyday life, for example, may vary both from some societies to others and sometimes from one section of the same society to other sections. Nevertheless, conceptions of time and the future exist – and have existed – in human consciousness everywhere.

The shift from space to time in utopian thought

Although there were precursors, Thomas More's *Utopia* published in 1516 was a watershed. By the end of the sixteenth century, the term 'utopia', coined by More and literally meaning 'no place', referred both to an entire genre of fiction and a conception of an ideal place. Until the end of the eighteenth century, utopias tended to be located geographically distant from, but contemporaneously with, existing societies. More's Utopia itself, for example, was situated well beyond the farthest known place from Europe. Typically, a fictional traveler arrives, often by shipwreck, at some distant place inhabited by some strange and different people, lives there for a period of time, and then returns to Europe to tell his fellow Europeans about the people, society, and culture of the distant land (Manuel and Manuel 1979). In so doing, the traveler, in effect, critically evaluates the known existing society, the inadequate 'what is' being contrasted with the more perfect 'what might be' or 'what could be' of the fictitious utopian society.

At the end of the eighteenth century, a significant shift from space to time took place in utopian writing. The typical setting of the ideal society (or its opposite, the dreadful society or 'dystopia') radically changed from some other geographical place at the same time to often the same place but at a future time. Condorcet, the aristocrat and supporter of the French Revolution, for example, using the social science of his day, accurately described many aspects of the coming future society, and Sebastien Mercier placed his fictional utopia in the year 2440. Thousands of writers have since followed their examples and placed the 'Other', more preferable – or more undesirable – society, in the future (Manuel and Manuel 1979).

Along with this shift from space to time as the location of the 'Other' came additional changes in utopian thought. One was that the perfect world could actually occur within a real society in this life on earth and not after death in heaven. Another was that change toward a more perfect world could be designed and directly brought about by human action. For More, only God could create perfection and it was not an earthly possibility. For Condorcet, humans could create a better world by their own actions here and now on earth.

Recent origins of futures studies

The modern futures field was clearly visible by the 1960s. The publication of *The Image of the Future* by F. L. Polak in 1951 was a major signpost and *The Art of Conjecture* by B. de Jouvenel which appeared in 1964 was another. Polak used the concept of 'image of the future' to analyze the rise and fall of civilizations and Jouvenel brought many of the principles of futures studies together under the same cover for the first time. Other signs of the new field included the creation of professional societies. In 1966, for example, the World Future Society was established by Edward Cornish and others and it has become one of the largest of the many futures organizations. In 1967, an international group that was to become the World Futures Studies Federation held its first meeting in Oslo, Norway. And in 1968, the late Aurelio Peccei and others founded the Club of Rome, which, although it has remained small, became one of the most influential futures groups during the 1970s. By 1977, when the World Future Society published *The Study of the Future*, Cornish was able to report on a considerable amount of futures research and to identify a growing community of futurists.

Many different paths of development led to contemporary futures studies. A few examples may illustrate their diversity. One path is found in the work of W. F. Ogburn and his associates on the analysis of social trends and on the role of technology in social change (President's Research Committee on Social Trends 1933). Among other things, Ogburn was a co-founder and the first president of the Society for the Study of Technology, a forerunner of the modern-day profession of technology assessment.

Another path was through national planning. Beginning with the national mobilizations of World War I, the ad hoc character of planning was replaced by full-time bureaucracies organized to attend to the details of planning for the future. Futures thinking through national planning continued during the Great Depression of the 1930s; was promoted by Communist Russia, Fascist Italy, and Nazi Germany; expanded with the military and economic mobilizations of World War II; spread to Eastern Europe after World War II; and, finally, diffused to third-world countries.

Another path of development was in the hundred or so new states that have been formed since the mid-1940s, mostly from the former colonial territories of European countries in Africa, Asia, the Caribbean, and the Pacific. In each of the new states, new national citizenries were formed and new national leaders came to power. They faced the decisions of nationhood, those choices that had to be made in order to create a politically independent nation-state and that were to establish the future character of the new nation. At the most mundane level, flags had to be designed, national anthems written, and national trees, flowers, birds, and even national heroes chosen. More important, geographical boundaries often had to be drawn (e.g. between India and Pakistan), forms of government decided upon and constitutions written and voted upon. New national histories were prepared in which history was re-interpreted in order to construct a past worthy of the aspirations of the new nation-states. At the most subtle level, within each of the new states the psychological character, the economy, the society, and the culture of the newly independent people were often debated, as to what they *ought to become* and why. The debate itself was both a struggle to be free of the past of colonial domination and a search for distinctive nationalist images of the future on which the future itself could be constructed.

Another strand in the development of futures studies was operations research and the 'think tanks'. Near the beginning of World War II, a team of scientists incorporated the then-new technology of radar into a system of air defense for Britain. Its tremendous success, along with other such military projects, led to the formation of other teams of scientists to deal with the problems of war management. In 1945, to keep such capabilities available to the US Army Air Corps, General H. H. Arnold arranged for a Research and Development unit to continue in operation.

The RAND Corporation became one of the most influential of the many institutes, centers, and other organizations that engaged in 'thought research' and that became known as 'think tanks' (Dickson 1972).

Most of what RAND produced had to do with futures thinking in some way: policy alternatives, designs, suggestions, warnings, long-range plans, predictions, and new ideas. By 1970, RAND had added nonmilitary projects to its agenda, and they accounted for about a third of its activities. RAND workers developed scenario-writing, computer simulations, technological forecasting, the Delphi technique, program budgeting, cost-effectiveness, and systems analysis. It was a school for futurists, including T. J. Gordon, O. Helmer, and H. Kahn. It spawned a number of other organizations including the Institute for the Future, Kahn's Hudson Institute (Dickson 1972), and Gordon's The Futures Group.

RAND, unintentionally, even aided the development of the new futures field by the negative reactions to itself, because some futurists were motivated to counter its presumed pernicious influence by moving into peace research and deliberately banning military topics and funding from their work (Jungk and Galtung 1971). There is a cautionary tale here that should not go unnoticed. From the beginning, RAND was mobilized to focus on military and largely establishment views and purposes. Despite its innovative contributions to futures research and the controversies among its own experts, RAND was a creature of its clients. It was narrowly restricted in its world views.

The Commission on the Year 2000 of the American Academy of Arts and Sciences marked another turning point in the development of futures studies. Chaired by D. Bell, it met in 1965 and 1966 and its participants were mainstream, establishment intellectuals who represented the elite American universities, government, some major corporations, and some of the largest foundations. Although the Commission itself did not continue in existence, it gave an impetus to futures studies, resulting in 1967 in the publication of a special issue of *Daedalus*, 'Toward the year 2000: work in progress', Kahn and Wiener's *The Year 2000*, and, eventually, additional futures work by some of its own members as well as by other people. Most important, it gave academic and scholarly respectability to futures studies.

Parallel developments in the policy sciences and in evaluation research also contributed to the futures field. H. D. Lasswell, D. Lerner and others proposed the formation of the policy sciences in 1951. The two purposes were (1) to study the policy and decision-making processes themselves and (2) to provide information to assist decision-makers in their tasks. Lasswell was among the first scholars to see that decision-making and policy-making necessarily rely on anticipations of the future and he formulated the idea of the 'developmental construct', which is somewhat similar to the concept of 'image of the future'. He called his method of futures research 'developmental analysis'.

Evaluation research is the attempt to assess the consequences of various organized social actions, such as social programs, after they have occurred. Have they, for example, achieved their goals effectively? The proximate origins of evaluation research go back to the 1930s, especially to the evaluation of programs designed to deal with economic depression. Today, it is a gigantic industry. The psychologist, D. T. Campbell, has likened the evaluation researcher to a person sitting on the stern of a ship looking backward and reporting to the captain where he has been.

But evaluation research has been merging with the policy sciences and becoming more future oriented. The reason is that the 'evaluation of any particular project has its greatest implications for projects that will be put in place in the future' (Cronbach *et al.* 1981: 7). In the new view, program development is a series of interactive cycles: planning, implementation, evaluation with feedback to planners, more planning, changes in implementation, re-evaluation with more feedback that results in policy modifications, etc. Thus, the evaluation researcher is becoming, contrary to Campbell's early view, more like a person sitting on the bow of a ship looking forward and reporting to the captain where he is going.

A NEW FIELD OF INQUIRY

The above brief review of some of the origins of the modern futures field is by no means complete. Many other precursors or sources of influence could be mentioned, such as the science fiction of Jules Verne and various writings of H. G. Wells; the counter-culture, anti-Vietnam War, and Black Power protests of the 1960s; and the environmental movement of the 1970s (Dator 1979). Soon after 1970, of course, when Alvin Toffler's best-selling *Future Shock* was published, concern with the future became fashionable.

The futures field is still young and developing, and some writers fear that it is too fragmented even to be called a 'field' at all (Marien and Jennings 1987a). It is, admittedly, diverse in its subject matter and in the backgrounds of its practitioners. The latter range from aeronautical engineering and physics to journalism and management consulting to, increasingly, political science, sociology, and other social sciences. Calling futures studies a 'multi-field', perhaps, or a field with a 'transdisciplinary matrix' might be most appropriate (W. Bell 1987).

Yet, today, futurists have formed themselves into loose communities of full-time scholars and professionals and their activities have been institutionalized within hundreds of organizations, such as business firms, government agencies, centers, institutes, university teaching programs, and professional societies. The last are many and farflung geographically, from the Association Internationale Futuribles (of France) and the Instituto

Neuvas Alternatives, SA (of Mexico) to the Japan Society of Futurology and the Chinese Future Society.

Abstracts of nearly 10,000 futures-relevant books, reports, and articles appeared in the volumes of *Future Survey Annual* between 1979 and 1989 – and this does not include futurist materials in languages other than English. Of the 324 active futures-relevant journals being published in 1986, 91 percent were begun since the end of World War II and 70 percent were started after 1970 (Marien with Jennings 1987b: 187). This is not to say that growth has been steady. Rather, there have been ups and downs, as illustrated by the membership of the World Future Society which had rapid growth from its inception in 1966, reaching a peak of more than 50,000 members in 1979, sliding to 22,500 in 1985, and coming up again to 26,000 in 1987. In 1980, over 5,500 people from 30-plus countries attended the First Global Conference on the Future in Toronto, Canada amid a sense of excitement and ascendancy. But, by 1986, the futures field had entered a new phase in the United States, according to some futurists (Toffler 1986), one of retrenchment, reflection, and a search for more solid foundations and accomplishments. Even so, there were signs of the continued spread of futures studies in China, Eastern Europe, and Russia and other territories of the former Soviet Union.

Because it is new and has diverse origins, futures studies still has somewhat fuzzy boundaries with a core of fulltime professional futurists and a more-or-less distant periphery of planners, economic forecasters, evaluation researchers, policy analysts, think tankers, special interest activists, and others who may not fully identify themselves as futurists. Yet, taking all of the evidence of professional growth into account, we can have little doubt today that futures studies has become a new field of inquiry (Dator 1986).

PURPOSES OF FUTURES STUDIES

The major purpose of futurists is to maintain or improve the welfare of humankind and the life-sustaining capacities of the earth itself. Futurists distinctively carry out this purpose by systematically exploring alternative futures. They engage in *prospective thinking*. They try to create 'new, alternative images of the future – visionary explorations of the possible, systematic investigation of the probable, and moral evaluation of the preferable' (Toffler 1978: x). The possible, the probable, and the prefer-able – these are what futurists seek to know: what can be, what might be, and what ought to be. Moreover, futurists' distinctive obligation to the future invites them to speak for the freedom and well-being of future generations, the coming as-yet-unborn people of the future who in the present have no voice of their own.

To carry out their tasks, futurists also seek to know what causes change, that is, what the dynamic processes are that underlie technological developments on the one hand and changes in the political, economic, social, and cultural orders on the other. Futurists seek to determine what anticipated changes may have to be accepted because they are beyond human control and what can be brought under human control. Also, they seek to discover the unanticipated, unintended, and unrecognized consequences of social action.

Thus, futurists attempt to clarify goals and values, describe trends, explain conditions, formulate alternative images of the future, and invent, evaluate, and select policy alternatives (Lasswell 1967). They also study images of the future held by various groups, such as national leaders or slum dwellers (Mau 1968), and they analyze the dominant societal images of the future and their implications for the rise and fall of entire civilizations (Polak 1961).

Of course, just as in any profession, there is a division of labor among futurists. Some futurists are primarily analysts, focusing their efforts on 'knowing', that is, on methods, theories, and scholarly issues involving assertions about the future. Other futurists are primarily activists, focusing their efforts on shaping the future itself. An example of the latter is the late Robert Jungk (1976; Jungk and Müllert 1987) who was often actively involved at the grassroots level, working to increase participation by ordinary people in the decisions that affect their lives.

Other activists work to disseminate alternative images of the future or even to advocate an image of some particular future. A successful example of spreading such images combined with the goal of increasing the participation of ordinary citizens in shaping them took place in Honolulu in 1982. Professors James Dator and Ted Becker of the University of Hawaii organized the first Honolulu Electronic Town Meeting (ETM). It had several different parts. There was a scientific-information-gathering part through the Hawaii Televote in which 700 persons selected by random digit-dialing were invited to be interviewed about economic and social policies affecting the future of Hawaii. There was also a disseminating-discussion part. Two daily newspapers, three commercial radio stations, Hawaii public radio, a commercial television station, Hawaii public television, and the island's largest cable television station all participated. Most of this was structured as phone-in programs, so that the public was both being informed about the issues and able to participate in the electronic discussion. There were also dramatic/satirical vignettes illustrating various points of view. Finally, there was a judgmental part. Before the end of the ETM, ballots were published in a newspaper and everyone was invited to vote on the issues. The culmination was a final hour-long television program with Dator, Becker, and the Lt Governor of Hawaii in which viewers could call in to ask questions or make comments (Dator 1983a).

Other purposes of futures studies involve the present. First, the action that takes place in the present is what shapes the future. Thus, present conditions must be studied, because futures thinking is largely about what to do now, that is, what action to take to create a future that will be as desirable as possible, given present conditions and hopes for the future.

Second, futures thinking plays an orientating role, letting people know where they are in the present. Often, the rapidity of change results in confusion about what is happening in the present and what did happen in the immediate past. Unless people have some perspective on where they have been, where they are going, and where they want to go, the present itself is largely unintelligible. For example, if you want to know if a glass is half full or half empty, it helps to know that it was full a week ago, two-thirds full yesterday, half empty today, and probably will be totally empty tomorrow (rather than empty a week ago, a third full yesterday, half full today, and probably totally full tomorrow).

Third, the results of futures research help people to balance the demands of the present against those of the future. For example, people can deprive themselves in the present for the sake of expectations of future payoffs that may never come. Thus, they may shrink and pauperize their present. But the opposite is also possible: People can deprive the future. People can borrow from the future so much that they mortgage it beyond its capacities. If they do, then, when the future comes, it may be hell, like a Faustian pact with the devil coming due (McHale 1978).

FUTURISTS' ASSUMPTIONS

In every field of inquiry many assumptions are made so that investigation can continue. Some of these assumptions are explicitly stated, but many are not. Most, perhaps, are simply taken for granted. Yet it is important that every field examine its foundational assumptions from time to time and re-evaluate their cogency. There are many assumptions underlying futures studies, some of the most central of which I'll try to state here.

First, there are some general assumptions, at least partially shared by members of many other fields. Two examples are the following:

1. People are project pursuers; they are acting, purposeful and goal-directed beings. They create projects for themselves and set about trying to achieve them.

2. Society consists of the persistent patterns of repetitive social interaction and the emergent routines of human behavior that are organized by time, space, memories, expectations, hopes and fears for the future, and decisions. Society is constructed and re-constructed daily as people act, react, and interact.

Second, there are a number of specific futurist assumptions that, although other fields may share them, are distinctively part of the futurist perspective. They include the following:

1. Time moves unidirectionally and irreversibly, from out of the past in a momentary present toward the future. There are a number of different arguments that support this assumption, such as the second law of thermodynamics (entropy – the tendency toward uniform inertness – always goes in one direction), biological development (people grow older with time, never younger), wave motion (radio waves, for example, are never received before they are sent), the history of the universe (residual black-body radiation supports the idea that time has a beginning, sequence, duration, and direction), and traces of the past ('footprints in the sand' remain in the present as evidence of past times, such as archeological remains, growth rings of trees, and geological layers of the earth).

2. Not everything that will exist has existed or does exist. Thus, the future may contain things that have never existed before that invite new thoughts, new understandings, and new reactions.

3. Futures thinking is essential for human action. 'Reaction' might be possible without futures thinking, but not action. For to act requires anticipation. Thus, images of the future (goals, objectives, intentions, hopes, fears, aspirations) are part of the causes of present action.

4. The future is not totally predetermined (Amara 1981). This assumption explicitly recognizes the fact that the future does not already exist out there in time bearing down on people in an inevitable way. The future is 'open'.

5. To some extent, future outcomes can be influenced by individual and collective action, by the choices people make to act in one way or another.

6. The interdependence of the world invites a holistic perspective and a multidisciplinary approach when providing information on which to act. Futurists view the world as so interrelated that no system or unit can be viewed as totally isolated. Rather, they argue that every unit that is the focus of futures research should be considered an open system.

7. Some futures are better than others. This is obvious and is often simply taken for granted in other fields, although such lack of scrutiny has resulted in a mish-mash of implicit and unjustified value judgments. For futurists, this is a salient assumption, because they explicitly explore preferable futures as well as possible and probable futures. People judge the consequences of their own and others' acts as more or less desirable. Values – the standards by which good and bad are defined – are part of the steering mechanisms both of individuals and groups as they make their way in the world. Thus, part of the futurist task is to study, explicate, evaluate, and even formulate the criteria people use to make evaluative judgments of alternative futures.

In addition, when they describe, criticize, or propose preferable futures, futurists need some methods by which to assess the values that they use to make their judgments and to justify them to other people (W. Bell 1993; Lee 1985). Futurists have appealed to values such as the quantity and quality of human life (both considerations of freedom and well-being), life satisfactions, and happiness on the individual level; social harmony and peace, sustainability, effectiveness, efficiency, and equity on the level of group or societal functioning; and the life-sustaining capacities of the earth itself on the level of the biosphere. Other candidates for worthy, and possibly universal, values include sufficient (but not enormous) wealth, knowledge, affection, opportunities for family life and sexual behavior, respect for authority, loyalty, courage, perseverance, cooperation, honesty, generosity, helpfulness, friendliness, trust and trustworthiness, and self-realization (W. Bell 1994; Kidder 1994).

8. In making one's way in the world, the only really useful knowledge is knowledge of the future. This assumption follows from the fact that the past no longer exists. The past is closed. Although we can learn more about the past as we dig up more facts about it and although we can reinterpret the past and change our thoughts about it, we cannot change the past itself. It is – and will always be – what it was. But the future is different, because it has not yet happened. The future might still be bent to human will and actions. Even coming events beyond human control may be adapted to successfully, if they can be anticipated.

People must speculate about the future in order to make their way through their daily lives intelligently and effectively. Consciously or subconsciously, they make contingent and corrigible predictions and act on them; generally, the better their predictions, the more effective their actions. They organize their lives by train, bus, and airplane schedules; by the ebb and flow of ocean tides; by when a football game or newscast is scheduled to be aired on radio or television; by the openings and closings of business establishments; by the schedules of schools and universities; and by the announced timing of civic events, such as public concerts or parades.

People act on their expectations about the future behavior of the weather, the stock market, the cost of housing, and interest rates on loans. They organize their own actions according to their anticipations of the day the garbage gets picked up, when church services will be held, and the chances of getting into medical or law school after college. For sensible action, even driving a car requires predictions about where other vehicles will be moving, whether, for example, an oncoming car will stay on its own side of the road. Hopes and fears, expectations for the future, estimates of future consequences of present behavior, and predictions of the behavior of other people and phenomena beyond human control help govern perceptions of the options for action that people have and the choices that they make among them.

Under some circumstances, lessons of the past can be used to help guide the future. That is, knowledge of the past is one source of learning something about the possibilities for the future, but it must be creatively transformed if it is to be useful. The transformation seems natural to people because they casually change their knowledge of the past into expectations all the time in their daily lives. But the transformation involves a speculative leap that may or may not be warranted. The past cannot be accepted uncritically as a good guide to the future in its raw and unadulterated form, because, contrary to the well-known aphorism, history seldom – if ever – repeats itself in exactly the same way. A lesson of history must be relevant and appropriate to the new present and coming future. Criteria of its applicability need to be examined. The speculative leap involved in transforming hindsight to foresight must be made explicit and questioned for its cogency. To fail to project past knowledge adequately into the future results in preparing for yesterday rather than tomorrow.

9. There is no knowledge of the future (Riner 1987). This is the paradox of futures research: Although the only really useful knowledge in making one's way in the world is knowledge of the future, there is, strictly speaking, no knowledge of the future. Although there are past facts, present options, and future possibilities, there are no past possibilities and no future facts.

It is this paradox that futurists aim to resolve: the need to know before the fact what is in some basic sense largely unknowable until after the fact. It is this gap that futurists attempt to fill with conjectural or surrogate knowledge. Futurists make contingent, corrigible, and only more or less certain assertions about the future: e.g., 'this may happen if you do nothing'; 'thus and so might happen if you do x, y, or z', etc. Futurists attempt to ground such assertions in fact and logic, trying to make them 'presumptively true'.

But futurists know that such assertions may not turn out to be 'terminally true' when the future becomes the present, because the future is uncertain. It is problematic. The future cannot be observed; it is not evidential. Reichenbach (1951: 241) expresses an extreme version of this view: 'A statement about the future cannot be uttered with the claim that it is true; we can always imagine that the contrary will happen, and we have no guarantee that future experience will not present to us as real what is imagination today.' Thus, futurists must face the paradox of the need for information about the future in order for people to act intelligently and the impossibility of obtaining knowledge of the future in the strict sense.

But all is not lost. At the level of a theory of knowledge, Musgrave (1993) has shown that conjectural knowledge – i.e. justified belief in a proposition – is possible. Moreover, within what he calls a 'critical realist theory of knowledge', justifying beliefs about the past and the present are not fundamentally different from justifying beliefs about the future. All depend on making serious efforts to refute propositions and tentatively accepting those that survive, i.e. that are not refuted. In sum, we can objectively and rationally justify our believing in a proposition, even if we cannot justify the truth of the proposition itself. If such a justified belief in a proposition – about the past, present, or future – turns out on new evidence to be wrong, we say, yes, the proposition is wrong, not that we were wrong to believe it.

At the level of practical techniques, futurists have adapted or invented a variety of methods of justifying their beliefs in assertions about the future. People can act on such justified beliefs *as if* they were true, even though they are provisional, contingent, conditional, and often multiple. The futurist task, of course, includes trying to show explicitly just how warranted such assertions are.

THE METHODS OF FUTURES RESEARCH

Many standard methods of research are used in futures studies, from sampling techniques and statistical analysis to data-gathering using laboratory experiments, surveys of opinions, and participant-observation. Because it is important to have an accurate and detailed description and analysis of past trends and 'initial conditions' of the present as a basis for both forecasting and designing the future, all such methods may be of use in specifying 'what was' and 'what is' as preparation for conjecturing about 'what will be', 'what might be', 'what could be', or 'what ought to be'.

Moreover, there are many aspects of past and present realities that have some bearing on the future and these, too, can be studied using the standard methods of science and social science. They include:

1 People's present images of alternative possible futures.
2 People's expectations of the most likely, i.e. most probable, future.
3 People's goals, values, and attitudes; their preferences among perceived alternative futures.
4 People's present intentions to act in particular ways, such as how they intend to vote, to invest, or to buy.
5 People's obligations and commitments to others (because they define expected behaviors and are often reinforced by social norms).
6 People's history, traditions, and experience with, and past decisions about given phenomena (not only because they are base lines, but also because they contain prescriptions and proscriptions for future behavior).
7 Trend analysis of time series data.
8 Present possibilities for the future. Such possibilities are real and can be studied just as any other present realities. Science, for instance, is

full of examples of the study of possibilities, or 'dispositionals' as they have been termed (Rudner 1966). For example, a fragile glass may never be broken, but it is a real present possibility that it could become broken. It really *is* breakable. Studying such possibilities results in an empirical basis for making warranted assertions about possible futures.

9 The restatement of explanations as predictions. Futurists can predict by making explicit assumptions, critically examined for their plausibility, and, then, by restating causal knowledge based on past evidence as contingent predictions. A scientific explanation has the same logical structure as a scientific prediction, except for one feature. That feature is the critical one of time perspective. Statements such as 'If, and only if, x, then y with some probability p under certain conditions c' summarizing past evidence can be used to make assertions about the future by changing the time orientation from past to future. Doing so, however, requires that such statements be evaluated for their applicability, just as any knowledge of the past must be so evaluated if it is used to make assertions about the future (W. Bell 1987).

Yet futurists have developed their own methods, too, either by adapting standard methods or creating new ones to achieve their special purposes (Gordon 1992). McHale and McHale (*c.* 1975) in their international survey of futurists identified more than 17 methodological approaches, often used in conjunction with each other. Such methods include extrapolation techniques using time series data, statistical models, brainstorming, scenario writing, simulation, historical analogy, probabilistic forecasting, Delphi techniques, operational models, cross-impact analysis, causal modeling, network analysis, relevance trees, gaming and contextual mapping. Additionally, there are newer methods that have come on the scene since the McHales did their survey, such as the innovative work of Textor (1980) in anticipatory anthropology in which the traditionally past-oriented field methods of anthropologists have been re-oriented toward the future.

Monitoring is another method that is increasingly used. It is a process of assessing events as they occur and immediately projecting them into the future. It is on-line data gathering and analysis combined with immediate extrapolation. For example, it includes scanning (i.e. searching the environment for signals), immediately specifying trends of relevant data and projecting them, continuously revising both the trends and their projections as signals keep coming in, and then, if the projections fall below or above certain levels, often reacting with some action designed to affect the future of the trends. Such things as the flows of electricity, food supplies in a supermarket, bank transactions, prices of stocks and bonds, air traffic, the arrival and departure of tourists in a country, and population growth and decline, all lend themselves to the technique of monitoring.

One example of the use of monitoring in futures studies is *Megatrends* (Naisbitt 1984), although it emphasizes the scanning, detecting, and projecting elements in monitoring and leaves most of the evaluating and reacting up to the readers of the book. As its name announces, the book is an effort to identify the megatrends or 'broad outlines' that will define the new society of the United States. The contents of *Megatrends* were largely taken from a quarterly publication then known as the Naisbitt group 'Trend Reports' and from the data base underlying them. The staff, says Naisbitt (1984: xxx), 'continually monitors 6,000 local newspapers each month' and aims to 'pinpoint, trace, and evaluate the important issues and trends'. The work, presented in a breathless and glitzy style, is often simple-minded or wrong. The 'megatrends', as Slaughter (1993b: 829) has pointed out, are not all 'mega' and not always 'trends' either. Even though the best-selling *Megatrends* contains unimpressive results, monitoring can be an effective and valid futurists method.

The Delphi technique is an example of a method specifically invented by futurists for the study of the future. Helmer and Dalkey (1983) were working on a RAND project when they co-developed it. It involves the use of experts ('oracles') as respondents in a series of repeated panel surveys. Initially, questions are asked about the nature and timing of future developments, and, then, questions are re-asked, perhaps several times, after the panel of experts has been told about other experts' responses in earlier phases of the survey. It is often combined with cross-impact analysis to study what would happen to one event, *if* something else changed in a certain way. With the growth of computer networks of experts, a Delphi exchange of information and a set of predictions can be done within hours.

Mention must be made of the famous report of the Club of Rome, *The Limits to Growth* (Meadows *et al.* 1972). Using the methods of modeling and simulation, the authors analyzed the capacity of the earth as a whole for population and economic growth. Starting with real data bases, they made some assumptions about the finite supply of fossil and mineral resources, the earth's limited capacity to absorb pollutants, and the finite limit of total possible food production. Then, they worked out the implications of their model through computer simulation. The authors concluded that both population and economic growth must stop. If they do not, then mass poverty will occur, because of the exhaustion of materials and food and the inability of the environment to absorb wastes.

Although *The Limits to Growth* has been subjected to withering criticism (Cole *et al.* 1973), it achieved its major purposes. It stimulated debate, discussion, and more research on an important topic involving human survival. That is, it raised the public's consciousness about the future, especially the awareness of the possibility of environmental disaster and the resource and food limitations that may face humankind, *unless people do something about it*.

The conditional feature of this conclusion should not go unremarked. In addition to being an example of computer simulation and the consciousness-raising function of futures research, *The Limits to Growth* also illustrates another characteristic of some of the futures literature: It is a prophecy of doom designed – or, more accurately, passionately hoped – to be self-defeating. That is, the forecasts or projections made by Meadows *et al.* give a picture of a future possibility so undesirable that people may be motivated to take actions that will prevent such a doomsday from occurring.

Surveys of behavioral intentions and images of the future, as noted above, are rather direct ways of studying the future. For example, studies of voting intentions, consumers' intentions to buy certain products, business-men's intentions to make capital outlays, or government's projected budgets have consequences for the future and investigating them has become a standard way of studying the future.

Finally, scenario-writing is a basic method of futures studies. Scenarios are stories or future histories of what might or could happen under certain circumstances, if current trends continue, for example, or if some specific courses of alternative action are taken. They can be combined with nearly any other method, from the most qualitative to the most quantitative, and they permit people to visualize and to explore alternative futures. Kahn's *On Thermonuclear War* is an excellent, though grisly, example. In a nutshell, Kahn asked his readers to think the unthinkable by considering the aftermath of World Wars III through VIII. On the one hand, he forced upon them the gory details of megadeaths and, on the other hand, the nearly-as-scary life after a thermonuclear war. Also, he forced them to consider the limited, chancy, and, perhaps, unlikely alternatives to it. Such a future war, he said, was possible, and the possibility wouldn't go away by not thinking about it. In fact, failure to think about it, he argued, might make it more probable.

THEORIES OF SOCIAL CHANGE AND THE FUTURE

There is no single, fully developed theory of social change and the future on which futurists have agreed. One reason is that many futurists work for clients who are mostly interested in practical results, not abstract theories. Thus, the driving force for futurists' work tends not to be the test of theory or the creation of knowledge for its own sake. Rather, it tends to be the search for solutions to recognized problems. No doubt futurists ought to give more concern to theory construction, because theory and practice are two aspects of the same principles. Good theory can produce good practice.

Another reason for the lack of comprehensive futures theory is that futur-ists deal with a wide range of subject matters. Anything in the world, after all, might have a future and might be of interest as a subject of study. In this respect, although one looks forward and the other backward, futures studies is similar to history. On the one hand, many futurists specialize in some particular subject matter such as population, health care, weapons technology, family life, business firms, government structures, economic development, international relations, or the environment. Each topic may require a special theory of its own. Yet, on the other hand, some futurists have made sweeping generalizations summarizing a global or macro-social future just as some historians have made grand efforts to formulate general principles summarizing human development throughout history.

Whoever their client and whatever their specific topic, all futurists necessarily are interested in social change. Although they often neglect theory, futurists have drawn – sometimes implicitly – on a wide range of existing theories of social change, including evolutionary, equilibrium, conflict, cyclical, functional, tension-management, technological, or others. Moreover, theories of Karl Marx, Max Weber, Emile Durkheim, Alexis de Tocqueville, and many other social theorists are occasionally encountered in the futurist literature, although none seems adequate to accommodate the various dimensions of futures thinking that futurists have elucidated.

There are, however, a number of theories dealing with social change and the future that have been suggested by futurists. Several overlapping sets of theories deal with population and economic growth and development, usually of the overshoot-and-collapse-doomsday forecasting similar to that of Meadows *et al.* Certainly, a key theoretical concept for futurists is the 'sustainability' of human society (Slaughter 1993a)

D. Bell's theory of the post-industrial society is another obvious example. Certainly, there is considerable evidence to support his speculations of the coming of the knowledge or information society: the shift from a goods-producing to a service economy, the rise of the professional and technical classes, the axial principle of the centrality of theoretical knowledge as the source of innovation and of policy formulation for the society, the spread of information technology, the increase in future orientations, and the increasing importance of the 'axial structures' of the university, research organizations and other intellectual institutions, among other things. 'Every modern society,' he says, 'now lives by innovation and the social control of change, and tries to anticipate the future in order to plan ahead. This commitment to social control introduces the need for planning and forecasting into society' (D. Bell 1976: 20). A major engine of social change for Bell is the growth of knowledge, especially theoretical knowledge, and a new intellectual technology, while a major steering mechanism for the direction of change is the character of the political managers who have the power of decision.

In *The Third Wave*, Toffler (1981) gives another, but not entirely different, theoretical perspective. He specifies six principles typical of all industrial societies: standardization, specialization, synchronization, concentration, maximization, and centralization. All, he claims, are under attack. The forces against them are found in the new industries arising from quantum electronics, information theory, molecular biology, oceanics, nucleonics, ecology and the space sciences. From home computers and talking appliances, to plans for asteroid mining and space cities, to biological solar cells and expanded consciousness, the organization of work, family, and politics is being transformed. What is resulting is a demassified society, individuation, electronic cottage industries in which many workers will own their means of production, home centeredness, community stability, reduction of energy requirements, new jobs, flexitime, self-help, production for one's own consumption, and the crackup of the nation-state, to mention just a few of the many developments that Toffler specifies.

Underlying Toffler's views are two interrelated theories of change, one dealing with the social consequences of new technology and another dealing with a theory of human choice. Both are part of an emergent theory of social change in futurist thinking that Etzioni (1968) calls 'a theory of societal guidance', that Dator (1983b) calls 'a theory of transformational society', and that W. Bell and Mau (1971) call 'a cybernetic-decisional theory of social change'.

Bell and Mau, for example, make explicit use of Polak's 'image of the future' which is a key theoretical concept of futures studies. Using it, we can state a general futurist theoretical proposition: Images of the future inform and shape individual and group action. Although the past may condition and constrain the present, images of the future help cause the present too, both because images mold crucial present acts and because such acts importantly create the coming present of times future.

Also, a theory of decision-making underlies much futurist work. Decision-making is action-oriented and is, thus, inherently future-oriented. It tends to make future projections of current social realities problematic and to ask how such realities could be maintained as they are or how they might be re-designed by deliberate human action. Bell and Mau combine the concept of 'image of the future' with decisional theory, bringing in other concepts in futurist theorizing, such as 'choice', 'decision', 'value', and 'action'. Clearly, this goes beyond a theory of social change and encompasses an action theory of human behavior.

Another general futurist theory, also still being developed, is based on the concept of the 'self-altering prophecy', which is a prediction that leads to changes in its own conditions and, hence, in itself. Such prophecies can be self-negating or self-fulfilling. An example of a self-negating prophecy is a prediction of coming empty classroom space that is negated because school officials, becoming aware of the prediction, 'simply decide to close some schools' (Berk and Cooley 1987: 260). A self-fulfilling prophecy is illustrated by the fact that children's performances in school are partly shaped by their teachers' expectations. Henshel and Johnston (1987) give many examples, both positive and negative, of the 'feedback loops' and 'bandwagon effects' involved in self-altering prophecies. It now seems clear that any complete futurist theory of social change must come to grips with the complex ways in which predictions themselves are taken into account by various social actors, both individual and collective, as they formulate their choices, make decisions among them, and design and take the actions that shape the future. For that matter, no adequate theory of human behavior and social change can safely ignore the role of self-altering prophecies.

Henshel (1976) has also done pioneering work exploring the theoretical relationship between prediction and control. He distinguishes, for example, between 'unaltered phenomena' on the one hand and more or less intentionally 'designed or engineered phenomena' on the other. For unaltered phenomena, natural scientists often have as much difficulty in predicting accurately as do social scientists, such things, for example, as the weather, earthquakes, or, to take a social example, the percentage of British Members of Parliament who are short. In the case of designed phenomena, however, prediction follows from having control, from the very fact of the design or engineering elements involved. While D. Bell stresses that control is made possible by the ability to forecast, Henshel emphasizes the reverse: forecasting is made possible by the ability to control. Both are true.

People in their everyday lives, as well as social scientists, can make reasonably accurate predictions some large percentage of the time partly because so many social phenomena have been more or less consciously ordered and controlled. Some examples are the side of the street on which people drive their automobiles; how many spouses a person can legally have at one time in a particular society; the year of the next presidential election in the United States; the total number of MPs in England five years from now; or a prediction that a woman will not marry her father or her mother. This is not to say, of course, that human decision and action cannot change constitutions, governing rules, or even the laws and traditions concerning eligible marriage partners (W. Bell and Olick 1989).

Despite these and other theoretical efforts, the futures field is relatively underdeveloped theoretically. Much futures research has been directed at specific practical problems with relatively little regard for theory, while macro-social futures work often has been done along atheoretical lines with a strong historicist bent. For example, Kahn and Wiener (1967) base their projections of a standard future world and its 'canonical variations' on projections of a basic set of past trends of Western society, with the explicit recognition that they use no formal theory of history (and, a critic would add, relatively little data). Clearly, there is an opportunity for new contributions to theories of social change and the future.

CONCLUSION: IMAGES OF THE FUTURE FOR OUR TIME

Futurists and others doing futures-related research have created a diverse and extensive literature. Taken as a whole, it contains discussions and evaluations of the dominant images of the future for our time. Whether they are likely or unlikely, desirable or undesirable, or small- or large-scale, these alternative images of the future constitute a rich tapestry of possibilities, probabilities, and preferences to inform the thinking, choosing, and acting both of ordinary people and of leaders as they attempt to steer themselves and their groups, organizations, and even entire societies toward what they regard as the best possible future.

Futurists have many different substantive concerns and each one contains implications for alternative and competing images of the future. There is, for example, the important topic of population growth. Already, the earth's population is more than five billion. Are we headed for an earth of 10 or 11 billion people before the end of the twenty-first century? Can all those additional people be accommodated without aggression and violent conflict? If not, can the growth be slowed? What is an optimal total human population for the earth in order to maximize the chances of a long and satisfying life for every living person? How can such a target population be agreed upon and how can the means to achieve it be negotiated among the diverse peoples of the earth?

Population growth, of course, is related to several other aspects of the future, such as abundant food for all or mass starvation, depletion or preservation of natural resources (from water and oil to forests and minerals), environmental damage or protection (from air pollution and acid rain to ozone loss and the warming of the earth's atmosphere and the flooding of coastal areas), a thriving and prosperous versus a collapsed and depressed economy, and a world spending its wealth on weapons of destruction or on human well-being, at war or at peace (Marien with Jennings 1987b). Can we create sustainable human societies?

The number of alternative possibilities for the future is enormous. Such possibilities include, in addition to the above, adequate health care for everyone, a decent level of living, opportunities to marry and have children, a job, ample and satisfactory housing, and opportunities for education and learning. They include, on another level of abstraction, the feeling of empowerment, enlightenment, a sense of personal well-being and happiness, material comfort, the opportunity to learn skills, giving and receiving love and affection, freedom of expression and other freedoms, justice and other ethical conduct, and the respect of others. And, of course, they include the opposite of all these things: torture, disease, degradation, humiliation, poverty, homelessness, loneliness, imprisonment, repression, hate, violence, ignorance, injustice and immorality, powerlessness, and despair.

The future could contain astounding advances in genetic engineering; information technology; communications; robotics that will reduce the dehumanizing routine and repetitive tasks that some people now have to perform; knowledge of the physical and social worlds; human potential, such as altered consciousness, control of emotions, body and mind control through bio-feedback, super-learning, greater longevity, deeper wisdom, and synergistic social organizations; abundant energy resources; fairness in human relationships; democratic participation and decision-making; guaranteed human rights and commensurate responsibilities for everyone; and the continued increase in the scale of society, including the evolution of human life into outer space.

What will the future bring? Futurists claim that it largely depends on the choices that people make and the actions that they take. Futurists try to contribute to the making of informed and wise choices by carrying out systematic studies of possible, probable, and preferable futures and by spreading information, formulating plans, and taking part in the public discussions about what constitutes the most desirable future and about what are the best ways to create it. Futurists aim to challenge people's thinking by encouraging them to examine critically their current routines of behavior, to consider alternatives, to search for currently unrecognized possibilities, to analyze their goals and values, to become more conscious of the future and the control they may have over it, and to care about the freedom and well-being of future generations. Clearly, futures education is needed, raising alternative images of the future to people's consciousness and spreading understanding of both their origins and their consequences (Riner 1991).

Whether or not the futurist message will be heeded in the years to come remains to be seen. What is without doubt is that the future is now being prepared, largely by the human actions that have been taken, that are being taken, and that will be taken – including your actions and mine. Although we do not know our destiny, some future for our small planet is coming whether we will like it or not. This Spaceship and Time Machine Earth travels on and we humans will share a common fate of our own making. Will the human experiment end in the hate, violence and destruction that now threatens us or can we seize our opportunities and write a human future of compassion, peace, cooperation, and justice in the book of time?

* This is a revised version of a paper first published in Italian as 'Futuro', in *Enciclopedia delle Scienze Sociali*, Vol. IV, Roma, Italia: Marchesi Grafiche Editoriali (1994). The author wishes to thank J. A. Dator, M. Marien, and R. D. Riner for comments on an early draft of this paper.

REFERENCES

Amara, R. (1981) 'The futures field: searching for definitions and boundaries', *The Futurist* 15, 1: 25–9.

American Academy of Arts and Science (1967) 'Toward the year 2000: work in progress', *Daedalus* 96, 3: 639–994.

Bell, D. (1976) *The Coming of Post-Industrial Society* (1973), New York: Basic Books.

Bell, W. (1987) 'Is the futures field an art form or can it become a science?', *Futures Research Quarterly* 3, 1: 27–44.

—— (1993) 'Bringing the good back in: values, objectivity and the future', *International Social Science Journal* 136: 333–47.

—— (1994) 'The world as a moral community', *Society* 31, 5: 15–22.

Bell, W. and Mau, J. A. (1971) 'Images of the future: theory and research strategies', in W. Bell and J. A. Mau (eds) *The Sociology of the Future*, New York: Russell Sage Foundation.

Bell, W. and Olick, J. K. (1989) 'An epistemology for the futures field: problems and possibilities of prediction', *Futures* 21, 2: 115–35.

Berk, R. A. and Cooley, T. F. (1987) 'Errors in forecasting social phenomena', in K. C. Land and S. H. Schneider (eds) *Forecasting in the Social and Natural Sciences*, Boston, MA: D. Reidel.

Cole, H. S. D., Freeman, C., Jahoda, M. and Pavitt, K. L. R. (eds) (1973) *Models of Doom*, New York: Universe Books.

Cornish, E., with members of the staff of the World Future Society (1977) *The Study of the Future*, Washington, DC: World Future Society.

Cronbach, L. J., Ambron, S. R., Dornbusch, S. M., Hess, R. D., Hornik, R. C., Phillips, D. C., Walker, D. F. and Weiner, S. S. (1981) *Toward Reform of Program Evaluation* (1980), San Francisco: Jossey-Bass.

Dator, J. A. (1979) 'The futures of culture or cultures of the future', in A. J. Marsella, R. G. Tharp and T. J. Ciborowski (eds) *Perspectives on Cross-Cultural Psychology*, New York: Academic Press.

—— (1983a) 'The 1982 Honolulu electronic town meeting', in W. Page (ed.) *The Future of Politics*, London: Frances Pinter in association with the World Futures Studies Federation.

—— (1983b) 'Loose connections: a vision of a transformational society', in E. Masini (ed.) *Visions of Desirable Societies*, Oxford: Pergamon.

—— (1986) 'The futures of futures studies – the view from Hawaii', *Futures* 18, 3: 440–45.

Dickson, P. (1972) *Think Tanks* (1971), New York: Atheneum.

Etzioni, E. (1968) *The Active Society*, New York: The Free Press.

Gordon, T. J. (1992) 'The methods of futures research', *Annals of the American Academy of Political and Social Science* 522: 25–35.

Helmer, O. and Dalkey, N. (1983) 'The delphi technique' (1963), in O. Helmer, *Looking Forward*, Beverly Hills, CA: Sage.

Henshel, R. L. (1976) *On the Future of Social Prediction*, Indianapolis, IN: Bobbs-Merrill.

Henshel, R. L. and Johnston, W. (1987) 'The emergence of bandwagon effects: a theory', *Sociological Quarterly* 28, 4: 493–511.

Jouvenel, B. de (1967) *The Art of Conjecture* (1964), New York: Basic Books.

Jungk, R. (1976) *The Everyman Project* (1973), New York: Liveright.

Jungk, R. and Galtung, J. (eds) (1971) *Mankind 2000* (1969), Oslo: Universitetsforlaget.

Jungk, R. and Müllert, N. (1987) *Future Workshops: How to Create Desirable Futures*, London: Institute for Social Inventions.

Kahn, H. (1960) *On Thermonuclear War*, Princeton, NJ: Princeton University Press.

Kahn, H. and Wiener, A. J. (1967) *The Year 2000: A Framework for Speculation on the Next Thirty-Three Years*, New York: Macmillan.

Kidder, R. M. (1994) *Shared Values for a Troubled World*, San Francisco, CA: Jossey-Bass.

Lasswell, H. D. (1967) 'Projecting the future', 25 September (mimeo).

Lee, K. (1985) *A New Basis for Moral Philosophy*, London: Routledge & Kegan Paul.

Lerner, D. and Lasswell, H. D. (eds) (1951) *The Policy Sciences: Recent Developments in Scope and Method*, Stanford, CA: Stanford University Press.

McHale, J. (1978) 'The emergence of futures research', in J. Fowles (ed.) *Handbook of Futures Research*, Westport, CT: Greenwood.

McHale, J. and McHale, M. C. (n.d. *c.* 1975) *Futures Studies: An International Survey*, New York: United Nations Institute for Training and Research.

Manuel, F. E. and Manuel, F. P. (1979) *Utopian Thought in the Western World*, Cambridge, MA: Belknap Press of Harvard University Press.

Marien, M. and Jennings, L. (1987a) 'Introduction', in M. Marien and L. Jennings (eds) *What I Have Learned: Thinking about the Future Then and Now*, Westport, CT: Greenwood Press.

Marien, M. with Jennings, L. (1987b) *Future Survey Annual* 1986, Vol. VII, Bethesda, MD: World Future Society; and (1988) Vol. VIII.

Mau, J. A. (1968) *Social Change and Images of the Future*, Cambridge, MA: Schenkman.

Meadows, D. H., Meadows, D. L., Randers, J. and Behrens III, W. W. (1972) *The Limits to Growth*, New York: Universe Books.

Musgrave, A. (1993) *Common Sense, Science and Scepticism*, Cambridge: Cambridge University Press.

Naisbitt, J. (1984) *Megatrends* (1982), New York: Warner.

Polak, F. L. (1961) *The Image of the Future* (1951), Vols I and II, trans. E. Boulding, New York: Oceana.

President's Research Committee on Social Trends (1933) *Recent Social Trends in the United States*, 2 volumes, New York: McGraw-Hill.

Reichenbach, H. (1951) *The Rise of Scientific Philosophy*, Berkeley and Los Angeles: University of California Press.

Riner, R. D. (1987) 'Doing futures research – anthropologically', *Futures* 19, 3: 311–28.

—— (1991) 'Anthropology about the future: limits and potentials', *Human Organization* 50, 3: 297–311.

Rudner, R. S. (1966) *Philosophy of Social Science*, Englewood Cliffs, NJ: Prentice-Hall.

Slaughter, R. A. (1993a) 'Futures concepts', *Futures* 25, 3: 289–314.

—— (1993b) 'Looking for the real "megatrends"', *Futures* 25, 8: 827–49.

Textor, R. B. (1980) *A Handbook on Ethnographic Futures Research*, 3rd edition: Version A, Stanford, CA: Stanford University Press.

Toffler, A. (1978) 'Foreword', in M. Maruyama and A. M. Harkins (eds) *Cultures of the Future*, The Hague: Mouton.

—— (1981) *The Third Wave* (1980), New York: Bantam

—— (1986) Remarks at the open plenary session, meetings of the World Future Society, New York, 14–17 July.

Chapter 2

Futures studies and the human sciences: the case for normative scenarios

James Ogilvy

Simply to be a human being is to be a futurist of sorts. For human freedom is largely a matter of imagining alternative futures and then choosing among them. Conversely, to be a good futurist, I will argue, one must at least aspire to being a good human being. One must care about the welfare of others. One's visions of the future must be informed by more than the science of what is or an imagination of what might be; one's visions of the future must also be informed by a sense of what *ought* to be.

The principal purpose of this chapter is to offer a justification for normative scenarios. But I have other goals as well, goals which are served by the way in which I reach the principal objective. In order to achieve a convincing justification for normative scenarios, we need to rethink the very nature of futures studies in the larger context of disciplined inquiry. If there is such a thing as futurology – a disciplined *logos* or discourse about the future – is it an art or a science or, as many suspect, nothing more than hopes and fears dressed up as science?

Put the question in a very concrete way: if futures research is indeed a legitimate field of disciplined inquiry, then why are there so few courses or departments of futures studies in our major universities? Why is futures research not recognized by academics as one among the many *disciplines*?

Let's face it: those of us who call ourselves futurists are not likely to wear this badge proudly when we are surrounded by academics. We are thought to be intellectual charlatans, soothsayers in business suits, tea-leaf readers and crystal ball gazers with little more credibility than astrologists. Where is our body of evidence? What is our methodology? How can we possibly claim a place at the academic high table when we have so little in the name of legitimate scholarship that we can offer? Go to the library today to do research on the future and you will not find one book copyrighted in the year 2000.

Faced with the slimness of our academic portfolio, we find ourselves on the defensive. We turn to our computers and our databases; we develop models; we debate methodology as if we were building the foundations for a science. We refine our polling procedures, twiddle our statistical techniques, and do our very best to make our trend analyses and technology forecasts look as thoroughly engineered as the technologies we are forecasting. In our defensive anxiety about the tenuousness of our academic credentials we are tempted to become holier than the Pope, more scientific than the scientists. And in such a mood, the last thing we want to hear about is normative scenarios. We want *facts*, not values. We want well-founded theory, not sentimental morality.

There is, consequently, a constant danger of bad faith in the work of most futurists. Eager to escape the charge of subjective bias, of claiming that what we want to happen will in fact happen, we do everything we can to make sure that our scenarios of what will happen have been scourged of every relic of what we ourselves might want to happen. Eager to escape the charge of issuing self-fulfilling prophecies, we do our best to articulate worst case scenarios. I call this bad faith, not because I think we are unsuccessful in scourging our hopes. I call it bad faith just to the extent that we *are* successful. To the extent that we mimic scientists in claiming value-free objectivity in our view of the future, we deny the very thing that makes us good human beings and good futurists. We deny that we *care*. But we must care. If we do not, we are doomed to a dreadful future.

All very well and good, you say. But so far we have only the makings of a windy commencement address. Where's the beef?

TWO STRATEGIES FOR LINKING THE TWO OBJECTIVES

I've mentioned two objectives for this chapter – justifying normative scenarios and rethinking the place of futures studies in the context of other academic disciplines. One possible strategy for linking these two objectives would be to argue, from accepted ideas about what constitutes a science, that futures studies is indeed a science, but that, because we are good, caring people, we will use this science for the betterment of humankind by developing normative scenarios. We might place futures studies on the firm foundations of accepted science and then, on the strength of that foundational maneuver, make the further argument that a good science must be an ethical science. This is precisely *not* the strategy I will follow.

Rather than defensively placing futures studies on the firm foundations of science, I want to pursue an offensive strategy. I want to show how very infirm the so-called foundations of science have become. Rather than dragging futures studies over into the camp of the sciences, I want to show how the so-called human sciences are moving in the direction of futures studies.

In short, *we* don't have to learn how to play *their* game; *they* are learning to play *ours*. The human sciences are moving through a paradigm shift that makes them much more amenable to the work of the futurist and far less pretentious about their place at the academic high table with the hard sciences. The burden of this chapter – and the reason it is so long – is to *show* this movement among the human sciences. It is not enough simply to *say* that the paradigm shift is here. And there is no brief way to demonstrate in the requisite degree of detail the very real movement taking place in the fields of anthropology, psychology, literary criticism, philosophy and sociology. At risk of running on at some length, I intend to demonstrate that the human sciences are moving toward a widespread recognition of the need for normative scenarios as an essential feature of their own epistemologies.

What a sad irony it would be if, just as these reinforcements from the human sciences arrived to support futures research, futurists themselves had decamped in the direction of the hard sciences! This is why I pursue this second strategy of linking my two objectives, and not the first.

BACKGROUND

Given the range of subjects to be discussed, and the conclusions yet to be reached, it may be more than merely incidentally informative to say a few words about how I came to the views I am expressing. I started my academic career as a philosopher. I taught for twelve years, mostly at Yale. Under the imperative to specialize, I found myself being backed into the corner of becoming a specialist on Hegel – the pre-eminent generalist. But my real ambition was to accomplish today something akin to what Hegel achieved in 1807: a totalized synthesis showing how all the parts of human endeavor relate to one another in the dialectical dance of history.

Then I moved to California, and, at the invitation of Peter Schwartz and Arnold Mitchell, spent seven years working at SRI International (formerly Stanford Research Institute) where it seemed easier to Hegelize than it turned out to be in an academic environment riven with departmental barriers maintained by an imperative to specialization – not a congenial environment in which to Hegelize, which is quite something else from specializing in Hegel. One of the first tasks I undertook at SRI was a collaboration with Peter Schwartz on a monograph entitled *The Emergent Paradigm: Changing Patterns of Thought and Belief.*[1] In that 1979 report we reviewed thirteen different disciplines to limn out the features of a new paradigm. To our surprise that report, which was not easy going for most readers, generated quite a bit of interest. But to our disappointment, it resisted two different attempts to turn it into a book for broader consumption. The present chapter represents a third-generation attempt to publish some of the ideas contained in that 1979 report.

At SRI, I wore two hats: I worked with the futures group using my training as an Hegelian to try to catch the momentum of the present toward the future. My second hat was also continuous with my training in philosophy. I spent three years as director of research for SRI's Values and Lifestyles (VALS) program, a survey-based segmentation system for dividing Americans into different groups distinguished not just by demographic characteristics but by their empirically verified values.

In 1987, Peter Schwartz concluded five years as head of long-range scenario development for corporate planning at Royal Dutch/Shell. We decided to form a company that would carry further some of the methods and techniques of futures research that had been developed at Shell and SRI over the past several decades. Our company is called Global Business Network. GBN is dedicated to gathering and applying the sorts of intelligence necessary for creating alternative scenarios to be used in strategic planning.

Our principal methodology is the generation and use of alternative scenarios that we develop around specific decisions being made by policy makers and strategists. We do not make predictions. Instead we think through several possible sets of consequences that today's decisions might have. By developing alternative scenarios that are explicitly linked to decisions facing managers, we guarantee that the differences that divide our scenarios from one another are differences that will make a difference to the decisions in question. We design our scenarios in such a way as to highlight the most important uncertainties surrounding the outcome of today's decisions.

Sometimes the most important uncertainties are technological: will battery technology move ahead fast enough to permit a light enough electric car? Sometimes the most important uncertainties are economic: will the growth of the economy in general be strong enough to sustain demand in a specific market? More often than many futurists may care to admit the most important uncertainties are social and cultural: the differences between the 1960s and the 1980s are best described in socio-cultural language rather than in technological or economic terms. The new values of the 1960s and 1970s, the anti-authoritarianism that drew strength from the resistance to the Vietnam war, the experiments with conscious-ness through drugs and mysticism, the rise of feminism, the awakening of awareness of the environment, and the preoccupation with self-realization that ranged from the quest for spiritual enlightenment to the narcissism of what Tom Wolfe called the Me-decade – each of these waves of social change that began in the 1960s is still rippling through the 1990s. But as these waves break on the shore of the next millennium, how will they give shape to the future?

Rather than trying to predict the future of values on the basis of some theory of social change, I believe that the best we can do is develop alternative scenarios. But these scenarios need not be completely neutral. I will argue that a case can be made for constructing scenarios that range from the utopian to the negative morality play; from a normative portrait of what ought to be to a negative portrayal of the punishments in store for us if we do not clean up our act. The case for normative scenarios, morality plays and abject utopianism needs to be made these days because the worship of science over the past century or so has led us toward embarrassment over our values.

I have seen big science, I have plowed the fields of the humanities, and I have experienced their uneasy union in the practice of contract research and corporate consulting. It is just the uneasiness of this union that provokes me to publish this chapter. The union of the sciences and the humanities is uneasy precisely where human beings with values try to be scientific about the values of human beings. This is a situation that is ripe for psychoanalytic examination. There are all sorts of opportunities for self-deception when the analyst and the analysand are one and the same consciousness. The resonances of transference and counter-transference are endless.

We cannot lift ourselves by the bootstraps up and out of the practice of revaluation we are purportedly studying. We are both the experimenter and the experiment; we are both the laboratory technician and the laboratory itself. But it is just this sort of self-referential, foundationless reflection that distinguishes philosophy from other well-founded disciplines. Just this sort of high wire act differentiates philosophy from the ever so much safer piling of fact upon fact – the masonry of historians or the carpentry of botanists or the engineering of physicists. Philosophy has no foundation and no safety net. It is a dance in mid-air which, if the dancer loses his balance, ends in a flailing fall.

In the following pages I hope to tease out some relationships between futures studies and philosophy, but this endeavor should not be confused with an attempt to give a philosophical *foundation* to futures studies. It is precisely the quest for foundations – whether philosophical or scientific – that current philosophy tells us is impossible. Rather than borrowing firm foundations from philosophy, it is just the recognition of foundationlessness in philosophy that I would take as a guide for learning how to do without the pretensions of scientific foundations for futures studies. In coming to terms with the role of values in confronting the future, it is important that we cut ourselves loose from the foundational security of solid facts and scientific theories.

In our work with alternative scenarios, we constantly come up against several inter-related questions having to do with human values. It is clear that one of the most important drivers of energy demand is people's willingness to conserve energy. Will people be willing to drive a 'green' car that is slow off the mark at stop lights? How much air pollution are they willing to breathe? How many homeless will they allow on their doorsteps? How much more *stuff* will materialism consume before a wave of asceticism sets in? Such a wave would be comparable to, but very different from, the counterculture of the 1960s. It would be a reaction against the 1980s, much as the 1960s could be read as a dialectical negation of the 1950s.

But will it happen? Who knows? The point is not to predict and say, yes it will, or, no it won't. The point is to imagine what it might be like as a way of anticipating possible moves for the human spirit. The several questions in the previous paragraph are all questions of values. They do not turn on questions of technological feasibility but on the very human question of what people will want in their lives in ten years' time. What part of a full human life will be most scarce and therefore of the highest value? And how will that skewing of the ecology of value tend to revalue other parts of life? For anticipating fundamental shifts in the economics of *value,* anticipating changes in *values* is essential.

But very difficult. Possibly impossible. Because if anything is a function of human freedom, you would think that the revaluation of human values would be a prime candidate. If our values are like a hard-wired, read-only program, then we are pretty mechanical creatures, hardly free at all. Only if we can write over at will, only if we can reprogram the human biocomputer can we be said to be free.

Precisely this primacy of freedom as definitive of the human means that the prediction of human values is in principle impossible. As Aristotle formulated the paradox over two millennia ago, if you can know the future, then you can't do anything about it; if you can do something about the future, then you cannot know it in advance. You can no more predict human values than you can predict movements in contemporary art. It is the artists that will do something about the future of art, and it is human beings who will revalue their values. If either one is predictable, then she is not an artist, he is not a human being. Both beauty and humanity share an inherent unpredictability.

Likewise in neither humanity nor in art can invention count on the force of novelty alone. New for the sake of new won't do. There must be some sense of continuity, some connection with eternal depths, even as there is a clear articulation of just why some break with tradition is so urgently required. It is always the old battle of the sons with the fathers, this rebellion that is creativity. Does it require a strong father for the struggle to be intense? Is intensity what one most wants out of this struggle? What about clarity of identity, which is, after all, what this struggle is all about? Who will we be ten or twenty years hence? What passions will most motivate us? *What is the future of desire*?

So one objective of this study is to deal with the question: What will our values look like in the year 2005? I say 'deal with' rather than 'answer' the question because my response is oblique. Rather than trying to forecast the evolution of values over the coming decades, I will tell you, as one among several possible scenarios, what I want and hope our values will become. And I will add to this normative scenario an account showing why such *advocacy is the only epistemologically authentic stance where values are concerned.*

I cannot predict the dominant values in the year 2005, not only because we lack a covering law to serve as the engine of prediction, but also because the very nature of valuation is to transgress all attempts at prediction. It would be nice to imagine that advances in sociology and anthropology would allow us to take some reading from our distant past, our recent past and our present and plot them on some theoretically grounded metric where we could apply some elegant covering law to project a series of readings for the near and distant future – with increasing plus or minus estimates of uncertainty for increasingly distant futures. It would be nice to imagine that futures research could aspire to reducing these plus-or-minus error factors, refining skill in prediction, minimizing risk. But this is not what our discipline is about. It is instead the articulation of risk so that we have some sense of *what is at stake* in our daily decisions.

To summarize the major point of this introductory section, the line of argument I am pursuing – away from a foundation on fact or scientific theory and towards a more creative and willful endeavor – drives futures studies toward becoming a kind of collectively practiced existentialism. The existentialist philosophers – Heidegger, Camus, Sartre – had a great deal to say about the importance of entertaining the various possibilities that open before the anguished individual entertaining his or her future. While I am eager to acknowledge the importance of the existentialists' emphasis on temporality and the future, I want to part company with their preoccupation with the finality of individuality. Camus' stranger is the quintessential solitary misfit. Heidegger's authentic *Dasein* may die alone, but is this any reason to believe that we must live alone? In his *Being and Nothingness* Sartre struggles to cross what can only be regarded as a self-imposed 'reef of solipsism'. All of this philosophical individualism is, I would argue, an artifact of the Cartesian-Kantian tradition in philosophy. Sartre saw as much late in his life but he had to lurch into Marxism to find a congenial medium for a collectivism to balance his early existential individualism. But Marxism is not the only medium for acknowledging the sociality of human existence. In steering futures studies toward becoming a *social existentialism* I hope to be able to avoid both the solipsistic extremes of existentialism as well as the juggernaut determinism of vulgar Marxism.

All these -isms are just ways of talking about that same uneasy union between the sciences and the humanities, the uneasiness I experienced moving from academic philosophy departments into contract consulting at SRI, the uneasiness C. P. Snow addressed in his famous essay on the two cultures;[2] the uneasiness that comes from the fact that science wants to be value-free but the future is very much shaped by values. This uneasiness is captured in the phrase 'the human sciences,' which some regard as an oxymoron. The human sciences seem to straddle the gap between the hard sciences and the humanities. This straddling act is not easy, as the following sections are intended to show.

What I hope to show by the following review of recent developments in the human sciences is this: rather than trying to found their own legitimacy on mimicking the hard sciences with their solid methodologies and confident access to objectivity, the human sciences are accepting their irreducibly semiotic and therefore inevitably ambiguous status. They are acknowledging their foundationlessness and accepting the finality of interpretations in place of facts. They are therefore waking up to the ineluctable *interestedness* of the human sciences, to the absurdity of claiming that sociology or social philosophy can conduct their inquiries in a wholly disinterested manner. To return to the opening paragraph, we must *care*. If we don't, then all is lost. But if we do, then we are hardly disinterested.

Thus do these several strategies and objectives come together: the first, a justification for normative scenarios; the second, the placement of futures studies in the context of the human sciences; the third, coming to terms with the risk of bad faith by ignoring our own values in shaping our visions of the future. These three strategies support one another. Having justified normative scenarios, it is easier to stop ignoring one's own values in the name of objectivity. And the claim to objectivity turns out to be empty in any case, if reports from the other human sciences are to be believed.

We begin with these reports from the human sciences, for there is where the criteria for scientific objectivity are tested. The basic criteria that define the difference between science and mere opinion can be said to make up a paradigm. While futures studies could not sit easily in the context of a positivist scientific paradigm, it can play a central role among the human sciences following a paradigm shift away from the positivist paradigm toward something new, something that lacks a name, something that might clumsily be described as a semiotic/existential paradigm.

The next section has more to say about the concept of a paradigm in general, the nature of paradigm shifts, and the outline of the positivist paradigm. Later sections then take a tour through recent paradigm-bursting developments in anthropology, literary criticism, philosophy, psychology and sociology. The concluding sections take a stab at what a normative scenario might look like. Given such a long running start, through the first six sections, the last three must take a long jump toward a value-driven vision of a better future and not just stumble through some trend analysis of our most plausible tomorrow.

1. THE EMERGENT PARADIGM IN THE HUMAN SCIENCES

During recent decades, a good deal of attention has been given to some fundamental shifts in assumptions about science and scientific method. T. S. Kuhn's *The Structure of Scientific Revolutions* is usually invoked as the source of talk about paradigm shifts.[3] But earlier sources arguing the perspectival and historical nature of science can be traced back to the philosophies of Kant and Hegel, and later sources are necessary to argue for a contemporary paradigm shift where Kuhn describes only past paradigm shifts.

For our present purposes, the point at issue is not so much the fundamental assumptions underlying any one discipline; rather, the point at issue is the nature of scientific explanation or inquiry in general. What counts as good science?

Scientists and philosophers of science have been working at cross-purposes during this century. While philosophers of science have been trying to codify the methods of scientists in earlier centuries as a way of arriving at a precise method for what counts as good science, physicists, chemists, biologists and many researchers in the human sciences have been merrily forging ahead using methods quite different from those of their predecessors.

Philosophy of science flourished under the banner of logical positivism, a school of thought founded by the Vienna Circle which included the young Ludwig Wittgenstein, Moritz Schlick and Rudolf Carnap. Their insights were anglicized by Bertrand Russell and A. J. Ayer. The essence of this worldview, and its implications for science, can be captured in a few propositions.

1 The world is the totality of empirically measurable atomic elements moving in space and time.
2 Motion in space and time takes place according to universal, deterministic, causal laws that cover all situations.
3 In order to explain complex phenomena like biological growth or human thought, it is necessary and sufficient to reduce those phenomena to their physical, constituent, simple parts and then plug state descriptions of those parts into equations representing well confirmed general laws.
4 One way to confirm general laws is to test their predictive power. Thus, if laws L1, L2, ..., Lr enable one to predict events of type E from antecedent conditions C1, C2, ..., Ck, then those laws are confirmed, and event E can be scientifically explained. In a classic statement by Carl Hempel and Paul Oppenheim:

> If *E* describes a particular event, then the antecedent circumstances described in the sentences C1, C2, ..., Ck may be said jointly to 'cause'

that event, in the sense that there are certain empirical regularities, expressed by the laws L1, L2, ..., Lr, which imply that whenever conditions of the kind indicated by C1, C2, ..., Ck occur, an event of the kind in E will take place.[4]

The import of logical empiricism for futures studies is as follows. If everything under the sun really can be described according to deterministic, predictive, causal laws, then the agenda for futurists is plain: take the past and present as antecedent circumstances C1, C2, ..., Ck, discover general laws L1, L2, ..., Lr, and set about predicting future events E1, E2 *ad infinitum*.

No one, of course, thinks this sort of cranking out of predictions is really possible. But debates over methodology in futures studies hinge on the precise reasons *why* the positivist program is not possible. Is it simply that we have not yet discovered the relevant laws of social change and technological diffusion? Or is it that we have not yet clarified the correspondence rules that would relate complex epiphenomena like thoughts or social change to their atomic, material constituents?

Any number of reasons could be given for the current failure of the positivist program. As long as the reasons given are of the type suggested, then the debate over methodology in futures studies will gravitate toward better measurement techniques, improved polling procedures, or statistical techniques and modeling tools that might uncover lawlike regularities amidst masses of data.

I would like to suggest that such efforts, however useful for particular purposes, are fundamentally misguided as putative answers to current questions about futures methodology. As an alternative to the covering law model of scientific explanation, I would like to suggest a new paradigm of scientific explanation. In short, futurists should borrow a few leaves from their colleagues in some other human sciences.

In the following sections, I want to take a brief tour through some new developments in the human sciences. The purpose of these brief explorations is not to glean new discoveries or general laws that can be exploited by futurists in their efforts to make predictions. To the contrary, the purpose is to see how researchers in several disciplines that may be regarded as more mature than futures studies have already abandoned their pretensions to the kind of predictive science to which some futurists still aspire.

Each of these sections will begin (a) with a discussion of recent paradigm-shattering developments in the field under review, then conclude (b) with a brief discussion of some direct implications for futures studies. Section 6 will then abstract from the human sciences taken as a group a set of features of an emergent paradigm.

2(a) ANTHROPOLOGY: FROM EXPLANATION BY LAW TO A SEMIOTIC DISCIPLINE

Once upon a time, the practice of anthropology was a pursuit of the origins of mankind. Grubbing about among the bones and broken crockery of ancient civilizations, anthropologists sought clues from which to reconstruct the social habits of prehistoric human beings. Among more than a few students of anthropology, this quest after origins was also a quest after *essence*: if we knew more about the advent of civilization, then perhaps we would better understand the deepest mysteries in the contemporary human heart. Perhaps the riddle of human nature, and the endless debate between nature and nurture, could be unlocked if we just knew more about the first humans. Were they noble savages? Were they social beings or loners? Loving or aggressive? Matriarchal or patriarchal? These questions were pursued as if their answers could tell us something important about contemporary society, e.g. the fate of feminism or the plausibility of a political ideology based on the perfectibility of the human heart. From Marx to Margaret Mead, arguments based on anthropology made claims about human nature that were based on anthropology's access to the first terms in the 'language' of human culture. Call it the Adam and Eve school of anthropology.

The achievement of structural anthropology was a breakthrough from a preoccupation with individual terms – first or last – to an articulation of structures and relations. And not just relations among terms, but relations among relations among relations.

Lévi-Strauss asserts that, 'The kinship system is a language',[5] but denies that the 'meanings' of its terms can be derived from some anthropological analogue to etymology. 'A kinship system does not consist in the objective ties of descent or consanguinity between individuals. It exists only in human consciousness; it is an arbitrary system of representations, not the spontaneous development of a real situation.'[6]

Also like languages, kinship systems reveal structures of relations so abstract as to defy any attempts at foundational analysis seeking an origin in some first term. In studying societies of the Cherkiss and Trobriand types, one finds, 'the relation between maternal uncle and nephew is to the relation between brother and sister as the relation between father and son is to that between husband and wife'.[7] Not originary or natural terms, but relations among relations determine the meanings of the resultant relata.

Structural anthropology, as developed by Claude Lévi-Strauss, made the move from atomic terms to 'molecular' relationships. But Lévi-Strauss tended to think of some relationships as fundamental, even universal. However varied and arbitrary the vocabularies of different myth systems, for example, 'The vocabulary matters less than the structure.' Further:

If we add that these structures are not only the same for everyone and for all areas to which the function applies, but that they are few in number, we shall understand why the world of symbolism is infinitely varied in content, but always limited in its laws. There are many languages, but very few structural laws which are valid for all languages. A compilation of known tales and myths would fill an imposing number of volumes. But they can be reduced to a small number of simple types if we abstract from among the diversity of characters, a few elementary functions.[8]

Lévi-Strauss moved anthropology away from the atomism of an original, essential human nature that could biologically dictate the structure of human society. But the structures of relations he put in place of elementary atoms came to play a role in anthropological theory that was not so very different from the role of Adam and Eve terms. To reach these unchanging essences – relational though they may be – all we have to do is, 'abstract from among the diversity of characters, a few elementary functions'.

More recently, anthropology has moved beyond the quest for universals of the sort that might be evident in first terms or first relationships. The problem is simply that the quest for universals leads toward insights that tell us less and less about more and more until we learn nothing about everything. It is always possible to say *something* that will be true of everything and everyone. But as the rich variety and distinctnesses of different cultures become evident with ever more research, the question arises: are the samenesses more essential to human nature than the differences? As Clifford Geertz puts the question:

> Is the fact that 'marriage' is universal (if it is) as penetrating a comment on what we are as the facts concerning Himalayan polyandry, or those fantastic Australian marriage rules, or the elaborate bride-price systems of Bantu Africa? . . . it may be in the cultural particularities of people – in their oddities – that some of the most instructive revelations of what it is to be generically human, are to be found.[9]

Geertz's contributions to anthropology manifest several aspects of a paradigm shift. Not only does he accept the move from primary terms to structures of relationships – 'In short, we need to look for systematic relationships among diverse phenomena, not for substantive identities among similar ones'[10] – but further, he argues that these systematic relationships, once revealed, have a different status from that of the laws of human nature anthropologists once sought. Geertz regards anthropology as, 'not an experimental science in search of law, but an interpretive one in search of meaning'.[11] The difference is immense.

The difference between the quest for law and the quest for meaning has implications that extend far beyond anthropology. The distinction extends throughout the human sciences to psychology, sociology and history. At stake in this distinction is nothing less than the nature and reality of human freedom.

Geertz calls his concept of culture 'essentially semiotic'. Semiotics is the theory of signs, of how they signify and mean what they mean. In regarding culture as semiotic, Geertz is treating the artifacts of culture like a language. The advantages of this approach are several. For one thing the old debate between subjectivism (culture is in people's heads) and objectivism (culture is patterned behavior) seems simply irrelevant since language is so clearly both. Another advantage lies in the quick end-run around the closely related issue: is culture public or private? 'Culture is public because meaning is.'[12]

The greatest advantage of the semiotic approach to culture, however, is the light it sheds on the role of symbols in constituting the human condition. According to an older view, symbols, sign systems, language and literature come only very late in the human story. First, it was thought, we had to deal with nature. Only later could we afford to dabble in culture. It is mankind, after all, that manufactures symbols.

But symbols manufacture man as well. We *are* our marriages, our wars fought beneath flying banners, our oaths cast in blood and language. We *are* the results of our dedications to our symbols. Human beings are unique among animals for this self-making evolutionary creativity that takes place alongside of strictly biological evolution. 'What this means is that culture, rather than being added on, so to speak, to a finished or virtually finished animal, was ingredient, and centrally ingredient, in the production of that animal himself.'[13] Our physical and cultural evolution is thus a kind of mutual bootstrapping operation in which nature and culture are interwoven into the web of meaning.

One hope of social science, to know the nature of man so well that optimal living arrangements could be computed, is a naive hope if Geertz is right. If cultures are objects for interpretation rather than calculation under laws, then the study of culture is endless. There is no hope of a definitive answer to the nature of human culture. It is always and forever up for grabs, ever subject to new creation through reinterpretation of what has become old.

Geertz tells a story, heard elsewhere in connection with William James. It is an old story that reappears here in the form of an Indian tale told to an Englishman who is asked to believe that the world rests on a platform which rests on the back of an elephant which rests in turn on the back of a turtle. When the English gentleman persists with the question as to what the turtle rests on, he is told, *another turtle*. And after that? 'Ah, Sahib, after that it is turtles all the way down.'[14]

So it now appears for the human sciences, with anthropology among them: *interpretations all the way down*. 'The fact is that to commit oneself to a semiotic concept of culture and an interpretive approach to the study of it is to commit oneself to a view of ethnographic assertion, as, to borrow W.B. Gallie's by now famous phrase, "essentially contestable".'[15]

Will we discover that collectivism as opposed to individualism is the most natural, and therefore essentially correct ideology for the optimal arrangement of human cultures? No. Nor will we discover that individualism is *the right answer*. To say that these interpretations are essentially contestable is just to say that there is no foundational essence or human culture that is incontestable. On this and other issues, rival interpretations will continue to contest the proper reading of whatever evidence is brought to bear.

Where meaning is concerned, it is not a matter of converging on closer and closer measurements. Where meaning is involved, alternative contexts can determine widely divergent significances for the same physical entity, whether it be a bone or a pun. And what finally stymies the positivist is the fact that the divergent contexts are determined in turn *not* by some secure and single basis, but by other interpretations which are the symbolic products of an unpredictable human creativity. Turtles and interpretations, all the way down.

In his work since *Interpreting Cultures*, from which all the previous quotations are taken, Geertz has become far more explicit about the semiotic, sign-interpreting nature of anthropology, and about the contagious spread of semiotic methods across the whole range of social sciences. Further, he has become more self-conscious about the significance of this movement *as a movement*, as a change of approach (or paradigm shift) reflecting a broadly recognized failure of earlier, more mechanical approaches that tried to mimic the hard sciences.

> Ten years ago, the proposal that cultural phenomena should be treated as significative systems posing expositive questions was a much more alarming one for social scientists – allergic, as they tend to be, to anything literary or inexact – than it is now. In part, it is a result of the growing recognition that the established approach to treating such phenomena, laws-and-causes social physics, was not producing the triumphs of prediction, control, and testability that had for so long been promised in its name.[16]

While the shift of method in anthropology is in part a function of the failure of the older laws-and-causes approach, it is in part also a function of a new blurring of disciplinary boundaries. Once upon a time, the articulation of different academic disciplines – mathematics, English, anthropology, sociology, and so on – was thought to represent much more than arbitrary conveniences erected for purposes of university administrators. The different disciplines were thought to represent the different branches of a naturalistic tree of knowledge. The differences between the disciplines rested, it seemed, on real differences in the world, like the differences between sheep and goats, or the organic and the inorganic, or the human and historical as opposed to the eternal laws of nature and mathematics.

In recent years, these lines between the disciplines have come to seem increasingly arbitrary, and it is this phenomenon within the working lives of researchers that is the subject of Geertz's opening essay in *Local Knowledge*, 'Blurred Genres: The Refiguration of Social Thought'.

> It is a phenomenon general enough and distinctive enough to suggest that what we are seeing is not just another redrawing of the cultural map – the moving of a few disputed borders, the marking of some more picturesque mountain lakes – but an alteration of the principles of mapping. Something is happening to the way we think about the way we think.[17]

In place of the laws-and-causes approach, three different metaphors now vie with one another in the methods and imaginations of anthropologists. The first is part of the legacy of recent discoveries in the physical sciences: *the game*. Just as Manfred Eigen finds games with rules a fruitful way to organize the play of determination and chance in a whole range of phenomena from genetics and evolution to economics and the arts, so some anthropologists use the game metaphor to describe cultures and the structure of everyday life. Erving Goffman is one of the chief proponents of the game metaphor. His analyses of institutions' social practices are peppered with references to implicit rules, strategies and 'moves', as if all of life were an elaborate board game. But, of course, *we* make up and maintain the rules, rarely consciously, but always conscientiously in our efforts to 'do the right thing' in whatever circumstances present themselves.

The second dominant metaphor, one which Goffman also exploits, is the metaphor of life as a stage, society as theater, history as drama. The dramaturgical metaphor has the merit of being particularly apt for the handling of rituals – weddings, funerals, coronations, and all sorts of pomp and circumstance whose stagings give clues to what matters to a society. Consider, for example, the Super Bowl as the indicator of what counts in American society, not only the nature of the competition, the players and their coaches, but also the details of the staging or frame: the role of television, the ads, the half-time show, and the fact that more than 100 million viewers around the world simultaneously participate in this event, a larger number than those joining in any other ritual with the possible exception of Christmas and New Year's Eve, whose celebrations tend to be more localized and customized in any case. Geertz's own studies tend to the dramaturgical, partly as a result of the fact that one of his targets, Bali culture, is a society where politics is very clearly enacted through theatrical rituals in which to perform a role is to play a part.

The third analogy following *game* and *drama* as model objects for the anthropologists is the *text*. This third analogy is the one that draws Geertz's attention most, and it is the one that most clearly opens up the boundaries between anthropology and literary criticism.

When looking at a culture as if it were an interpretable text, one is hardly limited to looking at literal texts. Geertz is hardly interested in a 'textual anthropology' on the model of a 'textual history' based on the readings of important written documents. The point is to look at all the pieces of a culture – not only its texts, if there are any, but its rituals, its ways of life – as elements in a larger 'text' that the anthropologist interprets much as a literary critic reads a poem or a novel. 'To see social institutions, social customs, social changes as in some sense "readable" is to alter our whole sense of what such interpretation is and shift it toward modes of thought rather more familiar to the translator, the exegete, or the iconographer than to the test giver, the factor analyst, or the pollster.'[18]

In his conclusion to another essay, 'Art as a Cultural System', Geertz further refines his description of the interpretive anthropologist in terms that emphasize the reading of living texts:

> It is not a new cryptography that we need, especially when it consists of replacing one cipher by another less intelligible, but a new diagnostics, a science that can determine the meaning of things for the life that surrounds them. It will have, of course, to be trained on signification, not pathology, and treat with ideas, not with symptoms. But by connecting incised statues, pigmented sago palms, frescoed walls, and chanted verse to jungle clearing, totem rites, commercial inference, or street argument, it can perhaps begin at last to locate in the tenor of their setting the sources of their spell.[19]

Text and context; the event or sign gains meaning through its setting in its social or literary surroundings. And because it is *meanings* that are sought, not measurements, the physical particulars, whether the type font or the details of the headdresses, may not be as important as the patterns of relationships linking particulars and their contexts. These patterns are read as the literary critic reads a text.

2(b) IMPLICATIONS OF NEW ANTHROPOLOGY FOR FUTURES STUDIES

These movements in modern and postmodern anthropology – Lévi-Strauss's structuralist turn, Geertz's interpretive turn – suggest similar moves on the part of futurists. Forget about the laws-and-causes approach toward a predictive science. Focus instead on multiple interpretations of the present. This, after all, is what a set of scenarios amount to: alternative interpretations of the present as the first chapter of several very different narratives. Today's decisions and events take on different *meanings* depending on the different tomorrows that are their possible consequences. Contemporary anthropology has made this shift from a positivistic emulation of the hard sciences toward a more literary, narrative approach – what Geertz calls *thick description:* a story-telling approach that stresses the narrative relationships among specific details more than general laws or universal principles. Again, this is just what good scenarios accomplish: a narrative synthesis of many details into a story about the future that makes sense of the present. And there are always several such stories for any given present.

As anthropologists and futurists alike make the move from a laws-and-causes positivism toward a more literary interpretive approach, both would do well to turn their attention from the methods of the hard sciences toward the methods – or is it madness – of literary critics. For it is the literary critics who are the experts at reading and interpreting texts.

But how do literary critics read texts these days? In reaching from the physical sciences to literary criticism to find a better model for the anthropologist's (and, by turns, the futurist's) task, Geertz can only find more turtles, for the foundations of literary theory are no firmer today than the foundations of anthropology.

3(a) LITERARY CRITICISM AND THE LEGACY OF EXISTENTIALISM

If it weren't for the fact that Geertz's inquiries steered us in this direction, literary criticism would qualify on its own for inclusion among contemporary disciplines reflecting a paradigm shift. In recent years, a paradigm war has been raging in the upper stories of that vast academic mansion known on lower floors simply as 'The English Department'. Some of the generals in this titanic battle of paradigms are actually from departments of French or Comparative Literature. The labels over the door don't much matter, though careers may be made or lost depending on whether the main heat of the battle moves from one flank to another. The major point of importance, whether your battalion talks French or English, is that the rules of the contest are changing. The reading of texts isn't what it used to be.

Surely there have always been fashionable -isms to complicate the unselfconscious act of reading a good novel. From Russian formalism to the New Criticism (now quite old) professors have earned their keep by telling us how the text was *really* working in ways far removed from our naive following of the yarn. But in recent years, particularly since the late 1970s, the cries from the attic have become particularly intense. From the floors below the esoteric squabbles often sound like the unintelligible babble of people who have read too much European philosophy. But one ignores these squabbles at one's peril, especially when words drift down with ominous connotations like 'deconstruction'. The literary critics have ganged up in an intellectual wrecking crew.

Deconstructive criticism works like a corrosive against all pretences at systematic explanation. The corrosion process works at both the foundational level and at the upper stories of theoretical abstraction. At the foundational level, deconstructive criticism shows that the simple elements that make up a text are not very simple after all, that each sentence, each phrase, each word is packed with complexities introduced by the several different contexts at play: social, economic, political, psychological, to say nothing of literary and historical contexts. And if the reader should want to take a foothold in any one of those contexts, say, by taking the political context as primary, then the deconstruction operation moves to the upper stories where the status of, say, Marxism as a theory will come under attack. Deconstruction challenges the very idea of seeing the world as neatly displayed beneath the gabled eaves of theoretical hierarchies with their unifying abstractions at the peak of the roof.

Though the project might sound anti-intellectual, the principal workers make up a very literate wrecking crew. If they traveled to work in a panel truck, its sides might bear legends with names like Nietzsche, Heidegger, and the current foreman, Jacques Derrida. The program is derived in part from Heidegger's project, teased out of Nietzsche, for the destruction of the tradition of Western metaphysics. What might such a program involve? And is it really necessary just for the purpose of reading a text, or a culture, or a decade of social change?

Just as Geertz proclaimed in his essay on 'Blurred Genres', the story starts to get very confused when anthropology reaches toward literary criticism for help only to find literary critics reaching toward philosophy. More turtles. 'The penetration of the social sciences by the views of such philosophers as Heidegger, Wittgenstein, Gadamer, or Ricoeur, such critics as Burke, Frye, Jameson, or Fish, and such all-purpose subversives as Foucault, Habermas, Barthes, or Kuhn makes any simple return to a technological conception of those sciences highly improbable.'[20] Kuhn, of course, is the great promoter of the concept of paradigm shifts. But how have some of the others taken part in the destruction of the Western tradition of metaphysics?

Heidegger's contribution was, among other things, to challenge the idea of philosophy as a quest after timeless truths. Existentialism, a mid-twentieth-century intellectual fashion that owes much to Heidegger, proceeds from the destruction of the Aristotelian view that essence precedes existence. An acorn's essence is to become an oak. The essence precedes the eventual existence of the oak tree. But people aren't like that. Their existence precedes their essence. What they actually do, the way they exist, determines their essence, who they really are.

(Existentialism is, socially speaking, an anti-aristocratic, very American philosophy.)

This textbook description of Heidegger's existentialism misses the more radical implications of his writings, however. By hurling humanity into time, Heidegger also hurls human categories, truths, the whole human world into time. Even the inquiry into Being – metaphysics – no longer appears under the guise of a precious glimpse into eternity, but becomes an historically bound activity in which the questioner must ever question his or her own situation, the power of the past, future possibilities, the aim of the questioning itself. Philosophizing *à la* Heidegger is an enterprise fraught with uncertainty and anxiety. Any attempt to escape that anxiety prematurely by hanging the enterprise on the skyhook of some lofty absolute, or by basing it on the firm foundations of objective 'facts', will not bring the inquirer closer to 'the truth', for truth, according to Heidegger, is not to be found by building a stable picture to correspond to a stable reality.

'Being', 'Truth' – each of the super-tools that theoreticians use to construct grand models of reality ultimately faces the corrosive power of deconstruction. Being has been bent by the tradition of Western metaphysics into the distorted image of mere presence, filling space here and now. The Cartesian view of the world through the cross-hatched lens of the Cartesian coordinate system turns time into just another dimension of a space whose every volume is the same as every other. The map for representing reality within the Cartesian coordinate system – graph paper – was supposed to assist in the picturing of reality; instead it became the model of the reality to be pictured. Time is leveled out onto the endless, meaningless moments whose tedium is captured by T. S. Eliot in 'The Love Song of J. Alfred Prufrock': 'I have measured out my life with coffee spoons.' One square block of Cartesian time is pretty much like another, and Being, reduced to presence in that time, is a dull business. Its model is matter, a bare, characterless substratum in which attributes coalesce to form things with shapes and boundaries.

The austere Cartesian metaphysics of matter and space and a spatialized time has very little in it of what Heidegger recognized in the writings of the Greek philosophers. There he saw a dynamic swarming of process and possibility, and an immersion of man in his environment quite different from the spectral distance assumed by later theoreticians. The separation of form from matter was all of a piece with the separation of observing subject from observed object. Descartes' separation of mind from matter has its roots in both an epistemology that separates knower from known, and in an ontology that separates Being from beings. For Heidegger, and for the pre-Socratic philosophers in which he claimed to find intimations of a livelier reality, these separations were less than tidy.

Being is not settled and measurable for Heidegger. The words we would use to describe Being are bound to reduce it to a mere presence that can be delimited on all sides. How to reveal the truth of Being when the usual tools of truth telling – words – are each matched with an attribute or property? If Being is that in which properties and attributes reside, but is not a property or attribute in itself, then words for properties and attributes will inevitably miss the mark.

Heidegger reflects on language, as does Wittgenstein. For both of these pre-eminent twentieth-century philosophers, the central drama of their philosophical careers consists in a constant struggle against the limitations of the tools of their trade: words. The early Wittgenstein thought through the old picture of language to its end. He hypothesized an ideal language, one for which true propositions would picture the facts. The later Wittgenstein deconstructs each part of that simple correspondence theory of truth: the form of the proposition, the relationship of perfect correspondence, and the givenness of so-called facts. Propositions need linguistic contexts in order to mean anything at all. Correspondence is often ambiguous: what geometric laws would prove the correspondence between 'Old Glory' and 'the Stars and Stripes'? Finally, 'the facts' don't come in the tidy bundles assumed by Wittgenstein's early *Tractatus*. Instead, our presuppositions and expectations always bend our selection of what is to count as 'the facts'.

Like Wittgenstein, Heidegger, too, challenged the simple correspondence theory of truth. Both tried to liberate themselves and their readers from the objectivist illusion that metaphor is a second-best way to represent reality. The very idea of a reality simply present behind our metaphors and linguistic attempts to picture, the very idea of an essence beneath existence, begins to crumble.

This mighty triumvirate of Nietzsche, Heidegger and Wittgenstein confronts the twentieth century with the disturbing news that the whole rationalist enlightenment, with its scientific triumphs and its philosophical systems, may rest on some drastic misunderstandings about the relationships between human inquirers, language, and the reality that inquiry would describe and explain with language and mathematics. These philosophers see their domain not as an inner sanctum of eternal truths to be sought by Promethean scientists and borne back to mortal men in pictures made with words and numbers. Instead, they see philosophy as, in large part, a matter of undoing the damage done by mistaking linguistic pictures for the reality they would represent – including those linguistic pictures that picture the relationships between speakers, language, and whatever is to be represented.

The later Wittgenstein rejects the whole picture theory of truth. The later Heidegger trades in the relatively professorial tone of his earlier tracts for an increasingly rhapsodic prose that evokes more than it pictures or describes. Poetry becomes the paradigm for a language that remains true to itself only by creating itself ever anew with neologisms and unexpected combinations. For the expected is always false to the unfolding of novelty that is non-Cartesian time.

The critique of static pictures of a static presence that follows from these reflections on being, time and truth has been extended from philosophy into literary criticism, where the mighty triumvirate are read more eagerly than in Anglo-American philosophy departments, where the news was too bad to be taken seriously. Most academic philosophers simply chose finer, harder pencils to draw their pictures with greater, if more specious, precision. Literary critics, less interested in precise truth to begin with, were more open to a frontal attack on aspirations to literal portraiture. After all, modern art had already shown the way to break free of literal representation. Perhaps the truth was to be found in fiction!

The corrosive force of deconstruction came into play against the calmly assumed categories of earlier critics. Categories like 'author', 'reader', 'text', might not be quite as grand as 'Being', but they were grand enough to assume a reified solidity in need of deconstruction.

In what seems at first more a pun than an argument, Edward Said deconstructs the *authority* of the *author*: 'authority is nomadic: it is never in the same place, it is never always at the center . . .'[21] Therefore, an author like Michel Foucault (among those genre blurrers mentioned by Geertz) is necessarily concerned with relationships of 'adjacency, complementarity, and correlation, which are not the same as the linear relationships of succession and integrity',[22] the simplicities of before and after or inside and outside.

Foucault's analysis of intellectual history amounts to a kind of cultural existentialism: the course of a culture is no more driven by some logical essence than is the course of a free individual's life. Instead Foucault sees worldview following upon worldview without any particular rhyme or reason. He calls each successive worldview an *episteme*. He could as well use the word, *paradigm*. Whatever the name, the theme is the same: a preoccupation with the influence of knowers on the known, not the other way around as various materialisms or scientific determinisms would have it.

Earlier philosophers like Kant and Hegel cut through the objectivist illusion to appreciate the role of consciousness in crafting experience. But for Kant the structure of consciousness was fixed: only one paradigm for all conscious beings. And for Hegel the successive order of the forms of consciousness followed a rational dialectic, a process of unfolding that, at least retrospectively, made some kind of essentialist sense. Foucault, however, sees sharp discontinuities between the several forms of consciousness that he finds in the last several centuries of European history. There is no clear foundation, and no clear rules by which successive stories have been added to that foundation.

Under the influence – one might say intoxicated by the genres – of philosophy and intellectual history, literary critics like Said see a similar exile from secure origins in the literary tradition. Said opposes the situation of the contemporary critic to that of a critic like Leo Spitzer, who was among the last of those to draw on an orally received training in a canonical tradition of world literature and languages studied in the original. The 'dynastic tradition' of interpretation could tell you where and how to begin; but the dynastic tradition has ended. So the contemporary critic is set loose in a sea of competing schools where none lays claim to the legitimacy enjoyed by received learning in the old dynasty. The foundations are lost along with essences, origins and simple presences.

Said distinguishes between *origin*, as a kind of passive foundation, and *beginning*, as both more ambiguous and more active, much like the free choice of the existential individual. There is a sense in which we do not know where to begin, but must instead find out what we meant to say by seeing, later down the line, what we have already said. As Roland Barthes describes his process of creation, 'I begin producing by reproducing the person I want to be.'[23] So, for Said, 'Beginnings, therefore, are for me opposed to originalities, or to those ideal Presences whose ideal originality Yeats called "self-born mockers of man's enterprise".'[24] Lacking a clear sense of origin, whether in a dynastic tradition or in a sense of personal essence, we must be enterprising!

3(b) THE IMPORT OF RECENT LITERARY CRITICISM FOR FUTURES STUDIES

What Said and others have done to literary criticism has direct import for the field of futures studies in several respects, one of which is as follows. Once upon a time literary criticism sought to ground the 'correct' reading of a text by tying it to the originary intentions of the author, who was considered as a kind of all-knowing and all-powerful God in relationship to the text. A second phase, the New Criticism, placed more emphasis on the creation, the text. Part of the force of deconstructionism has been to demonstrate that the text is no less ambiguous in its meaning than the intentions of an originary author. Consequently, contemporary criticism now finds itself stressing neither the author, nor the text, but the reader. As the fog of French deconstructionism begins to clear, the healthiest survivor on the literary critical horizon appears to be Reception Theory, a school of criticism that reframes the goal of criticism by emphasizing neither the author nor the text, but the role of the reader.

An instructive parallel to these stages in the history of literary criticism can be found in three analogical stages in the history of futures studies. Once upon a time the study of the future was literally an attempt to uncover God's intentions. With the advent of secular science, teleological accounts of God's design gave way to scientific attempts to trace causal chains in the manifest text of physical reality. If the plot of the present could not be told by reference to God-given purpose, then the plot of the present could be completed by predictions of the future; e.g. today's struggle could be justified by dialectical materialism's 'scientific proof' of what life would be like after the revolution.

But predictability in the social sciences now lies in the dustbin alongside aspirations to unambiguous validity of interpretation via text-based New Criticism. In place of prediction, future studies might borrow a leaf from literary criticism and develop its own analogue to Reception Theory. As I shall argue at greater length in the conclusion to this chapter, scenarios developed at the grassroots by those who will live one future or another may fill the bill as a close analogue to Reception Theory in literary criticism.

Just as a text finds its multiple meanings in the multiple readings of its readers, so the present has a range of possible meanings. These are not to be interpreted solely by reference to the will of a creator God, nor by reference to a single future that could be predicted by a deterministic social science. Instead, the meaning of the present is a function of the future, yet the future that in fact unfolds will be very much a function of human choices based on several different 'readings' of the present. Both the interpretability of the present and the multiplicity of future goals and values introduce uncertainty and human volition into the process of history. Multiple scenarios can reflect both the descriptive and evaluative dimensions of uncertainty. Like Reception Theory in literary criticism, multiple scenarios locate the leverage for describing the future where it belongs: with the human beings who will 'receive' a future they hopefully chose. So we need to know more about human beings – the human factor and its influence on the future.

4(a) THE IMPORT OF PSYCHOLOGY FOR THE EMERGENT PARADIGM

Evidence of an emergent paradigm can be found in other disciplines besides anthropology, philosophy and literary criticism. Contemporary psychology is in ferment. Freud's metapsychology, with its echoes of a nineteenth-century physicalism and reductionism, is regarded as an embarrassment to be set aside by practitioners and clinicians. Developmental psychologists see a dynamic unfolding of personality that is not utterly determined in the first three years of life. Jungian psychologists engage in semiotic interpretations of symbols whose meanings are always over-determined – too rich in possible meanings to be reduced to one unambiguous interpretation of significance. Finally, the object relations school – Melanie Klein, D.W. Winnicott, Ronald Fairbairn and Harry Guntrip

– sees the self as a structure of evolving relationships, not as a substance or thing with clearly defined boundaries. Their theories and their therapies treat the development of personality as a succession of relationships beginning with the primary relationship between parent and infant. Just as structural anthropology turns away from the attempt to build a kinship system out of atomic elements and locates structure in the lattice of kinship relationships, so psychology no longer begins with the assumption of a self-contained, atomic ego, but regards the self as established – successfully or unsuccessfully – through its relationships.

This shift in emphasis from *things* to *relationships* is important. Its significance extends from the abstractions of ontology to concrete decisions about everyday life. In ancient philosophy, especially in the influential writings of Aristotle, to be is to be an individual, and to be an *individual* is to be a *substance*. Relations were regarded as ontologically secondary or derivative, as added by the perceiving mind. If A is to the left of B, that relationship depends in turn on the relationship between A, B, *and an observer*. Substance, on the contrary, was defined as that which is self-sufficient.

This Aristotelian ontology of self-sufficiency was rendered even more explicit by Spinoza, who defined substance as 'that which is completely self-sufficient and needs no other in order to exist'. It doesn't take a card-carrying feminist to identify the *macho* presuppositions underlying the ontological priority of substance so defined. Nor does it take a degree in psychoanalysis to see the import of Spinoza's – and behaviorist psychology's – attempt to reduce human subjectivity to a set of observable behaviors and properties of physical substance. The reduction of subject to substance, and the privileging of self-sufficiency over relatedness, are part and parcel of a positivistic paradigm that puts facts before values, objects before subjects, and matter before mind. Even as his psychology opened up the symbolic dimensions of subjectivity and mind, Freud's metapsychology – his tacit and sometimes explicit beliefs about what counted as science – constantly dragged him back toward materialistic metaphors for describing the vicissitudes of the unconscious. Especially in his earliest work – *Project for a Scientific Psychology* – he held out the hope of reducing all psychological explanation to neuro-physiological descriptions of electronic and chemical reactions – reductionism rampant. Like some futurists, he felt that he could never get a fair hearing for psychology unless he turned it into a step-child of the hard sciences.

According to nineteenth- and early twentieth-century criteria for what counts as scientific inquiry, psychology often comes up short. William James and Freud based many of their insights on introspection. But if observer and observed are one and the same person, claims to objectivity are likely to be tainted by the subjectivity of the observer. Where does fantasy leave off and reality begin? Is the child's experience of the primal scene of parents making love based on fantasy or actual experience? Freud vacillated on this very question. But how could one ever know if one has only verbal reports to go on?

In an effort to live up to the requirements dictated by the physical sciences, behaviorist psychology eschews the evidence of introspection. Only observable behavior counts as evidence, thus leading to the quip that one behaviorist psychologist greeted another with the remark, 'You're fine. How am I?'

The behaviorist rigor with respect to observability leads to suspicions about all 'inner' phenomena – not just how to describe them, but whether they even exist. The constraints of rigorous theory construction forbid hypotheses that cannot be tested by experiments in which predictions are verified or disconfirmed in laboratory conditions involving controls and repeatable observations of carefully isolated independent variables. These constraints drove academic psychologists ever further away from clinical therapy with complicated human beings, and ever closer to laboratory experiments with rats and rabbits, who are plentiful enough to allow statistical significance, and uncomplaining in their submission to repeated experiments. Meanwhile, clinical psychologists seemed to be relegated to the role of latter-day priest-confessors, or scientific charlatans.

In his review of the object-relations school, Harry Guntrip takes up the challenge of the scientific status of clinical psychology, but he does so very differently from the behaviorists. Rather than reducing human experience to an interplay of theoretical entities – instincts, drives, or the 'mechanisms' of repression, displacement, sublimation, etc. – his best defense is a strong offense. He challenges the adequacy of the nineteenth-century scientific paradigm.

After describing a case history 'so utterly individual and unique that no possibility would exist in practice of finding an adequate parallel case to serve as a control', he observes: 'Such a case points out a fact that we must never ignore, that in psychoanalysis science is for the first time challenged to understand and thereby explain the unique individual, and that this must lead to a new development in our concept of what is science.'[25]

The problem of understanding unique phenomena is not unique to psychoanalysis, of course. History has a similar liability in its attempt to become a science: no era, no decade, no war is quite like any other. Nor does history yield easily to testable predictions or readily available control groups. Yet events might be predictable and still add up to a history. The subject of psychoanalysis – a person – is in principle less predictable. 'In fact, the more possible it is to predict consistently exactly what a human being will do, the less a real person he has become, and the more he presents what Winnicott calls "the false self on a conformity basis".'[26]

It is tempting to retreat to the position that psychoanalysis is an art, not a science. A work of art is, like an individual person, unique. But the goal of psychoanalysis is neither entertainment nor edification. Psychoanalysis uses knowledge to achieve a particular purpose – mental and emotional health. Art is supposed to be devoid of external purposes, an end in itself. But in the last analysis the categorization of psychoanalysis as an art or a science is less interesting than the use of psychoanalysis as an example showing the inadequacy of our understanding of what makes any discipline an art or a science. Rather than trying to learn more about psychoanalysis by glibly categorizing it as an art or a science, Guntrip leads us to learn more about science by assuming that psychoanalysis is a science and then revising our idea of science to accommodate psychoanalysis. In dealing with unique individuals, he writes, 'We are dealing with a different order of reality, which cannot be dealt with by orthodox traditional scientific methods.'[27]

Part of the difference between 'orthodox traditional scientific methods' and a new paradigm for science lies in the stress on (local knowledge of) the unique individual rather than the laying on of the universal and repeatable. But part of the difference lies in a closely related phenomenon: the difference between reductionism and holism. Reductionist analysis sees the individual as an assemblage of separable elements, each of which can be characterized by permanent properties. Magnesium is always magnesium, and it retains its atomic structure wherever you find it. Likewise, a carburetor is always a carburetor and can be transferred from one automobile to another of the same make and model. But Alice's paranoia is not just like John's. Despite the use of the same diagnostic label, the treatments appropriate to Alice and John may benefit more from an appreciation of how their paranoias are different rather than the same. Why are they different? Because paranoia is not a precisely repeatable, unchanging element like magnesium, but a syndrome whose nature is determined more by its relational context in a given character than by some list of intrinsic properties. This is the meaning of holism: that the whole determines the part more than the part, through its intrinsic properties, determines the nature of the whole.

Working within the 'orthodox traditional' scientific paradigm, 'Freud did not start with the concept of the whole person. Psychoanalysis became obsessed with distinguishable aspects functioning as parts needing to be fitted together',[28] like so many elements or unchanging, replaceable parts of a machine.

Working within the emergent, holistic paradigm, both existential therapists and those in the object-relations school stress the importance of seeing the whole person before reducing him or her to an assemblage of syndromes, neuroses or elemental instincts.

Their holistic perspective carries over into their view of the relationship between psyche and soma, or mind and body. 'It has been assumed hitherto that mind (that which enabled the scientist to create his science) is a kind of secretion, if anything, of the body. But now we have to think in terms of developing psyche as the vital stimulating factor evolving a body to meet its needs.'[29]

Neither the body nor the so-called primitive instincts can be regarded as fixed elements always exerting the same pressures or constraints. Just as Geertz objects to the idea that culture is a layer of refinement that is added on top of more archaic levels of physical determinants, so the relational and existential perspectives object to the idea that archaic elements lie unchanged beneath newer layers of mental or cultural refinement. 'The equation of "mature" with "up-to-date" and "infantile" with "archaic" is a misleading error perpetuated by the idea of evolutionary layers of the psychosomatic whole. It needs to be replaced by the concept of an evolutionary whole in which every constituent is appropriately different from what it would have been in a different kind of whole.'[30]

4(b) IMPORT OF OBJECT RELATIONS PSYCHOLOGY FOR FUTURES STUDIES

This last sentence could be grafted directly onto a description of the way scenarios should replace predictions. Scenarios are precisely those narrative wholes whose logics cast each part into a significative context different from what it would have been in a different kind of scenario. For example, the rapid diffusion of computing technology may contribute to social decentralization in one scenario or to the spread of invasive Big-Brotherism in another scenario. Ripped out of context and viewed – artificially – as an isolated element, the rapid diffusion of information technology cannot carry its meaning or significance on its own face. Only by embedding that technology in a larger text or context – a set of scenarios – can its several possible meanings be explored.

Neither culture, psyche nor mind is added on top of physical nature or body or technology taken as unchanging elements. From a holistic perspective, in the evolved organism of psyche and society, matter is informed and altered by mind 'all the way down'. There is no fixed foundation beneath holistic turtles, no unchanging elements into which organisms can be analyzed and reduced for purposes of explanation and prediction.

5(a) FROM CRITICAL THEORY TO EXISTENTIAL SOCIOLOGY

To the extent that sociology uses the cultural and intellectual artifacts of a society – a culturally bound set of categories – to understand that very society, it is just as suspect as introspective psychology: do we trust a psychotic to offer his own best diagnosis? No, individual introspection is almost bound to be warped by the biases of self-deception. Often too much is at stake for an individual subject to see him or herself clearly. Likewise, subjective bias on the grander scale of ethnocentrism is the original sin of sociology: *thou shalt not use one's own ethnic customs as the standard for judging other societies.*

As a consequence of their suspicious origins, the claims of sociologists are often subjected to close scrutiny for tell-tale signs of self-serving biases. For this reason, sociologists have often attempted to be utterly objective and scrupulous in their methods. Knowing that they are stained by the original sin of subjectivism and ethnocentrism, they have sought to be holier (that is, more objective) than the Pope (in this case, the natural sciences).

For the founders, Weber and Durkheim, sociology was supposed to be 'value free' (*wertfrei*). Weber's studies on the relationship between religious beliefs and economics allowed a distance between the subjectivity of the sociologist and the object under study by using evidence drawn from a safe distance. Chinese Confucianism and Indian Hinduism could be correlated with economies and societies separated by centuries and miles from his own perspective. Durkheim's landmark study of suicide attempted to base its findings on cold statistics that had nothing to do with subjective variations among individual suicides. Behavior, not subjective intention, was the object of study. Hence there was less danger that the social scientist's own intentions would cloud his understanding of the object under study. Simply by seeking correlations between actual numbers of suicides and other objective measures like economic performance and demographics, the social scientist could seek out laws that might describe the past, predict its future, and thereby explain the present. By treating society as if it were an aggregate of atomic individuals whose contrary intentions average out under the law of large numbers, sociologists might discover certain valencies, certain tendencies to aggregate and divide, certain iron laws that would unlock the secrets of social organization just as elegantly as the table of the elements unlocked the secrets of the atom. Humanity, though an aggregate of subjects, could be treated as an object after all.

A case could be made for taking Boltzmann's statistical thermodynamics as the paradigm of science to which sociology aspired. Subjective intentions, about which the sociologist could make no truly unbiased claims, could be cancelled out as so much Brownian movement. Human thought is no more than thermal noise: random perturbations at the micro-level of society. Just as the behavior of gasses at a macro-level can be predicted statistically without reference to the mechanics of forces and impacts among individual atoms, so the behavior of a society should be predictable from some of its macro-level features without reference to micro-level human intentions. Thus the paradigm of science for sociology is not exactly Newtonian, not a mechanics of individual forces and impacts. Yet the paradigm of positivistic sociology is still thoroughly objectivist. Even if society could not be treated like a clock or other complex machine, its movements might nevertheless reveal a *statistical* determinism that makes a mockery of reasoned intentions at the helm of history.

Reasonable people tend to be offended by arguments that wrest their fates from their own hands. Consequently there has been no lack of critics of positivist sociology. The romantic reaction against positivism – 'Yes we *can* choose our destiny! We *do* have free will!' – unfortunately misses the point. Positivism need not deny the efficacy of intentions at the micro-level. The romantic reaction falls into a myth of subjectivism which, by its own one-sidedness, tends to keep objectivism alive – as dialectical antitheses so often do. By missing the point, by confusing statistical with mechanical determinism, the romantics offered the positivists targets for legitimate criticism. As is the case in so many paradigm wars, the parties talked past one another, neither side satisfied that it had been heard, neither side convinced that it had been justifiably criticized. In their eager attempts to find each other's dirty linen, they ended up taking in each other's wash.

As long as the romantic reaction continued to distance itself from positivism's insights as well as its failings, the world studied by sociologists remained divided by a conceptual Maginot line that separated the two camps in the ongoing paradigm war. As Richard Harvey Brown draws the lines in an essay entitled, 'Symbolic Realism and Sociological Thought: Beyond the Positivist-Romantic Debate':[31]

On the side of science	On the side of the subjective/ Romantic reaction
truth	beauty
reality	symbols
things and events	feelings/meanings
'out-there'	'in-here'
objective	subjective
explanation	interpretation
proof	insight
determinism	freedom

Any sociology adequate to the task of comprehending a complex society will have to integrate both columns. During the last several decades sociology has shown signs of moving beyond the old paradigm war toward a new synthesis that bears many of the marks of the emergent paradigm.

One of the crucial players is Jürgen Habermas. Heir to the throne of the influential Frankfurt School of Critical Theory, Habermas has achieved a subtle synthesis of Marxism, psychology and communications theory. Complex to the point of being nearly impenetrable, his prose defies easy simplification. But as is often the case with German academics, a good deal of the obscurity owes more to pomposity than to the subject matter itself. The basic insights are not all that inaccessible.

Habermas begins from a distinction between two kinds of human interest: theoretical and practical. Theoretical interests include elements in the left-hand column above; practical, the right-hand column. Human beings are not interested in just one or the other column, but both. Because our knowledge serves both sets of interests, the criteria for an adequate social theory cannot exclude either set of interests.

One of the themes of his book, *Knowledge and Human Interests*,[32] is ferreting out the 'hidden objectivism' in the works of social theorists like Wilhelm Dilthey, C. S. Peirce and John Dewey. Though firmly rooted in the Marxist tradition, Habermas does not save his criticisms for those outside that tradition. Marxist positivism – claims for an objective science revealing the iron laws of a dialectical unfolding of history – comes in for a thorough critique. After all, Marx was not a disinterested academic in search of an elegant theory. He was a revolutionary, passionately interested in the liberation of the oppressed. But what is necessary for liberation? Is the truth enough to set men free? And what *is* the truth about human potentiality? How can we know until 'after the revolution'?

Habermas grapples head-on with a basic riddle of human society: to the extent that humans are free, the object of sociology is to some extent indeterminate. If ever you pin them down under the glass of theory, what you've got is like a butterfly that cannot fly – or a humanity that isn't free. Habermas is acutely aware of the extent to which humanity makes up its nature as it goes along – and must continue to do so.

What is necessary to assure social freedom? For Habermas the answer is an unconstrained exchange of ideas: 'undistorted communication', to use Habermas's often repeated phrase. Call it freedom of speech – an important if not very novel idea. But Habermas's attention to the free-flowing exchange of ideas marks an important break in a Marxist tradition that had often discounted the autonomous power of ideas.

Marxism has often fallen into its own form of positivism – a belief that the objective world of economics determines everything in human experience. As Marx himself wrote in *The German Ideology*, in a passage that directly contests the significance of paradigms in general: 'The production of ideas, of conceptions, of consciousness is at first directly interwoven with the material activity and the material intercourse of men, the language of real life. Conceiving, thinking, the mental intercourse of men appear at this stage as the direct efflux of their material behavior.'[33] Lest there be any doubt about the reach of this proclamation, Marx goes on to add: 'Morality, religion, metaphysics, all the rest of ideology and their corresponding forms of consciousness [for example, paradigms] no longer retain the semblance of independence. They have no history, no development; but men, developing their material production and their material intercourse, alter, along with this their real existence, their thinking, and the products of their thinking.'[34] Finally, in an oft quoted sentence that leaves no mistake about the order of causality between the objective and the subjective, 'Life is not determined by consciousness, but consciousness by life.'[35]

Against this solid foundation of economic determinism underlying the entire Marxist tradition, Habermas has taken pains to acknowledge two related points. First, that epistemology is important: the theory of knowledge, the dynamics of consciousness, cannot be ignored in the name of a science that could deduce consciousness from a science of objects, whether that science calls itself psychology, economics, sociology, or some combination of the above. None of these theoretical descriptions of objects can fully capture the choices of subjects. The categories and applications of these disciplines are themselves partly a function of individual and collective choices made by subjects to serve their practical as well as their theoretical interests. In other words, there is always something at stake. So-called disinterested inquiry always serves some interests. Habermas acknowledges the original sin of sociology as inescapable. Marxists have no special dispensation or claim to redemption.

Second, just as the life of the individual or the research of some limited intellectual community is always tainted by the interests and predispositions that color its consciousness, so the policies that guide nations are not purely the result of economic determinism. This, Habermas argues, is more true today than ever. Governments now play an active role in manipulating the economy: through tax policies, tariffs, monetary manipulations and interest rates. Given the extent to which ideas like Keynesian economics or supply-side economics are used to steer the economy, it seems a little backward to say that the forces and relations of production work as independent variables driving the production of ideas. The evolution of consciousness may be very much influenced by economics, but the economy is likewise directed by ideas. Hence, according to Habermas, the importance of a free and unconstrained exchange of ideas.

To put it in a polysyllabic nutshell that captures the relation between these two central points in Habermas's thinking: *social policy is the public epistemology underlying economic policy.* To unpack: liberating the oppressed is not just a matter of taking from the rich and giving to the poor. It is instead a matter of increasing the degree of truly human self-consciousness in society so that each individual and society as a whole make the kinds of choices that serve the human interests of each individual and society as a whole. An individual compelled by an obsession or compulsion to make certain 'choices' is not a free individual, rich or poor.

Likewise, a society driven by economic or technological imperatives is not a free society. Both in the case of the individual and in the case of society, *deliberation among options is a characteristic of freedom.* But social deliberation is no more free than the individual deliberation of a psychotic if social deliberation is compelled by some overriding, determining force.

What the fetish is to the obsessed individual, some comparably unquestioned object of desire might be to a society. If a society forbids an exchange of ideas about some social goal – whether the MX missile, AIDS, or racial equality – then the behavior of that society turns out to be just as compulsive, just as unfree, as the obsessed individual's.

To the extent that sociologists like Habermas and Alvin Gouldner have rescued consciousness from its role as a merely dependent variable in the social equation, they have achieved a paradigm shift in sociology. Like other instances in the emergence of a broad-based paradigm shift, it is a bootstrap operation with resonances within resonances. The paradigm shift that accords more significance to consciousness is a paradigm shift that points to the importance of paradigms and their shiftings. Further, the paradigm toward which they have shifted is one that underlines the significance of thought in determining the course of the world, which in turn exercises *its* mundane and material influence on further thought (Marx was not *all* wrong).

Habermas and Gouldner have been labeled 'reflexive' sociologists for their sensitivity to the feedback loops that confound all attempts to describe society as a machine obeying simple, linear, deterministic laws. This reflexivity plays an important role in their thought about society. Further, it marks their contributions with the *self-referential* feature of the emergent paradigm, and does so with all the dizzying resonances usually found when one plunges into the hall of mirrors that modern consciousness has become. Reflexive sociology has forsworn firm foundations.

The main point of distinguishing practical from theoretical interests is to acknowledge that we are (or at least can be) free to choose what we are. Objective, theoretical science does not have the last word when it comes to humanity. We are (or can be) a bootstrap phenomenon. Always within the context of very real constraints, some historical, some biological, humanity can frame its own laws. This is a liberating lesson.

Curiously, however, Habermas himself remains trapped within several other aspects of an old paradigm, both in the form and in the content of his sociological research. Its form is very much the model of scholarly, abstract, and – ironically – highly distorted communication. He's almost unreadable. Further, the content supports an unproven assumption of universal laws underlying language and communication. Like Lévi-Strauss and unlike Geertz, Habermas seems to harbor the hope that just around the corner of the next research grant, someone is going to come up with the universal, unified field theory of language and communication, and that from that theory we are somehow going to be able to deduce the legitimacy of a universal ethical order. 'Tis a consummation devoutly to be wished. But if it turns out to be an academic's pipedream perhaps this abstract universalism will do more harm than good.

A new school called 'existential sociology' fulfills the need for an alternative to the universalism implicit in Habermas's extension of critical theory. In a series of books, several published by Cambridge University Press, a group including Jack Douglas, John Johnson, Richard Brown and Stanford Lyman are developing an approach that has all the earmarks of a new school held together and reinforced by a common paradigm.

Like Habermas, they confess their values, their interestedness in practical uses to which their researches may be put. But unlike Habermas, they will come out of the library and enter into the concrete situations they study. The paradigm case that best illustrates the impossibility of the researcher retaining a distance from the subject under study is the book by Jack Douglas and Paul Rasmussen *Nude Beaches*.[36] Imagine the value-free social scientist strolling out onto the southern California sand clad in the white coat of the laboratory technician, clipboard in hand. The phenomena under study would escape him or her.

The existential sociologist is willing to enter into the lives he or she is studying. 'Our emphasis on the problematic and situated nature of meaningful experience contrasts both with the structuralism of Alvin Gouldner's "reflexive sociology" and Jürgen Habermas's "critical theory"'[37] declare Douglas and Johnson. And in their situatedness, they are not afraid to acknowledge the role of feelings. They thus distance themselves from all of the more or less parallel distinctions between the practical and theoretical; between thoughts and feelings; theory and practice; contemplation and action; form and matter; universal and particular.

Richard Harvey Brown and Stanford M. Lyman pull together many of the elements of the emergent paradigm in a virtual manifesto issued as an invitation: 'Symbolic Realism and Cognitive Aesthetics: An Invitation', the essay with which they introduce a paradigm-defining anthology of essays by the school of existential sociologists. These statements deserve to be quoted at length, not only as rich *evidence* of an emergent paradigm; just as important, they are eloquent and original statements *defining* the emergent paradigm.

> In general, it might be said that the current awareness of a crisis in sociology focuses on three main issues. First, no available paradigm has achieved dominion in the discipline. Instead a plurality of approaches rooted in different and even opposed epistemologies, compete for regency. Second, none of these paradigms appears to have attained internal consistency with respect to its own ... assumptions. Finally, despite sociology's lack of preparedness, a host of moral and political

issues demand from it both explication and resolution. As in earlier crises, the task confronting sociology is complex . . .

Much of the writing in this volume is informed by what might be called a 'symbolic realist' or 'cognitive aesthetic' perspective. The two terms are not quite synonymous. Symbolic realism stresses ontology; cognitive aesthetics stresses epistemology. The first focuses on the possibility of our having symbolic worlds; the second provides criteria of adequacy for judging whether such worlds constitute knowledge. Cognitive aesthetics is not the romantic aesthetic of the nineteenth century, but instead a critical theory of interpretation and judgment that has much in common with dialectical hermeneutics and semiotics.[38]

What has been gained by allying cognitive aesthetics with dialectic hermeneutics and semiotics? *Dialectical hermeneutics* refers to a school of thought nourished in the tradition of Hegel, Dilthey, Heidegger and Gadamer, with or usually without a little Marx thrown in. *Hermeneutics* is the theory and practice of interpretation. To the positivist its importance is restricted to timid exercises in academic literary criticism or biblical studies. To those who grant a plurality of interpretations, each including slightly different experiences of the same (or ostensibly the same) objects, then the theory of interpretation becomes very important. Dialectics enter in with the play of *rival* interpretations – or *alternative* scenarios.

Semiotics, once again, is the theory of signs. The word came into use with the need for something broader than 'linguistics', which seems restricted to the more literal languages like 'English', 'French', 'German', or 'Swahili'. What about music, or fashions in clothes, or body language? The word *semiotics* also serves as a convenient net for containing syntax (on the relationships among the parts of a sentence), semantics (on the relationships between words in language and things in the world), and pragmatics (the uses to which words are put).

The fact that Brown and Lyman ally themselves with dialectical hermeneutics and semiotics marks their thinking as *perspectival* rather than objective. This next passage combines the exemplary with the elegant in stating and contributing to the definition of the role of perspectives or frames of vision in an emergent paradigm:

Thinkers from Giambattista Vico to Wilhelm Dilthey to George Herbert Mead have told us that man is the symbol making animal. Unlike animals that merely live, we have lived experience. The world is apprehended and organized through the mediation of our concepts, categories, and structures of thought. To say this is to say that all knowledge is perspectival. Anything we know is known *as* something; it is construed from some point of view. A library, for example, becomes a different object of experience for the accountant, the scholar, and the custodian. Likewise the rules of baseball define what will be seen as a ball or a strike, much as the rules of psychopathology or of sociology respectively define what is to be apprehended as schizophrenia or role conflict. In this view we cannot know what reality is in any absolute or objectivist fashion; instead, all we can know is our symbolic constructions, the symbolic realities that are defined by our particular paradigms or frames of vision . . .

[A] cognitive aesthetic framework draws attention to the central role of paradigm innovation in the development of science. Both the artist and the scientist, as well as the politician or citizen who is seeking to create a new mode of public discourse, are seen as having a basic affinity: They are creating paradigms through which experience becomes intelligible.[39]

Lyman and Brown not only acknowledge the importance of paradigms and their construction; they also see the inevitability of paradigm wars – the struggles between rival paradigms over whose map provides the best guide to reality. These paradigm wars are not mere academic quibbles. To the extent that their outcomes determine the very meaning of human and social behavior, they amount to titanic struggles over the future of humanity.

The practice of sociology, anthropology and the other human sciences ceases to be a disinterested study of distant cultures. Instead it becomes a poetizing of human purposes: whither humanity? Shall we become more like machines?

[T]he spokesmen for cybernetic systems theory argue that society is (or is like) a great computer, with its input and output, its feedback loops, and its programs; this machine – society – is in turn guided by a servo-mechanism – the techno-administrative elite. To see this imagery as a metaphor, however, is to reject it as a literal description, to unmask it as a legitimating ideology, and to provide a basis for criticizing its rhetorics. By doing a close textual analysis, it becomes clear that in the rhetoric of social cybernetics, there is an atrophy of the very vocabularies of citizenship, moral responsibility, and political community. In place of these, the machinery of governance, initially conceived as serving human values, becomes a closed system generating its own self-maintaining ends. The polity – the arena for the institutional enactment of moral choices – dissolves upward into the cybernetic state, or downward into the alienated individual, whose intentionality is now wholly privatized and whose actions, uprooted from their institutional context, are bereft of social consequence and deprived of moral meaning.[40]

Strong stuff! And their final sentence caps it off: 'Our recognition that social order is a construction invites us to actively reconstruct our worlds.'[41]

In another essay, Brown is explicit about the implication of multiple realities:

> Symbolic realism holds that all social reality is symbolic, including sociology itself. In the symbolic realist view there are multiple realities, including those of social scientists, and none has absolute priority over others. The task of the sociologist becomes that of describing these various realities, their structures, their processes of change, and their coming to be. Such analyses are not copies or blueprints of 'reality', however. Instead they represent a kind of decoding or translation by which the realities constituted by peoples are reconstituted into the reality that is social science.[42]

5(b) IMPORT OF EXISTENTIAL SOCIOLOGY FOR FUTURES STUDIES

Once again we arrive at multiple realities underlying multiple scenarios. Anthropology sought a foundation in semiotics and literary criticism. Literary criticism reached toward psychology in its attempt to grapple with the multiplicity of motives of both author and hero. Psychology explodes into sociology with the realization of the relational character of psyche and the importance of social context. And now, sociology, like the anthropology with which we began this tour of the human sciences, loops back into semiotics.

In discipline after discipline the attempt to find some bedrock of unambiguous empirical research, some solid objectivity, dissolves in a confrontation with ambiguity and 'essentially contestable' interpretations. Reality refuses to show a single face. Instead the world of human beings insists on being ever interpretable from different perspectives, no one of which can claim definitive priority over others. The old positivistic worldview, where the physical sciences played the role of secure foundation, gives way to a circular, self-referential process of inquiry where the *coherence* of several disciplines within a single paradigm is more persuasive than any claim to *correspondence* between a conceptual model and reality. For our models, our metaphors, our paradigms define what we take to be reality.

6. TOWARD AN EMERGENT PARADIGM

Having now hurtled through several of the human sciences in sequence, and having lain down their linear movements on the loom of my strategy, I would like to cross this warp with the woof of a few cross-disciplinary comparisons. This weaving maneuver will identify some features of an emergent paradigm that are common to these several disciplines. The point of this exercise, once again, is to guide the argument toward the outline of normative scenarios that cash in on recent achievements in the human sciences rather than trying to emulate the hard sciences.

The endgame strategy for this overlong essay is as follows: first, to abstract a set of features characteristic of the new paradigm emerging from the human sciences by following their woof across the warp of the disciplines already summarized; second, to clarify what might be meant by *normative* scenarios in an era when the very idea of norms seems suspect, or, at best, weakened by cultural relativism; and finally to sketch the outlines of a scenario that reflects the features of a new paradigm that is emerging in the human sciences and is also normative in a sense that can survive postmodern critique.

Since each of the features of the emergent paradigm has already been discussed several times and at some length in the several contexts of the disciplines that make up the warp, their review on the woof will be brief. The point is to pull the threads of the warp together by weaving this woof across the different disciplines so that a set of conceptual tools will be available for fashioning, first, a new paradigm, and second, a normative scenario. But the application of these tools is not simple or obvious. Indeed there is a danger of using these new paradigm tools in an old paradigm way. That is why, before their application to the fashioning of normative scenarios, there must be an intervening section on norms and values. Like our understanding of the structures relating facts to one another, our understanding of values is also subject to paradigm change.

Here, then, is a short list of features of a new paradigm emerging from the human sciences, together with some hypotheses about what these features *might* imply for a normative scenario. As we shall see in the next section on a new approach to the normative, these first hypotheses can be misleading. Not until the final section will the true import of these features be fully evident.

1. The semiotic turn

Geertz described anthropology as a semiotic discipline in search of meaning, not a science in search of laws and explanations. Philosophers, particularly Richard Rorty, speak of the linguistic turn in characterizing the significance of Wittgenstein and Heidegger. But Roland Barthes and Michel Foucault apply the tools of linguistic analysis to a wider domain of signs than words alone. Likewise psychologists have liberated themselves from Freud's materialistic meta-psychology to give full weight to Freud's real contribution: his emphasis on the power of symbols. Finally, existential sociology embraces a 'symbolic realism' that accords efficacy and power to symbols. In each of the disciplines reviewed we see a turn away from a materialistic ontology that would reduce symbols to the role of epiphenomena – pale reflections of material presences following physical laws. In each of these disciplines there is an acknowledgment of the way symbols can motivate action without relying on a reduction to physicalistic causes to account for their efficacy.

The simple but wrong application of the semiotic turn to normative scenarios might run as follows: as opposed to a nominalist reduction of norms to mere conventions of speech, we can now depend on norms that are resistant to nominalistic reduction. We can identify symbols of values that transcend mere conventions. We can locate standards for the Good, the True and the Beautiful in a semiotic order that replaces Plato's realm of Ideas as the locus of normative standards.

Just as I earlier declined the temptation to build the edifice of future studies out of towering stalagmites based on the purportedly firm foundations of the hard sciences, so I now hesitate to hang futures studies on a series of normative stalactites reaching down from the lofty heights of some transcendent order, whether semiotic or idealistic. For it is the achievement of recent studies in semiotics to show that *we have no independent access to a transcendent signified beyond the signifiers*. Instead the distinction between signified and signifiers is a 'floating' distinction. Each signified becomes a signifier of some further signified. The distinction between signifier and signified is real and useful in particular cases, but when you press for an ultimate signified, Sahib, it's signifiers all the way out. So the Semiotic Turn should not be used in the service of some new idealism that would substitute language for Platonic Ideas.

2. Difference over identity

Geertz invites us 'to look for systematic relationships among diverse phenomena, not for substantive identities among similar ones'. He is less interested in what we all share than in how we differ. Likewise linguists are less interested in the identities that abide through the evolutionary changes traced by diachronic etymologies than in the differences that define the synchronic structure of a language at a particular point in time. Words mean what they mean, not by virtue of some one-to-one link between self-identical symbol and self-identical thing. Rather, words mean what they mean by virtue of the usage-place they maintain in a structure of differences, the lattice-work of an entire language. In Guntrip's review of the object relations school of psychologists, he criticized Freud's preoccupation with universals. Instead he focused on the differences that make each individual unique. Finally, in the symbolic realist view of existential sociology, 'there are multiple realities, including those of social scientists, and none has absolute priority over others'.

At the risk of engaging at a level of abstraction that fades off into the vacuous, I cannot resist a very simple observation. Physical things impress us with their self-contained identity. Apples, rocks, chairs, tables – all the pieces of furniture of the physical world – come in clearly contained bundles with definable borders. Identity is easy for physical things, and to the extent that we are preoccupied with physical things, we take identity as a tacit criterion of existence. To be is to be a clearly identifiable individual. When it comes to symbols, however, identity – and therefore ontological status – is less obvious. What about the number 3? Or Beethoven's Fifth Symphony? Or the gross national product? Or the cause of the Civil War? Philosophers wax scholastic about such things just because categories like identity, borrowed from a common sense schooled on the physical, turn out to be inappropriate and hopelessly clumsy when applied to such symbolically mediated 'entities'.

Just because there are so many different kinds of difference, and my simple observation abstracts from all those second order differences, I feel at risk of broaching the obvious or the vacuous; nonetheless, I think there may be a non-trivial relationship between this second feature of the emergent paradigm and the first feature – the semiotic turn. My very abstract point is just this: preoccupation with the physical will lead one to focus on identities; preoccupation with the semiotic order of symbols demands that one focus on differences. To know a physical thing is to know what is inside its boundaries: its shape, what it is made of, its material. To know a symbol is to know how it relates to what is outside: its grammatical and syntactic relationships, the place it maintains in a logical space, what it is *not*. As the linguist Ferdinand de Saussure discovered with his insight into 'the arbitrariness of the sign', it matters not at all what a word is made of, its letters, the ink on the page, the sound of the syllables. What matters is the pattern of relationships that differentiate the usage of that word from all other words.

This preoccupation with difference rather than identity in the semiotic order might also be prematurely elevated into a Platonic ideal for application to normative scenarios. We might rush off in praise of the organic and unique as opposed to the mechanical and the standardized. We might insist on schooling that treated every student as completely unlike every other. We might demand healthcare that treated every patient differently. We might oppose every attempt at bureaucratic standardization as an obsolete holdover from an industrial order that achieved economies of scale by stamping out the same, same, same from the drill-presses of the industrial economy.

As we shall see in the concluding section, there is something important to be gleaned from correlating the metaphysics of identity with the industrial era, and the metaphysics of difference with the information era. But an over-hasty idealization of difference will get us into just as much trouble as an habitual preoccupation with identity.

3. From explanation to narration

In each of the disciplines reviewed one finds increased attention to narrativity as the form of redescription most appropriate to the human sciences. Whether it is Clifford Geertz giving thick descriptions of the plots that make sense of the rituals of different cultures, or psychologists referring to archetypal myths, or sociologists seeking the meaning of social behavior in the contexts of stories with beginnings, middles and ends, the importance of story, plot and narration is now recognized well beyond the boundaries of literary criticism where it was always acknowledged. Among philosophers probably Paul Ricoeur, author of the monumental three-volume *Time and Narrative*,[43] has done most to show how narration does a better job of capturing the meaning of human actions than explanations that would reduce those actions to the interactions of simpler elements described by the hard sciences.

The implication of narrativity for normative scenarios is obvious: scenarios are narrations with beginnings, middles and ends. Narrativity distinguishes scenarios from predictions, which merely give a state description at some future date. This implication is so straightforward it need not wait for a subtler development after the next section's new look at norms. The narrativity of scenarios isn't something that will be added after an appreciation of new developments in the human sciences. Narrativity is essential to scenarios. The human sciences are emulating those futurists who use scenarios to the extent that the human sciences embrace narrativity. Here we have a clear instance of the potential irony mentioned in the introduction: what a shame it would be if futurists decamped in the direction of the explanatory hard sciences just as reinforcements were arriving from the human sciences bearing justifications for story-telling.

4. The fall into time

Once upon a time there was no sense of historical time. Aristotle regarded the number of species as fixed for all eternity. Neither Platonic Forms nor Aristotelian species were subject to change and evolution. The very idea of historical progress was an invention of thinkers like Vico and Herder. Then Darwin altered the place of humanity in nature. But still the hard sciences followed the paradigm of mathematics: just as two plus two always and everywhere equals four, so the truths discovered by physics and chemistry should be true for all time.

The principal figures discussed – Hegel, Nietzsche, Heidegger, Wittgenstein, Foucault, T. S. Kuhn – transport us *from* a world where we could plant our feet firmly on the ground of foundations laid in the concrete of scientific materialism, then train our gaze upward toward the fixed stars of timeless values ... *to* a world where we float or fall (in relativistic space it's hard to tell the difference) and never come to rest on firm foundations. Things change. Nations crumble. Ideologies that had been likened to religions suddenly lose credibility.

Hegel awakened us to history. Nietzsche and Heidegger worked out the significance of history for the individual: a certain amount of despair and confusion at the transience of things and their lack of a clear direction. Wittgenstein and Foucault offer different but equally unsettling perspectives on the semiotic turn: the realization that almost all of our distinctively human experience is mediated by symbols, almost never raw or immediate, always culturally and linguistically tinged and therefore never entirely innocent.

These lessons of the last century or so of philosophy – about time and history and the gradual displacement of the solid by the semiotic – leave us today just a little tentative about our commitments. We know better than to believe that we can catch a quick express called the Absolute. We know that the best we can expect is a local ride on the relative. The Absolute left the station long ago. And we know that we are likely to switch trains a few times before we get to wherever it is we are going.

Rather than suggesting new norms, the Fall into Time seems to undermine the very idea of the normative – at least to the extent than norms are thought to transcend mere fashions. The Fall into Time and the next feature of the emergent paradigm, the Democratization of Meaning, both threaten a Platonic commitment to timeless norms. These two final features of the emergent paradigm therefore make a transition to, and compel us to entertain, an alternative to the Platonic interpretation of normative values.

5. The democratization of meaning

From Reception Theory in literary criticism to communicative ethics in philosophy and sociology, the logic of legitimation is shifting from a dependence on transcendent norms to the immanent process of dialogue among writers and readers and speakers of the language. The *real* meaning of love or happiness or justice is not there to be discovered like diamonds or oil, trapped beneath layers of sediment just waiting for someone with enough intelligence and resources to find it. To a significant extent we are making it up as we go along. Human virtues are renewable resources. They are created and sustained by practices. Reception Theory locates the ultimate authority for interpreting the meaning of a text neither with the author, nor in an autonomous text, but in a community of readers. Likewise futures studies might draw a lesson from Reception Theory by locating authority over the future neither with God nor with policy-makers, nor with scientific futurists, but instead with the citizens of today who 'vote' through a range of symbolic transactions for the shape of tomorrow.

But this prospect of democratization raises a problem, the same problem democracy has always posed: *What if the people are wrong?* There is an abiding and intrinsic tension between the process of democracy and the concept of transcendent norms. To the extent that we surrender arbitration of norms to the will of the people, there will always be some aristocratic voices who protest a descent to the lowest common denominator. Ever since Socrates debated with Thrasymachus (who said that justice was the will of the stronger), ever since Thomas Jefferson defended the need for more direct representation against Alexander Hamilton's support for a more aristocratic Senate, the old debate between transcendent norms and the immanent will of the people has been with us under one rubric or another: the ideal vs. the real, high standards vs. popular opinion, norms (as ideals) vs. the normal (taken as median or average). Even the language of the normative is subject to this dialectical ambivalence. So let us turn to a more focused reflection on a new approach to this very old debate.

7. A NEW LOOK AT NORMS

In both a pre-modern religious context, and in a modern, liberal, progressive context, the idea of a normative scenario is likely to connote some common understanding of some transcendent values. In the pre-modern context those values would be derived and legitimized by reference to the will of God. What is good, everywhere and for all time, is what conforms to the will of God. In a more modern, secular, humanistic regime, norms are legitimized by reference to a science of human nature. The secular enlightenment substituted the universality of science for the universal reach of the will of a monotheistic God. In both contexts – pre-modern religion and modern science – there was a way to legitimize norms that could transcend the particular interests of private individuals or local customs and practices. There was a way of referring to a higher authority, an Absolute that transcended the relative perspectives of different individuals or different cultures.

But now, for better or worse, we live in a postmodern era. Part of what defines the postmodern condition is the lack of definitive criteria – religious or scientific – for progress toward a more perfect humanity. In place of the Christian heaven on earth we are confronted with a plurality of religions: Muslim, Buddhist, Christian, Jewish, and any number of other sects. In place of the modern idea of secular progress we find a plurality of standards for a more perfect humanity: feminist, multi-cultural, indigenous peoples, you name it.

So it's hard to name a norm and claim that it applies to everyone everywhere. And if a putative norm does not apply to everyone everywhere, then perhaps it is not a norm at all, but just one more custom peculiar to a particular tribe. Jews don't eat pork. Southern blacks like pigs' feet. WASPs cultivate the stiff upper lip, and so on.

To reduce the normative to the sociology of taste seems to rob the normative of the obligatory, imperative power that pre-modern and modern norms possessed. These postmodern 'norms' seem pale and impotent by comparison to the commandments of the Lord or the universality of science.

No wonder normative scenarios seem out of date. No wonder that reference to norms seems naive. No wonder that futurists are tempted into the bad faith of suppressing their wishes for a *better* tomorrow and devote their best efforts to worst-case scenarios. The pre-modern and modern sources for legitimizing transcendent norms have been de-legitimized by a more sophisticated recognition that we live in postmodern times when absolutes like God or secular humanism have lost their credibility.

How, then, is it possible to reconstruct a normative discourse after the deconstruction of transcendent absolute values? How can we justify normative scenarios when norms are essentially contestable? The answer, I believe, is by *entering the contest*. A normative scenario can articulate the force of widely accepted values without requiring either the omnipotence of a Lord of lords or the universality of mathematics. Norms need not be absolute in order to transcend the relativity of individual opinion. Norms need not be completely unambiguous in order to exercise some force of obligation.

Let me give some examples. There are legitimate grounds for differences over the degree to which a government should guarantee the welfare of all of its citizens. Yet some sympathy for the sufferings of under-privileged children seems to be a normal response of most mature adults. Is this because they feel constrained to obey some religious command to act as their brothers' keeper? Is it because some sympathy for other members of the species is part of human nature? It is less important that we prove the superiority of the religious or the naturalistic explanation than that there be an actual *experience* of sympathy and compassion. *Why* the experience occurs is less important than the fact *that* it occurs.

I lack a convincing theory for justifying the source of moral obligation. But the lack of a meta-ethical theory does not preclude the possibility of ethical practice. Having given up God as well as nature as foundations for values, I am well aware of the tenuousness of my grasp on morality. I have no knockdown drag out proofs for the validity of the norms I would invoke. Yet it is my belief – and it is only a belief – that the normative dimension of human existence *necessarily partakes of such tentativeness*.

It is my belief that what would count as a *better* humanity must necessarily differ from actual humanity in ways that are speculative, creative, risky, artistic, and never definitive or obvious. The gap between what ought to be and what is cannot be closed by the force of law or the force of mere familiarity. It can only be closed by a human will that could have acted otherwise.

Things change. Appeals to tradition are not always sufficient for invoking norms. Nor is it wise to throw out all the wisdom gained by earlier generations. It is not easy to improve upon the way life is lived. The lessons of history are not to be despised. Yet if we are to give any credence to *the fall into time* then we must grant the obsolescence of the Platonic correlation of the Good with the Absolute and Eternal. We must acknowledge that the price of holding onto that Platonic correlation is nihilism: we would throw out the baby of morality with the bathwater of absolute, eternal Truth. The only way to preserve the force of morality is to decouple it from a Platonic correlation with timelessness.

Now that we have fallen into time we must figure out how to moralize in time – how to find, create and maintain norms that are appropriate to the times. Rather than imagining that norms must derive their obligatory force from some timeless foundation that would transcend any particular conditions, we must see how the moral dimension of our existence is intrinsically tentative – stretched across a gap between what *is* in any given present, and what *might be* in a better future.

The definition of what would count as a better future cannot be read off from the past or from some great blueprint in the sky that would transcend past, present and future. Instead the criteria for what will count as a *better* future, like the criteria for what would count as better art, are bound to contain some reference to the recent past and present. Like all cultural movements, the evolution of ethics will depend on an interplay between individual creativity and an evolutionary selectivity that operates on a level that transcends the individual.

Knowing this much about the necessary tentativeness of norms, what can we derive from the recent past and present of the human sciences? What hints toward a normative scenario can be drawn from recent developments in the human sciences? The Semiotic Turn suggests the importance of *meaning* in all its ambiguity. Rather than relying on the force of law or aspiring to the grip of necessity, a semiotic anthropology shows us how the values derived from ethnic origins can be constitutive of meaning *inside* a given culture without necessarily having obligatory power over those *outside* that culture.

Salman Rushdie got into trouble by trying to straddle two cultures. As a Westerner he embraced the value of free speech and the liberty of the individual; but as a Muslim he committed blasphemy. He now claims obedience to Islam. It is hard to see how his piety toward Mohammed can be squared with the words that he has written and published so freely.

Most of us do not span radically different cultures in most of our day to day activities. Our values derive from the interplay between the norms of the culture we were reared in and our awareness of a larger, newer world that calls to our sense of concern. To say that we derive our sense of morality from the culture we are reared in is to admit a vast panoply of influences, given the range of texts we may have been exposed to in our formal education and the range of stories we have internalized from years of television and movies.

The influences that determine one's sense of morality cannot be said to constitute a well-ordered, internally coherent whole. We inherit a dialogue that posits the rights of the individual even as it posits the need for social justice. The dialectic of individualism and collectivism is not about to be settled once and for all, even after the demise of Marxist ideology. So Salman Rushdie's guilt in the eyes of Islam cannot be redeemed by an equal and opposite innocence in the eyes of a Western tradition preaching the right of the individual to free speech. For even in our Western tradition we acknowledge the needs of the collective and the demands it can make for individual sacrifice.

Am I arguing for the death of Salman Rushdie? No. I am only pointing out the *difficulty* of ethical debate across cultural boundaries. For those who acknowledge the cultural relativity of values, there can be no simple appeal to standards that transcend all cultures. One can appeal to norms that operate within and work to constitute a culture. But once one steps outside that culture, or tries to stand between two cultures, then one risks the betrayal of one culture for another. Once you become a cultural double agent, the rules become very messy – which is not to say there are no rules; only that they will often conflict with one another.

To summarize the significance of the Semiotic Turn: we now know that the sources of *meaning* to be found in the myths and values of a given culture can be called upon to give form and structure to an individual life; but further, we know that these sources of meaning can transcend the individual without being absolute or eternal. Norms can be obligatory and contestable at once. This is how norms *are*. They are not to be confused with will o' the wisp opinions at one extreme, or necessary laws at the other. The human sciences show us how to move beyond a laws-and-causes approach to human nature, and still hold onto the role of culturally conditioned *meaning* as constitutive of an individual life.

Literary criticism then helps us to read the text of our culture to determine the inventory of meanings that we can draw upon. By deconstructing the authority of the author, literary criticism reminds us of the shared work of constituting and maintaining meanings within a culture. Reception Theory reminds us of the importance of a literary selectivity in which readers participate in the evolution of meaning.

Critics are the pre-eminent *prosumers*, Alvin Toffler's term for proactive consumers who influence the shape of a product by making sure the producers know what they want; or, through the wonders of modern technology and information processing, actually participate in the production of a product by feeding their preferences into the design and production software. Critics have been doing as much ever since Milton read Virgil. Critics help to determine the shape of the literary 'product' of a society. But the rest of us participate as well each time we 'vote' with the purchase of a book, or contribute to an opinion survey, or tune in to a particular show on television. In the metabolism of the symbolic economy, we all play a role every time we engage in dialogue, read a newspaper, respond to a new movie.

As with the literal ballot box, so also the symbolic ballot box of cultural metabolism – the production and consumption of images – elects only those options it can understand and appreciate, whether candidates or referenda. Part of the role of futurists in this system of cultural metabolism should therefore be to articulate in an understandable and appealing way images of a better future. We need an antidote to *Blade Runner*, a foil for *Clockwork Orange*, a better sequel to *1984*, a truly humanized *Animal Farm*.

It may be too late to talk about utopia. 'Utopian' has become a pejorative term. Pragmatism is in better favor than utopianism. But there are times when pragmatism, the philosophy of *whatever works,* doesn't work. There are times when business as usual is doomed, when even incremental reforms are inadequate, when discontinuities are inevitable and radical alternatives the only way out. At such times it is irresponsible to refuse to be utopian, for only on the other side of a seemingly unbridgeable gap can conditions be once again stable.

Think of utopia as a new equilibrium, as a new constellation of the same old stuff, but now so arranged that everything works where before everything seemed to be at odds with everything else. Vicious circles turn virtuous. Think, for example, about the relationships between education, state budgets, cultural conflict, and the high costs of high technology. It is easy to see a vicious circle driving ethnic minorities further into poverty because they lack access to expensive new technologies only available to white kids in rich schools. Yet one can also imagine a scenario in which individually paced instruction software allows ethnic minorities to learn better than in crowded classrooms with inadequate numbers of well-intentioned but unwittingly racist instructors. After using the instructional tools of a color-blind technology, a more educated work force improves productivity, super-charges the economy, which pays for better schools with better technology for improved education of ethnic minorities ...

What can tip the vicious circle over into its virtuous reversal? If Reception Theory is right, the reversal might happen as quickly and easily as the reversal of figure and ground on one of the famous psychological tests like the vase/face diagram. Now you see it as a vase, now you see two facing faces; now you see a vicious circle, now you see a virtuous circle that is well nigh utopian.

But it sometimes takes someone to point out the utopian possibilities in an otherwise wretched situation. I have some friends, two noted futurists who shall remain nameless, on whom I can always count for the darkest of perspectives. They are experts in the development of worst-case scenarios. Once, upon seeing them walking down the hall together at SRI International, I saluted them as the Brothers Grim. I value their contributions to the list of warning signals, but their voices are too predictably Cassandran to be balanced or, therefore, trustworthy when it comes to anticipating some of the better possibilities.

Given all of the very real problems facing humanity today it is not easy to see how some of them might be solved. It is easier to see how what has been invented can come unravelled than it is to see how unsolved problems can be solved. It is easier to take apart something that exists than to build an incredibly complex working organism never before seen on earth. So it is understandable that futurists find it easier to draft devolution scenarios than to imagine transformative solutions that would turn vicious circles into virtuous systems of mutual support. In order to draft optimistic scenarios that are plausible, the futurist must be able to imagine solutions and inventions that no one else has yet imagined. This is a tall order that would require the futurist not just to hope for such inventions but to actually invent them.

I, for one, do not feel adequate to the task. I have no solution to the crisis of escalating costs for healthcare or declining standards in our nation's schools. I don't know how to organize an ecologically sustainable market economy. I have no elegant answer for housing the homeless or feeding the hungry. Yet I am convinced that if we futurists are to pursue our calling responsibly, we must try to imagine scenarios in which some of these problems have been solved so that we can then get on to dealing with other problems without engaging in the denial of deeply held values.

8. EARTH MIGHT BE FAIR . . . A NORMATIVE SCENARIO

Despite my own postmodern waverings between secular atheism and pagan polytheism, I am nonetheless drawn to the sheer poetry of the Christian hymns I was forced to sing in compulsory chapel at school. 'Earth might be fair and all men glad and wise . . .' What a wonderful idea, even in its sexist formulation. 'All persons glad and wise' wouldn't exactly scan.

Earth might be fair: the richness lies precisely in the ambiguity as between ethical and aesthetic interpretations of 'fair'. We could certainly do with a little more justice; and we could also do with more beauty, the Shakespearean meaning of 'fair'.

Imagine a world without lawyers, a world where disputes did not have to be settled in court because there were so many fewer disputes to begin with. Imagine a world where generosity and good will were the norm rather than suspicion and defensiveness. Imagine a world where all the resources now devoted to processing and adjudicating insurance claims were instead devoted to preventive health maintenance. Imagine a world where all the resources now devoted to advertising were instead devoted to quality improvements in products. Just as we are now learning to live in a world where the cold war is over and we can entertain the distribution of a peace dividend, imagine a time when we could entertain the distribution of a litigation dividend, an insurance dividend, an advertising dividend.

But what would all the lawyers and insurance salesmen and advertising copywriters *do?* What will all the soldiers do if peace breaks out in earnest? But is it any justification for existing practices that place a high burden on other human beings that the human beings who practice them don't have anything else to do? Let them play. I'm serious. Let me explain.

One of the problems of a postmodern economy is to find alternatives to the industrious productivity of work as a measure of economic health. What if we are working to produce too much of the wrong stuff? Throughout pre-modern and modern times, productivity was a legitimate measure of economic strength. People did not have enough of the basic necessities and we depended on natural science and technology to improve our ability to get more out of less in less time. But now there is general agreement among the techno-elite that the remaining pockets of hunger are caused not by a lack of agricultural capacity but by social and political snafus that leave food rotting in the field; homelessness is caused not by the lack of raw materials for dwellings but by policies that force foreclosures on people who cannot cope with the complexities of a global economy.

At risk of gross over-simplification I want to say that our most vexing problems today are not problems that can be solved by science and technology; they are human problems that call for a degree of social invention that we have not seen since the creation of democracy and the writing of the American Constitution. We don't yet know how to organize our human interactions. Some of us haven't even learned how to play together; or if we have, we've grown up and forgotten. Consequently we try to make up for a lack of joy by enjoying the material possessions that science and technology and the market economy can spew forth with abandon.

Take the nuclear family, one of the principal means for organizing human interactions. Recall poet Philip Larkin's famous line: 'They fuck you up, your mum and dad.' But they had their problems too: Victorian upbringing, a culture of possessive individualism that has evolved from what social critics called alienation to what a more psychoanalytically oriented critique calls narcissism – learning to live with alienation and love it by loving only oneself.

Surely there must be a better way to raise hairless monkeys. But what might it be? Maybe if mom and dad were less alienated, less over-worked, less tired at the end of the day . . . then earth might be fair. If more fathers and mothers raised children who retained a sense of wonder, and a sense of humor; if mom and dad could avoid the descent of their own love into squabbles over what he said she said about what he did . . . then earth might be fair. But until then we will remain locked in the same old Freudian/Frankfurt School family drama that extends from exploitation in the workplace to oppression over the breakfast table . . . if there is a breakfast table and not a staggered grabbing for Fruit Loops and Pop Tarts on the way to work.

Despite the wonders of modern science there never seems to be enough: enough love, enough attention, enough respect, enough dignity. So we make too much of the things we know how to make: war, toxic waste, bad television. Perhaps there is a better way to organize our lives and our relationships, one that does not pit the demands of work against the delights of love. Perhaps there is a way to reconstruct our world, as Brown and Lyman invite us to do. But in doing so we cannot base our reconstruction on the firm foundations of science. Nor will we be able to depend on transcendent norms as a measure of the better. Instead, like sailors rebuilding our ship at sea, we must fashion our new world from what we have at hand: our existing legal system, our existing healthcare system, our existing educational system, our existing families. So the job is not altogether utopian.

But let us not forget that radical change for the better *is* possible. Dictatorships in Haiti, the Philippines and Nicaragua *have* been toppled in the last decade – which is not to say that their successors are without problems. Real per capita disposable income in the United States *has* grown over ten-fold in the twentieth century – which is not to say that we know what to do with the money. Nor should we ignore real declines in the same figure over the past fifteen years for the lower quintiles of the population. Finally and most emphatically, the fall of the iron curtain and the end of the cold war must offer lessons of hope regarding other seemingly intractable issues.

I can recall spending a week at a retreat in Wyoming with a very brainy group from the John F. Kennedy School at Harvard, plus assembled experts like Robert MacNamara, Representative Les Aspin, and a former ambassador to Austria, all gathered in the early 1980s to entertain alternatives to nuclear deterrence fifty years into the future. I had been asked to help with the methodology of alternative scenario development. But in the course of five days of intense discussion I was unable to bend the collective wisdom of that group to entertain seriously any scenario that would contain less than 50 percent of the then current force structure over the next fifty years – still enough megatons to make the rubble bounce and render the earth uninhabitable. Less than ten years later we now take for granted what was then unthinkable to some very good thinkers. Surely there is a lesson here somewhere about the impotence of hope among intellectuals when confronted by the power of entrenched acceptance of the intolerable. We intellectuals would err on the side of pessimism rather than be accused of naivety. World-weary pessimism seems so much more intellectually respectable than even the best educated hope.

But I would argue – and it has been the aim of this chapter to do so – that the fashionable face of all-knowing despair is finally immoral. Granted, the bubble-headed optimism of Pangloss and Pollyanna are equally immoral. A refusal to look at poverty or oppression can contribute to their perpetuation; but so can an intellectual commitment to their inevitability.

So let us entertain, at least for a moment, a scenario that builds on what we are learning from the human sciences – a scenario that exhibits some of the features of an emergent paradigm. Imagine, if you will, a *sublimation of the economy.* In fact it is already happening if you can see it as such. The industrial economy of the production and consumption of material things is giving way to an information economy of ephemeral entertainments and services. This is not news. But the *interpretation* of this epochal shift in the way we earn our daily bread has not yet been fully developed in terms of the Semiotic Turn evident in the human sciences. Instead the slogan, *All that is solid melts into air,* has been interpreted, from Karl Marx to Marshall Berman,[44] as a lament over the loss of normative meaning that the process of modernization has wreaked upon stable cultures. But once we decouple the normative from the eternal, once we fully accept *the fall into time,* then there is a possibility – worth entertaining as one among several scenarios – that the statement, *All that is solid melts into air,* might cease to be interpreted as a lament for lost certainties and become instead an announcement of the advent of the sublime.

Sublimatio was the term the alchemists used for the process by which the philosopher's stone was heated to a point that it melted into vapor – air – without ever passing through the intermediate liquid state. Sublimation was later taken by Freud to mean the process by which erotic and aggressive instincts are redirected into the creation of art, culture and religion – thus allowing him, under the influence of a mechanistic-physicalistic paradigm, to then *reduce* the products of culture to *nothing but* redirected instinctual energy – art as so much smeared shit. But the metaphor of sublimation – and, like the alchemists, I take it only as a metaphor – can just as well be taken as an access to the sublime. When the mechanistic-physicalistic paradigm is shifted by the Semiotic Turn, then there is an opportunity for reinterpreting the efficacy of the sublime *all the way down* rather than reducing culture to the redirection of base instincts all the way up.

In talking this way about the sublime, I know I risk gaining allies I don't want. I do not want the support of New Age enthusiasts who think that the sublime is some esoteric realm that can be accessed by incantations, crystals, or yet another seminar on the Course in Miracles. Nor do I hope to please supporters of that ole' time religion. Virtually every form of orthodox religion – with the possible exception of Zen Buddhism, whose supporters deny that it is a religion – seems to me to be subject to charges of childishness, wish fulfillment, and an indulgence in magical thinking that is inconsistent with the real contributions that science has made to our interaction with our environment. Whatever religions may have contributed to social organization and psychological well-being in the pre-modern world, in our postmodern world their multiplicity means that they are in danger of doing more harm than good. We don't need more *jihads.*

No, the process of sublimation we are now undergoing owes little or nothing to an already completed, eternal sublime. Nor can it be reduced to a redirection of instinctual or material foundations. Instead it is a self-referential, emergent, creative lifting by the bootstraps that generates meaning *where there was none*. It is not impossible, nor are there any guarantees. This is the bane and the blessing of human freedom in the realm of the sublime.

Imagine a scenario in which educational reform was finally taken seriously, not as the imposition of some new religion on the young, but as the cultivation of human potential. The tools are at hand, but today we have not yet applied those tools in our schools. Instead we expose our children to teachers who are drawn from the lowest quintile of our universities' graduating classes. As they say, those that can, do; those that can't, teach. But imagine what could happen if education became the cause of the opening decade of the new millennium, much as civil rights and the Vietnam war preoccupied the 1960s, or feminism and the environment motivated so many in the 1970s, or greed obsessed the 1980s, or globalism and information technology the 1990s. It could happen. Social agendas do change.

If education became the cause of the 1990s, if teachers' salaries were raised and the respect paid to educators enhanced, then by the turn of the century we might be graduating students who were truly skillful, not just in the manufacture of physical goods, but in the creation and consumption of the sublime. And how much lighter on the earth such an economy would be!

The spread of industrial manufacturing to produce more *things* puts our environment at severe risk. This is not news. But only now are we beginning to see that economic growth need not be correlated with energy demand or the exploitation of non-renewable resources. In our work with one of the nation's largest electric utility companies, Pacific Gas and

Electric, Global Business Network has helped to fashion scenarios that show PG&E's future as dependent not on generating and selling *more* energy, but on building profitability by helping their consumers consume *less* energy. PG&E can sell what Amory Lovins calls *negawatts* rather than megawatts. PG&E can sell conservation and still stay in business. Paradigm shifts are possible, even for upper management.

Better education can lead to more efficient use of energy. And there are technologies under development that can help clean up the mess we have already made. Nano-technology – the technology of manufacturing at the molecular level – may be able to generate mini-machines that eat toxic wastes or transform them into useful resources. It is possible, according to Eric Drexler, author of *Engines of Creation*.[45] The possibilities were at least sufficiently intriguing to motivate Peter Schwartz, president of Global Business Network, to host the first international conference on nano-technology. Peter, by the way, wasn't paid for this task. He did it because he saw in nano-technology the possibility of a better future. He cares. This is what makes him a good futurist.

Bio-technology promises similar breakthroughs. Of course it is possible that we will release some horrible mutation on the face of the earth. Negative scenarios must be developed as cautionary tales. There is a Faustian hubris to scenarios that depend solely on techno-fixes. But there are some techno-fixes that will be required if this scenario is to advance from its beginning through its middle toward an end.

If this scenario's beginning depends on vast improvements in our educational system, its middle would chart the application of intelligence to many of our more or less technical problems: energy, the health of the environment, the health of individuals. There are feedback loops in this scenario, vicious circles that turn virtuous. Today too many children show up at school too sick and malnourished to learn anything at all. Tomorrow's students might be better fed, healthier, and therefore better able to learn how to stay healthy. It is possible.

It is also possible that the sublimation of the economy will lighten the burden on the earth that our industrial economy creates in the first place. *Pace* Paul and Anne Ehrlich, who trace most of the earth's ills to over-population, perhaps a human species less bent on material possessions and material consumption might be able to raise rather than lower the carrying capacity of the ecosphere. In order to contemplate such a scenario one must pass through a paradigm shift from a mechanistic-energetic physics of reality, through the Semiotic Turn, to the economics of the sublime. For only on the other side of that paradigm shift does one begin to escape the law of the constant conservation of matter and energy. So I want to return to the centrality of the Semiotic Turn as an interpretation of the information revolution, and to the fall into time as an aspect of our self-understanding of human freedom.

I know of no law of the constant conservation of laughter, or any limitation on joy. I see no reason to limit our sense of what is possible for the distribution of delight. These human *goods* need not be subject to a law of constant conservation. If I have more, you needn't have less. Quite to the contrary, there might be a virtuous circle of mutual reinforcement in the spread of sublime delight, like a ripple of laughter that gains momentum in a crowd. According to the economics of the sublime, there *can* be *enough* for all.

I know that this scenario is beginning to sound impossibly utopian, like something sprouted from the shores of California where the loco-weed grows. So I will hasten to add something about the problems that have *not* been solved by the middle of this scenario.

There is no universal understanding of the best way to live a deeply fulfilling human life. On the contrary there is a rich and variegated ecology of customs and mores. Further, there is a constant risk of *transgression*. Precisely to the extent that people have learned that *being good* is not necessarily about conforming to timeless norms, but rather more about exercising human freedom in the service of creativity and delight, there is a constant danger of decadence. For like creativity in art, creativity in life sometimes requires a bending of the rules for the sake of beauty. But not all novelty in art is successful. Some slides over into the decadent and ugly. The enlightenment rationality of the Minuet will slip over into Wagner, and from thence to jazz and rock 'n' roll. Next thing you know you get heavy metal. I love the Grateful Dead but I draw the line at Metallica. How is one to know where to draw the line?

There are no rules for how to break the rules safely, though *games* can be seen in this context as ways of limiting play to only those moves that are safe, moves that limit risks to contestants. The spread of human freedom means a spread of risk taking, and risks are not risks if they never fail. There will be failures, and there will be the need for means of insuring that failures are not too disastrous for too many people. Maybe we will never get a full insurance dividend, not unless we can avoid experiments on the scale of the USSR. Experiments in new systems of social and economic organization should be smaller, and fail-safe mechanisms far beyond my imagination will need to be built in, checks and balances to rival the inventiveness of the Constitution. For, as I've said, the spread of human freedom means a spread of risk taking, and risks are not risks if they never fail.

This scenario is not utopian because evil will not have been eliminated. On the contrary, the close bond between freedom and transgression means that some confrontations with evil are virtually inevitable. Though it may sound as perverse as Freud's uncovering of infant sexuality, I see the origin of evil in the play of innocents, in the horsing around that got too rough, in the joke that went wrong. 'I didn't mean it that way,' he said. The Semiotic Turn can end in tears.

Watch the play of cute little kittens and you will see a rehearsal for the brutality of the tiger. See in the tussling of adorable little puppies the vicious attack of the wolf. But there is no viciousness or brutality in the animal kingdom, really. The moral overtones come only from minds that can add an interpretation of cruelty to what, in nature, is a mere act of survival. It takes a twisted mind to turn nature's metabolism into acts of evil. It takes a Semiotic Turn to add cruelty to nature.

It takes a twisted parent to convince a child that he is 'being mean' to his younger sister when all he was doing was playing. This move is called 'attribution' among psychologists. It's one of the ways that mum and dad can fuck you up. 'Don't pinch your sister' is one thing. 'Don't be mean' is another. By the latter I may learn not only how *not* to be mean, but also that, deep down, I *am* mean. Innocence disappears so quickly.

So the very thing that renders the sublimation of the economy possible – the Semiotic Turn – also renders transgression unto evil virtually inevitable. Earth might be fair, and almost all glad and wise, but human beings will not be angels, and evil will not be eradicated.

But human beings can be more truly human, more free, more creative, and less subject to the uniform necessities of nature. We have struggled up through the realm of necessity and now stand, more and more of us, on the brink of the realm of freedom. The shift to an information economy, the sublimation of the economy, is the crucial instrumentality for this transition.

Precisely because the very nature of information is to differentiate, precisely because information theory defines information as a difference that makes a difference – news, not noise or redundancy – an information economy can thrive only where mass-market conformity breaks up into highly differentiated niche markets, even unto markets of one.

There was a fine match – a paradigmatic coherence – between industrial mass-manufacturing and the conformist values of the mass market. If keeping up with the Joneses meant having the same car, and the genius of the industrial economy lay in producing lots and lots of the same car, then the match between supply and demand was, as it were, made in heaven. But this match is coming unglued with the transition from the industrial to the information economy. As Arnold Mitchell, creator of SRI's Values and Lifestyles program, used to put it, the Belongers (we used to capitalize the names of our lifestyle segments) liked to 'fit in', but those who lead the new lifestyles 'prefer to stand out rather than fit in'. Individuation is the name of the game in the new economy. But individuation is (a) precisely what becoming more human is all about according to every wise psychologist from Jung to Eric Ericson, and (b) precisely what an information economy, as opposed to a mass-manufacturing industrial economy, is prepared to deliver.

The VALS program was all about charting the breakup of the mass market into segments or lifestyles that were not, strictly speaking, better or worse than one another, just different. But now the segments are shattering still further as individuals internalize the chaos of postmodern mores into the depths of their souls. There was a time when Achievers could be trusted to behave in all situations like Achievers, and Belongers would remain true blue Belongers, and the try-anything-once crowd, the segment we called Experientials, could be trusted to shop around. But now you see people who are Achievers by day and Experientials by night; ladies who shop at Bloomingdales one day and Price Club the next; men who wear black tie one night and a black motorcycle jacket the next. In short, people aren't staying true to type. A marketer's nightmare: people are becoming less predictable.

But this unpredictability should be cause for joy among humanists because it is precisely this unpredictability that we can just as well interpret as freedom flexing her muscles. The old shell of oppressive conformism is breaking. All that is solid melts into air? The constriction of Smalltown's norms for behavior is being broken all over the globe and, one by one, individuals are emerging from the realm of necessity – what nature or nurture tells them they have to do – and they are stepping forth into the realm of freedom. And a new technology, a technology whose essence is to differentiate, will be there to greet them.

This is where we will get the advertising dividend. The old style of advertising depended on broadcasting, a one-to-many communication that blared the same message, over and over again, at everyone. Stage two – the stage that VALS was there to accommodate – was the stage of the partial breakup of the mass market into segments. The first application of the information revolution to mass manufacturing allowed for shorter production runs. Economies of scale could be chopped into smaller pieces that, still economically, could satisfy niche markets. Advertising was then customized to tailor the right message about the right product to the right segment through the right medium. This was called narrowcasting. Advertise MacDonald's and pick-up trucks on Saturday afternoon network telecasts of the bowling championships. Save the BMW ads for the reruns of *Brideshead Revisited*.

We are still at a stage somewhere between broadcasting and narrowcasting, somewhere between an industrial and an information economy, somewhere between what I have arbitrarily labeled stage one and stage two. But a perfectly plausible normative scenario can be drawn for stages three and four. People, human beings, are pressing beyond mass conformity, and on beyond niche segmentation, to segments of one. Individuation. And information technology is capable of following them there. Computers are perfect for the task. Orwell's *1984* was wrong in this respect. Assembling and recording lots of information about individuals need not mean Big Brother's invasion of your privacy. Instead it can mean the careful tailoring of the traffic of marketing information so that I receive information about all and only those things that my purchasing behavior shows I'm interested in.

We already see the first signs of this transition, albeit in a form that any fool can see through, namely, the junk mail that shows up announcing that, yes, you James Ogilvy have been chosen ... But this is just the first adolescence of information technology at work. Stage three follows broadcasting to the mass (stage one) and narrowcasting to the few (stage two) with communication to segments of one (stage three). The American Express bundles of one-page catalogs are subtler than the mailings from Publishers' Clearing House. Amex doesn't plaster your name all over everything. But your bundle is not the same as my bundle. Computers have seen to that.

Soon, I don't know how long it will be, I will no longer receive the Sears catalog, or even more specialized product catalogs. I will receive the James Ogilvy catalog. Stage four: narrow-catching (a word Stewart Brand came up with). This is what American Express is trying to give me. They just haven't got enough information about me yet. But when each of us can receive our own personalized catalog, then we will be ready to distribute the advertising dividend. Then the offensive blare of persuasion will give way to the quieter hum of real information – differences that make a difference to individuated individuals. Then earth might be fairer when fewer billboards deface the countryside or the city skyline. It is possible. This is the direction in which information technology is taking us, and human freedom, I think, wants to go there.

Of course human freedom is very playful, even capricious. And as I've mentioned, in the play of innocents the seeds of evil and transgression are born. But as playwright and philosopher, Friedrich Schiller pointed out in his *Letters on the Aesthetic Education of Man*, 'Man is most truly human when he plays, and when he plays, most truly man.'[46] In our playfulness we will keep remaking human life as we go along, better and better for the most part, but occasionally worse.

The fall into time will be more widely acknowledged. Imagine a world where people were able to swim in the tides of change rather than drown in confusion. Employers will be looking for swimmers, people who can keep up with time's current. They are the best at coping with change. In a scenario where most people were comfortable with a certain amount of change there would be less reactionary insistence on the sanctity of tradition, and less certainty about the justification for punishing transgressors.

The democratization of meaning in this scenario will take the form of an evolutionary survival of the fittest interpretations of family life, romance, success. There will not be just one pattern of perfection toward which all would aspire in some recrudescence of industrial standardization. Instead the paradigmatic preoccupation with difference over identity will encourage differentiation and experimentation, if not transgression. There will not be one best way of being human, but a rich ecology of species in the gardens of the sublime ...

There is no clear *end* to this scenario just because embracing the fall into time means that there will be no finality, no goal which, once reached, would mark a conclusion. In this sense, too, this scenario is not utopian. I have not drawn a blueprint for an ideal society. Instead I have tried to reinterpret parts of the present – e.g. the information revolution – through the lenses of a paradigm shift already taking place in the human sciences. I believe that some of the phenomena that others lament – the decline of traditional orthodoxies, the melting into air of firm foundations – can be reinterpreted in ways that could contribute to a *better* future. But it is clear to me that this better future cannot be seen in terms of incremental improvements of the commonplace. A paradigm shift is required if we are to reinterpret the present as the prelude to a better future.

What we futurists must do if we are to contribute to the story is not invent a new paradigm out of whole cloth. Rather, we need only look around and see what is already happening in the human sciences. There we find the semiotic turn already accomplished, a preoccupation with difference over identity already evident, the fall into time already acknowledged, and the democratization of meaning well under way. What we must do is weave these threads into scenarios that have normative import, scenarios that carry the transition from explanation to narrativity further into a future we would like to leave to our grandchildren. Truly, Earth might be fair, and almost all glad and wise. We must just use our imaginations to spin out scenarios of better ways to play.

NOTES

1 Peter Schwartz and James Ogilvy, *The Emergent Paradigm: Changing Patterns of Thought and Belief*, privately printed by Stanford Research Institute, The Values and Lifestyles Program, report no. 7, 1979.
2 C. P. Snow, *The Two Cultures*, Introduction by Stefan Collini. Canto edn, London and New York, 1993.
3 Thomas S. Kuhn, *The Structure of Scientific Revolutions*, Chicago, 1962.
4 Carl G. Hempel and Paul Oppenheim, 'The Logic of Explanation', *Philosophy of Science*, 15, 1948; reprinted in *Readings in the Philosophy of Science*, ed. Feigl and Brodbeck, New York, 1953, p. 324.
5 Claude Lévi-Strauss, *Structural Anthropology*, trans. Jacobson and Schoepf, New York, 1963, p. 47.
6 Ibid., p. 50.
7 Ibid., p. 42.
8 Ibid., p. 203f.
9 Clifford Geertz, *The Interpretation of Cultures*, New York, 1973, p. 43.
10 Ibid., p. 44.
11 Ibid., p. 5.
12 Ibid., p. 12.

13 Ibid., p. 47.
14 Ibid., p. 29.
15 Ibid.
16 Clifford Geertz, *Local Knowledge*, New York, 1983, p. 3.
17 Ibid., p. 20.
18 Ibid., p. 31.
19 Ibid., p. 120.
20 Geertz, *Local Knowledge*, p. 3f.
21 Edward Said, *Beginnings*, Baltimore and London, 1975, p. 12.
22 Ibid., p. 290.
23 *Roland Barthes* by Roland Barthes, trans. Richard Howard, New York, 1977, p. 99.
24 Said, *Beginnings*, p. 380.
25 Harry Guntrip, *Psychoanalytic Theory, Therapy, and the Self*, New York, 1971, p. 177.
26 Ibid., p. 182.
27 Ibid., p. 193.
28 Ibid., p. 93.
29 Ibid., p. 37.
30 Ibid., p. 91.
31 Richard Harvey Brown, in *Structure, Consciousness, and History*, ed. R. H. Brown and Stanford M. Lyman, Cambridge, 1978, p. 15.
32 Jürgen Habermas, *Knowledge and Human Interests*, trans. Jeremy J. Shapiro, Boston, 1971.
33 Karl Marx and Friedrich Engels, *The German Ideology*, in *Marx & Engels: Basic Writings on Politics & Philosophy*, ed. Lewis Feuer, New York, 1959, p. 247.
34 Ibid.
35 Ibid.
36 Jack D. Douglas and Paul K. Rasmussen, with Carol Ann Flanagan, *The Nude Beach* (*Sociological Observations*, vol. 1), Beverly Hills, 1977.
37 Jack Douglas and John Johnson, *Existential Sociology*, Cambridge, 1977, p. xiii.
38 Richard Harvey Brown and Stanford M. Lyman, in *Structure, Consciousness, and History*, Cambridge, 1978, pp. 1, 2, and 5.
39 Ibid., p. 5.
40 Ibid., p. 6.
41 Ibid., p. 9.
42 Richard Harvey Brown, 'Symbolic Realism and Sociological Thought: Beyond the Positivist-romantic Debate', in *Structure, Consciousness, and History*, p. 14.
43 Paul Ricoeur, *Time and Narrative*, trans. Kathleen McLaughlin and David Pellauer, Chicago, 1984–88.
44 Cf. Marshall Berman, *All That is Solid Melts into Air*, New York, 1982, especially Part II.1. Berman takes his title from Marx's formulation in *The Communist Manifesto*, ed. Samuel H. Beer, New York, Appleton-Century-Crofts, 1955, p. 13.
45 K. Eric Drexler, *Engines of Creation: The Coming of Nanotechnology*, New York, 1986.
46 Friedrich Schiller, *On the Aesthetic Education of Man* (in a series of letters), trans. with an Introduction by Reginald Snell, New Haven and London, 1954.

Chapter 3

50 key works: a beginner's guide to the futures literature

Kjell Dahle

This chapter presents 50 key works within futures studies, dealing with possible, probable, desirable and non-desirable futures. It also provides information about what kind of background authors of such works have.

Some of them may not use labels like 'futures studies' or 'futures research', not to mention 'futurology', about what they have written. But they have all developed or converted knowledge in order to contribute to long-term planning, the formulation of visions, or social change. And that is what futures studies are about.[1]

The literature has been categorized, to make it easier for newcomers to browse amongst the rich offerings. The categories are: Classic introductions, Looking back – and ahead, Trends, Scenarios, Utopias, The world problematique, and Change. As mutually exclusive categories are hard to find in this field, the categorization will to some extent be arbitrary.

CLASSIC INTRODUCTIONS

Earlier chapters in this book have shown that the notorious 1960s was also the decade when futurist organizations popped up around the world. Futurists then started to get their own tools in the shape of serious techniques and methodologies. I will thus present some sources to the state of the art of the 'new' field of futures studies around 1970.

The dynamic spirit of new academic fields can result in good introductory textbooks. So too in the case of futures studies. Some books from the 1960s and 1970s are still among the best introductions to the field. (This embarrassing truth is, in fact, one of the reasons why the collective efforts behind the present book have been made.)

The Study of the Future. An Introduction to the Art and Science of Understanding and Shaping Tomorrow's World is a classic that is still available,[2] edited by the president of the World Future Society, Edward Cornish. It was designed to meet the need for a brief, readable, general-purpose introductory book.

Basic principles of futurism are discussed, as well as the American and international development of the field. Futurists are seen as persons interested in the longer-term future of human civilization, using non-mystical means to identify and study possible future occurrences. The book presents methods and case studies, as well as future-oriented organizations and the ideas of a dozen leading futurists. It was written with the broad assistance of members and staff of the WFS, and evolved from the extensive project 'Resources directory for America's third century'. Serving as a contribution to the US bicentennial celebration in 1976, this project was a result of grants from the National Science Foundation and the Congressional Research Service.

Handbook of Futures Research, edited by Jib Fowles, is another classic of the 1970s. It contains about 40 articles, mainly written by Americans, about various aspects of the new field. Among the topics are the international growth of futures research (with a broad survey of institutions, literature, and people associated with futures research), problems related to futures research (methodology, ideology, self-fulfilling prophecies, and values), approaches/methods, controversies in the field, and challenges facing futures research.

As early as in the middle of the 1960s, a major study was carried out for the Organization for Economic Cooperation and Development. OECD felt the need for an account of the state of the art of technological forecasting as well as practical applications. The work was done by an Austrian, Dr Erich Jantsch, and resulted in the classic *Technological Forecasting in Perspective. A Framework for Technological Forecasting, its Techniques and Organisation.*

One of the major findings was that, in spite of adoption on an increasingly wide scale in industry, research institutes and military environments, technological forecasting was not yet a science but an art. The development of special techniques was, however, found to have gained a great deal of momentum in the past few years. The book thus includes a thorough discussion of more than 100 distinguishable versions of forecasting, grouped under some 20 different approaches in four broad areas. Those are intuitive thinking, and exploratory, normative and feedback techniques. Like other basic terms, Jantsch defines them in ways that are still highly relevant.

The same year, in 1967, a quite different classic, *The Art of Conjecture*, was published in English. The author, Bertrand de Jouvenel, was the founder of Futuribles International in Paris. Educated in law, biology and economics, he worked as a journalist and author. Later, he became the first president of the World Futures Studies Federation.

Baron de Jouvenel mistrusted pretentious terms such as 'forecast', 'foresight', 'prediction' and 'futurology', especially since prognosis-makers are often credited with aspirations they do not (or should not!) have. He wanted futures studies to be taken seriously, and thus preferred the unpretentious term 'conjecture', stressing the uncertainty of the field. Like Jantsch, he regarded the intellectual formulation of possible futures (*futuribles*) as a piece of art, in the widest possible sense. By linking historical examples to current problems, the book shows the complexity and unpredictability of society when it comes to making models of the future.

The year 1967 also saw the first global conference of futures studies, held in Oslo. The meeting and its participants were used as a source for the book *Mankind 2000*, edited by the two main initiators, Robert Jungk[3] (Institute for Futures Research, Vienna) and Johan Galtung (PRIO, Oslo). Robert Jungk was a German journalist, researcher and political activist. He inspired the creation of many futures institutions around the world, both academic and non-academic. The Norwegian Galtung has a diverse background, holding university degrees in both mathematics and sociology, having worked in five continents, being an adviser for ten UN organizations and a guest professor at more than 30 universities. He succeeded Bertrand de Jouvenel as the president of the World Futures Studies Federation. Galtung's contribution discusses what is new in futures research. It rejects the traditional division of labor between ideologists who establish values, scientists who establish trends, and politicians who try to adjust means to ends. Futures research develops a more unified approach to the three fields.

In a postscript, Jungk and Galtung advocate an internationalization and a 'democratization' of the field, which should not be allowed to become 'the monopoly of power groups served by experts in the new branch of "futurism"'.

In the early 1970s, the thorough report *To Choose a Future* was presented by a Swedish Government committee, led by Cabinet member Alva Myrdal. Its task was to give advice on the development of futures studies in Sweden, and it turned out to be most influential.

The book describes a risk that futures studies will become the private preserve of influential specialists, thereby eroding the democratic and political element in the shaping of the future. Advice is given on how to avoid this, for instance always to present several possible futures. According to the Commission's recommendations, the Secretariat for Futures Studies was established the following year, attached to the Cabinet office.

LOOKING BACK – AND AHEAD

Time has passed since many of today's futurists became active, and looking back can be most valuable. Even for futurists. Michael Marien and Lane Jennings asked prominent Americans from the 'futures vogue' of the 1960s and 1970s to reflect on how the reality of the 1980s differed from what had been anticipated, and on what had been learned about social and technological change since the 1960s. The answers resulted in the book *What I Have Learned*.

Some of the 17 contributors focus on updates and revisions of their previous thinking. Others summarize lessons learned, rather than updating published thinking from a long time ago. Several acknowledge that predicting the future is harder than once believed. But they all agree that thinking about the future can be useful, not only in anticipating certain developments, but also in asking better questions and learning more about one's self.

The German futurist Ossip K. Flechtheim took his look back a little earlier. From his US exile, he introduced the word 'futurology' as early as 1943, searching for a logic of the future in the same way as history searches for the logic of the past.

History and Futurology (1966) is an adapted collection of this frontrunner's most important articles since the 1940s. He tries to assess the fate of mankind in the coming centuries as objectively as possible, and has been criticized for his belief in this kind of approach. Flechtheim, a professor of political science at the Free University of Berlin, is still an active figure in the public debate.

Rick Slaughter, the founder of the Futures Studies Centre in Australia, represents a new generation of futurists. He sees foresight in the 1990s as conscious work to complete the transition to a more sustainable world, while there is still time to achieve it. According to his latest book, *The Foresight Principle*, foresight is not the ability to predict the future, but a contribution to desirable changes.

A brief look is taken at the origins and development of the Western industrial worldview, considering some of its costs. The author sees analysis and imagination as key words for foresight, and discusses how institutions of foresight can secure better implementation at the social and organizational level. Strategies for creating positive views of futures with young people are also discussed by the author, who holds a PhD in the role of futures studies in education.

In their book *Zukunftsforschung und Politik* of 1991, Rolf Kreibich *et al.* analyze the development of German futures research, which reached its peak in the late 1970s. After a decade of low activity, they find that the situation now looks more promising. This new generation of German futurists has moved the focus from quantitatively oriented prognostics to more normative studies of desirable futures. Comparative analyses of futures studies in France, Sweden and Switzerland are included in the book, which is a result of a project financed by the regional authorities of North Rhine-Westphalia.

Far more critical voices than those mentioned above have also taken their look back. There has been a Western hegemony in futures studies as in most other fields, and the diversity and 'unpredictability' of the actors did not correspond very well with, for example, state Marxism.

Georgi Shakhanazov's book *Futurology Fiasco. A Critical Study of Non-Marxist Concepts of How Society Develops* is a translation of a Soviet work, published in Moscow in 1982. He saw the field of futures studies as a 'bizarre mixture of valuable observations, quasi-scientific nonsense, and anti-communist fabrications of the foulest'. Different approaches are discussed, but according to the author they all had in common that they 'in no way refute the Marxist-Leninist postulate that socialism is inevitable'.

From his Third World point of view, Ziauddin Sardar has a somewhat more elaborate critique of the development of futures studies. In his essay 'Colonizing the Future', he analyzes the evolution of futures studies, and claims that it is increasingly becoming an instrument for the marginalization of non-Western cultures from the future.

Even those futurists who are inspired by non-Western cultures tend to produce 'a grotesque parody' of non-Western thought, according to Sardar. His article was published in the international journal *Futures*, a must for anyone who wants to get an idea of what serious futures studies are about. Rick Slaughter and Sohail Inayatullah responded to Sardar's essay in the same issue.

Being a consulting editor of *Futures*, Sardar himself is an example of the fact that futures studies also has room for critical people born in the Third World. One of the latest editions is a special issue on African futures studies, edited by Colin Blackman and Olugbenga Adesida.

Adesida is an economist/information systems analyst working with the United Nations Development Programme's project 'African Futures', based in Abidjan. According to him, there is no place today where a change from ancestral worship to worship of future generations is more necessary than the African continent. This special issue of *Futures* takes stock of progress in the use of futures studies concepts and methodologies in Africa, and discusses how such studies could be better integrated into decision making and planning. A long-term view and a participatory approach are seen as essential in this respect.

Also within the old Eastern bloc there were futurists who, to some extent, could operate within the main international network of futures studies. A prominent example is Igor Bestuzhev-Lada, a professor of sociology who has experienced all the changes of post-war USSR. His article 'A Short History of Forecasting in the USSR' in the American Journal *Technological Forecasting and Social Change*, gives a most thrilling description of problems and achievements in different phases up till 1991.

For the further development of forecasting in his area, Bestuzhev-Lada recommends a normative approach, dealing with global imbalances. The task is to outline an alternative civilization able to overcome them, and the transition thereto.

TRENDS

Some of the most famous futurists in the public eye mainly deal with trends; they try to predict which futures are the most probable. Post-Industrial Society, Future Shock, and Megatrends are only a few of the widely diffused 'trend' concepts originating from futures studies.

In his popular book *The Coming of Post-Industrial Society*, Daniel Bell presented the thesis that in the next 30 to 50 years there would emerge a post-industrial society, representing a dramatic change in the social framework of the Western world. The creation of a service economy, the primacy of theoretical knowledge and the planning of technology are among the central dimensions of this new society.

The United States is used as a unit of illustration. The book appeared in 1973, but Bell, a Harvard professor of sociology, launched the concept of 'post-industrial society' as early as 1962.

Alvin Toffler launched his famous concept, 'Future shock', in 1965. His goal was to describe what happens to people who are overwhelmed by change, how they manage – or fail – to adapt themselves to the future. His international bestseller *Future Shock* of 1970 was a result of subsequent conversations between the author (a former journalist) and researchers from a wide range of disciplines as well as industrialists, psychiatrists, doctors and hippies.

Unlike many other futurists he emphasizes soft, everyday aspects of the future. A main conclusion is that the speed of change can often be more important than the direction of change. The time frame of planning must be extended if we are to forestall technocracy, and the growth of futures research is therefore seen as one of the healthiest phenomena of recent years.

Yoneji Masuda, a Japanese professor of information science, published his bestseller, *The Information Society as Post-Industrial Society*, in 1980. He saw humanity standing on the threshold of a period when information values would become more important than material values. This was a result of a new societal technology based on the combination of computer and communications technology.

The first part of the book deals with the question of when and through what stages the 'information society' will be created. The second part presents the author's theoretical and conceptual studies on the information society. The discussion ends with 'Computopia', the author's vision of a preferred global society in the twenty-first century, dominated by self-realization and freedom of decision.

Taichi Sakaiya's *The Knowledge-Value Revolution* has become another Japanese bestseller. Sakaiya is an economist, essayist and novelist, and the author of more than 30 books. Like so many others, he claims that the industrial society has reached its zenith. In the coming age, people will no longer be driven to consume more, but will turn towards values created through access to time and wisdom.

'Knowledge-value' is the worth or a price a society gives to what it at the moment acknowledges to be 'creative wisdom'. People will pay a high price for items that correspond to the demands set by the social subjectivity of the group to which they believe they belong. For the industrial world, matching the social subjectivities of the times will thus be the most important production factor.

John Naisbitt sold as many as 9 million copies of his book *Megatrends*, published in 1982. Here, the USA was described as a society in between two eras. Those who are willing to anticipate the new era will be a quantum leap ahead of those who hold on to the past. Ten empirical, mainly quantitative 'megatrends' are presented, including the transition from Industrial Society to Information Society, and from Hierarchies to Informal Networking. The findings are based on content analysis of local newspapers, as trends are found to be generated from the bottom up.

An English-American professor of history, Paul Kennedy, shifted his main interest from the past to the future in the late 1980s. As a result, his international bestseller on trends was published in 1993: *Preparing for the Twenty-First Century*.

After giving a generalist view of some important global trends of our time, he discusses how prepared the world's regions and nations are for the challenges that seem to be coming. However, in spite of the book's title and dimension, there is no real analysis of practical solutions or of general worldviews. This is a key example of the elegant and successful futures writer; the book has a broad appeal, but Kennedy lacks the futurist tools that could have enabled him to say something more meaningful about preparations for the next century.

Willis Harman's *Global Mind Change* of 1988 is a completely different kind of 'trend book'. The author predicts a societal transformation in the form of a paradigm change towards the end of the twentieth century. This may be just as radical as the earth-shaking shifts in view of reality that took place when the 'modern' worldview began to take shape in the seventeenth century.

According to Harman, the origins of present global problems are to be found in the belief system supporting our whole economic structure. The establishment's solutions just deal with symptoms instead of accepting the need for fundamental change. Within the coming worldview, we will accept reality both through physical sense data (like today) and through a deep intuitive 'inner knowing', being part of a oneness.

Harman's point is not to accelerate or resist changes that take place, but rather to help our society understand the forces of historical change. Dialogue and caring can make us go through the process with as little misery as possible. The author is a veteran within American futures studies, with a background in electrical engineering and systems analysis as well as psychology.

Lester Brown *et al.*'s *Vital Signs. The Trends That Are Shaping Our Future* is a new annual series from the Worldwatch Institute in Washington, DC, representing still another kind of trend studies. In text and easy-to-read graphs, the latest version analyzes 37 key indicators that track change in our environmental, economic and social health. In addition, it examines seven special features on important trends for which global historical data are not available. Topics covered include food, agriculture, energy, atmosphere, economy, transportation, environment, social and military trends.

SCENARIOS

The most unpredicted rise of OPEC in the 1970s (in many places better known as the oil crisis) had consequences for the futures literature. There was a shift in interest from the realm of trends and predictions to the choice between alternative futures, in the form of scenarios or utopias.

Scenario-writing had, however, also been used by many trend researchers, like the highly controversial Herman Kahn. Independently of what one thinks of his political analysis, it has to be admitted that he was a key figure behind the development of today's scenario analyses. His 1967 book, with Anthony Wiener, *The Year 2000* will remain an important classic.

It includes scenarios both for the world society and for the USA, inspired by methods from military studies. Kahn, a scholar of mathematics and physics, strongly believed in future economic growth and prosperity, and that ecological problems would be solved by technological innovation. This book, produced at the Hudson Institute, was the first volume from the 'Commission on the Year 2000' project, sponsored by the American Academy of Arts and Sciences. Basic concepts like 'surprise-free scenarios' and 'standard world' were introduced to the public.

Michel Godet, a professor of industrial prospective at the Conservatoire National des Arts et Métiers (CNAM), represents a more modern tradition. He has defined a scenario as 'the description of a possible future and the corresponding path to it'. His article, 'Introduction to La Prospective', of 1986 describes a French approach based on action and non-predetermination using specific methods, such as scenarios.

Godet presents three objectives of the scenario method: to detect the priority issues for study; to determine the main actors and their strategies; and to describe a development by taking into account the most probable evolutionary path, using sets of assumptions about the various actors' behavior. By assessing the consequences of different measures, scenarios can then be used to prepare action plans for companies as well as for organizations and governments.

A growing number of studies on the year 2000 were initiated during the 1980s, taking advantage of the scenario method. Their aim has been to analyze long-term alternative futures of nations or regions. To promote such efforts, the Institute of 21st Century Studies was established.

Martha Garrett of that institute edited *Studies for the 21st Century*. This book, published by UNESCO in 1991, provides an overview of about 50 projects from all continents. Both normative and exploratory studies are included. In addition to reports from the different projects, the book presents methodologies used and discusses lessons learned. Professional and national backgrounds strongly influence the approach that teams have taken in their studies. Still, there is a high degree of agreement on certain points, like sustainability being the key to a continuing future for humankind, and the foundation of new public attitudes being a prerequisite of changes in action.

An example of a twenty-first-century study is Jim Northcott's *Britain in 2010*. The main forecasts are on a 'most probable' basis, although the authors know that 'the one thing that can be predicted with certainty is that some of the forecasts will turn out to be wrong'. Three different scenarios are thus added, identifying potential areas of choice.

The first one is market-oriented, the second presents a left-wing, interventionist alternative, and the third illustrates an environmental-oriented approach. The report was produced in 1991 by a multidisciplinary group at the Policy Studies Institute (PSI) in London, in cooperation with Cambridge Econometrics. It was funded by a consortium of private sector companies and government departments.

James Robertson's *The Sane Alternative. A Choice of Futures* shows a far more qualitative approach. The author, with a background in the British Cabinet Office and banking, sees the period up to about 2010 as a critical period in the history of humankind. He briefly presents five very different futures, all assumed to be realistic.

The scenarios are 'Business as Usual', 'Disaster' (giving up in advance), 'Authoritarian Control', 'Hyper-Expansionist (HE) Future' (even bigger toys and more important jobs for the boys), and 'The Sane, Human, Ecological (SHE) Future' (a decentralized alternative). Robertson is now a central figure within New Economics.

Kimon Valaskakis *et al*.'s *The Conserver Society* is a result of 14 Canadian government agencies' wish to study the implications of different policy options. Five separate scenarios are presented, including three 'conserver societies'. These are 'Scotch gambit' (do more with less), the 'Greek' ideal (do the same with less), and the 'Buddhist scenario' (doing less with less and doing something else). Two mass-consumption scenarios are added, the 'Squander society' (do less with more), reminiscent of a Roman orgy, and 'Big Rock Candy Mountain' (do more with more). The project was carried out by the futures research institute Gamma; 15 experts from as many different disciplines took part.

The ideas developed are thought to have had significant influence upon the development of environmentally based arguments in a number of areas such as health and agriculture, as well as providing a general context within which to cast environmental arguments in general in Canada.

Ove Sviden and Britt Aniansson's *Surprising Futures* presents notes from a workshop, where about 20 leading researchers from different countries and disciplines (including Michel Godet) drew up five global and regional scenarios up to the year 2075. Four of the scenarios were deliberately given a 'surprising' content, although they need not be more unlikely than the fifth, 'surprise-free' scenario called 'Conventional Wisdom'. The workshop was run in 1986 by the Swedish research council FRN and the International Institute for Applied System Analysis (IIASA) in Laxenburg, Austria.

We now move from the comparing of probable (more or less desirable) futures, on to works that focus on the 'ideal society'.

UTOPIAS

'Those who rule, decide what is reality and what is utopia.' These words from the German feminist journalist and author Carna Zacharias,[4] make it clear that the literature under this heading does not necessarily discuss something unrealistic or unattainable. In fact, instead of 'Utopias', it might just as well have been called 'Visions' or 'Images of the Future'. The Germans also use the term 'Zukunftsgestaltung' (futures design).

But, as the pragmatic Chinese Deng Xiao Ping once said, the important thing is not whether a cat is black or white, but whether it catches mice. In this chapter 'Utopia' means more or less fictional literature that describes a particular community, desired by the author. The main theme is the structure of those fictional communities.

So, does this kind of literature catch mice? That is, has it had any influence on societal development through the times? According to the late Dutch professor Fred Polak, the answer is yes. In his classic study *The Image of the Future*, he demonstrates that idealistic and inspiring visions of the past have greatly influenced later developments.

Utopias (and dystopias) are first considered from the history of Western civilization. The author then describes what he sees as a unique lack of convincing images in our own times. His hope for our cultural survival was in a new development of both utopias and dystopias.

The book demonstrates the advantages of a most interdisciplinary background. During his academic career, Polak was active within law, economy, philosophy and sociology. In addition, he was a central figure in Dutch culture, business and politics.

Probably the most thorough survey of utopian literature is Frank E. and Fritzie P. Manuel's *Utopian Thought in the Western World*. In chronological order, they identify historical constellations of utopias, bringing us from the ancient Greeks via Christian utopians and Thomas More to more modern utopians like Saint-Simon, Karl Marx, Edward Bellamy, William Morris and Herbert Marcuse.

The authors believe in the revival of utopias. They predict 'Man the innovator' coming up with the unthought-of, leaving model-builders and futurological predictors 'holding their bag of forecasts and facile analogies in embarrassed irrelevance'. Frank Manuel, a Harvard professor of history, and Fritzie Manuel, an art historian, wrote the book after more than 25 years' work on utopian thinking.

Krishan Kumar's book *Utopia and Anti-Utopia in Modern Times*, focuses particularly on the ability of utopias to capture the popular imagination or become the center of public debate. The bulk of the book is about English and American literature of the period from the 1880s to the 1950s. Works of five authors (Edward Bellamy, H. G. Wells, Aldous Huxley, George Orwell and B. F. Skinner) were selected for detailed study within the intellectual and literary tradition of utopias.

The last part considers the decline of utopia and anti-utopia in the second half of this century. Special emphasis is put on critical discussions of socialist ideology, ecology and the relations between utopia and research. Kumar, a Trinidad-born professor of sociology, claims that 'Futurologists' of the 1960s and 1970s were convinced of the imminent realization of their expectations, and thus saw their task as one of scientific analysis and policy prescription rather than of utopian picturing.

The success of Niels Meyer *et al.*'s *Revolt from the Center* in the late 1970s, showed that new visions may still capture the public imagination. This book triggered a broad public debate in Scandinavia, and sold more than 100,000 copies in Denmark alone (a country with 5 million inhabitants).

It was written by a professor of physics, a liberal politician and an essayist. They analyze weaknesses of the current social system, describe their utopia of a humane society in ecological balance, and discuss ways and means of achieving it. An important reform is the introduction of a guaranteed basic income. Those who want a higher material standard are given the right to a certain amount of paid work.

Visions of Desirable Societies, edited by Eleonora Masini, is a book most of whose contributors come from the Third World. It is a collection of images of the future from different ideological, philosophical and cultural perspectives, presenting the process of thinking within a United Nations University project of the same name.

The aim was to understand contradictions within and between different visions, and to find ways in which they may become more compatible in a diverse world. The book is based on papers presented at two conferences in Mexico in 1978–79, arranged by the World Futures Studies

Federation and CEEM (Centro Estudios Economicos y Sociales de Terces Mundo).

Whereas some authors have asked for more visions in our times, Michael Marien divided the existing ones into two categories. In his classic article 'The Two Visions of Post-Industrial Society' of 1977, he distinguishes between those who go for a technological, affluent, service society, and the proponents of a more decentralized and agrarian society that is ecologically conscious.

Marien is the editor of World Future Society's eminent (although most US-dominated) newsletter on literature, *Future Survey*. It is thought-provoking that he, probably the best expert we have on futures literature, found 'no evidence that any writer holding either of the two visions of post-industrial society has any appreciable understanding of the opposing vision'.

A collection of essays published 15 years after Marien's article leaves a quite different impression. Sheila Moorcroft's *Visions for the 21st Century* consists of essays from 21 invited international contributors, dealing with where we are and where we might want to go. Their topics are as varied as the cultures and academic disciplines they themselves represent.

The analysis differs as much as the proposed solutions, but the text still coheres. Most approaches are, in all their diversity, parts of the same problematique. It is up to each reader, though, to synthesize and assess which ideas could be parts of the same solution. Interconnectedness, interdependence and diversity are key words for this anthology.

THE WORLD PROBLEMATIQUE

Poverty in the midst of plenty, degradation of the environment, loss of faith in institutions, uncontrolled urban spread, and insecurity of employment. Those are some of the interacting parts of what the Club of Rome has called the 'world problematique'.

Donella Meadows *et al.*'s bestseller *The Limits to Growth* of 1972 (9 million copies in 29 languages) was the first report commissioned by the Club of Rome. Financed by Volkswagen Foundation, an international research team at the Massachusetts Institute of Technology (MIT) investigated five basic factors which limit growth on this planet: population, agriculture, resource use, industry and pollution.

Data on these factors were fed into a global model. A conclusion was that if present growth trends continue, the limits to growth will be reached some time within the next hundred years. To alter these dramatic trends, the report advocated striving to reach a state of global equilibrium.

A number of alternative world models were drawn up in the wake of the discussion following this highly controversial study. Herrera *et al.*'s

Catastrophe or New Society? A Latin American World Model was the first to take the explicit viewpoint of the Third World, but gave less attention to the environment.

The report proposed measures which should ensure that everybody's basic needs for food, housing, health care and education would be met by the year 2000 (except in large parts of Africa and southern Asia, where it was not seen as possible before 2050). The study was made by Fundacion Barriloche, an Argentine research foundation, with support from, among others, the UN system.

The Science Policy Research Unit at the University of Sussex, England, became a center of the critical debate on 'The Limits to Growth'. SPRU found little or no basis for the pessimism of the report. In Freeman and Jahoda's *World Futures* of 1978, methods and assumptions from the debate are used to sketch other possible profiles of world development in the next 50 years.

Combinations of high or low economic growth, and strong or weak international equality result in four different profiles. Future supplies of food, energy and non-fuel minerals are discussed in relation to these profiles. An assessment of possible technical change is also made. The main problems were found not to be physical limits, but political priorities.

The confrontation between the 'Limits' and 'Sussex' groups was intense, and at some conferences it is said to have come closer to physical confrontation than intellectual debate.

In the 'boom' of world models of the late 1970s, even President Carter ordered a report. *The Global 2000 Report to the President*, edited by the physician Gerald Barney, deals with probable changes in the world's population, natural resources, and environment. The relationships between the three issues are emphasized, since there is no lack of separate studies of them.

The Global 2000 Report indicates the potential for global problems of alarming proportions by the year 2000, and claims that the efforts underway around the world fall far short of what is needed.

Even more important was the work in the 1980s of the UN World Commission on Environment and Development, headed by Norway's Prime Minister Gro Harlem Brundtland. Its task was no less than to re-examine the critical environment and development problems of the planet and to formulate realistic proposals to solve them.

The Commission's report *Our Common Future* was published in 1987, after four years' work. 'Sustainable development' is the main concept of the report. As with *Global 2000*, the main importance is not in the innovativeness, but in the official status of the analysis and proposals.

The work of the Brundtland Commission was generally well received, but the report became highly controversial among environmentalists for its positive attitude to 'a new era of economic growth'. The discussion of the report led up to the huge World Conference on Environment and Development (WCED) in Rio in 1992.

WCED was held 20 years after the first UN conference on environment (in Stockholm). The year 1992 was also the 20th anniversary of *The Limits to Growth*. Donella Meadows *et al.* wrote a sequel, using the same computer model as in their first book. In spite of this, *Beyond the Limits* has been far less controversial than *The Limits to Growth*.

Although much more well received, the sequel has not attracted the same large readership as the first book. Thirteen scenarios for the period from the year 1990 to the year 2100 are sketched. In the recommended one, the population levels out at just under 8 billion people, family size is limited to two children and the material standard of living is roughly that of present-day Europe.

CHANGE

The perspective of change has been more or less involved in the categories already presented. But although authors dealing with desirable futures should especially be expected to accentuate processes of change, this is not very often the case. Some exceptions will be presented here. But first we should again stress that not all futurists focus on the need for major changes. Some warn against the implications of too much and too rapid change. In spite of, or rather because of, his experiences from social reform, the Egyptian intellectual and public figure Mirrit Boutros-Ghali is an example.

In his book, *Tradition for the Future. Human Values and Social Purpose* of 1972, Boutros-Ghali (a relative of the UN's present Secretary-General) finds a general tendency in futures literature to accept the idea of unlimited alteration of everything. He argues for the importance of preserving some absolute and unchanging human values, without which the future will not be worth living in an overcrowded and technological age.

Rajni Kothari's *Footsteps into the Future* of 1974 has a different focus. It deals with how to make a 'minimal utopia' feasible. The basic issue is how to move from a world in which there is a growing 'divorce' of scientific and technological progress from the freedom and well-being of human beings, to one in which the two are harmonized. Justice, self-realization, creativity and non-violence are important elements.

The author does not believe in fully worked out models, and therefore warns against 'catastrophic reversals of existing arrangements that may or may not produce the desired results'. Kothari's strategy is that of 'ever widening circles'; stepwise attempts at a number of levels. The intellectual task is simultaneously to stimulate new attitudes and major institutional changes.

The book belongs to a series of volumes entitled 'Preferred Worlds for the 1990s', initiated by the transnational World Order Models Project.

Kothari is director of the Center for the Study of Developing Societies in Delhi.

In *Envisioning a Sustainable Society. Learning Our Way Out*, Lester Milbrath describes why today's modern society cannot lead to sustainable development. After elaborating a vision of a sustainable society, the author discusses the transition from modern society to a sustainable society. Social learning is seen as the most viable route to social change.

Milbrath, a US professor of political science and sociology, does not believe that elite change can be very thorough, as true social change must affect the everyday behavior of the people. His prescription is to prepare for the moment when things get 'bad enough to force us to cast about'. Then we can make changes that would be beyond the realm of possibility in 'normal times'.

But is today's realm of possibility that narrow? Less than a year before becoming the US Vice-President, Al Gore published *Earth in the Balance*. A conclusion of his analysis is that we must make the rescue of the global environment the central organizing principle of our civilization.

He proposes a new global Marshall Plan, consisting of five strategic goals. These are stabilizing world population, developing and sharing appropriate technology, a new global 'eco-nomics', a new generation of treaties and agreements, and education for a new global environmental consensus.

Gore is an example of important elements within the establishment who want to bridge the gaps between the dominating worldview and policy, and today's ecological knowledge. The key, seen from his point of view, will be a new public awareness of how serious is the treat to the global environment. There will be no meaningful change until enough citizens are willing to speak out and urge their leaders to bring the earth back to balance.

The Group of Lisbon's *Limits to Competition* of 1993 shows that Gore is not a loner within the establishment. The group consists of 19 prominent professors, bureaucrats, cultural workers and industrialists from Western Europe, North America and Japan.

They are concerned with the role of competition in the process of economic and social globalization. Instead of praising competitiveness, they call for co-decisions in the form of 'global social contracts'. Here all concerned parties conclude that the benefits of 'going together' are greater than the inconveniences.

If we are to move towards the contracts, the initiative has to come from the three dominant global powers: Western Europe, North America and Japan. The target is a global society that will satisfy the basic needs of 8 billion people inhabiting the planet by the year 2020. Common endeavors will be the key, and this makes the global civilian society a powerful tool. The report stresses the importance of systematically recognizing and supporting local actions, behaviors and experiments at the global level.

The demand for a 'new economics', or a 'green economics' is common to both oppositional green movements and more established thinkers. Paul Ekins' *Wealth beyond Measure* of 1992 is a highly illustrated guide that presents the state of the art in laypersons' terms.

Contrary to the view of mainstream economists and politicians, the new economics movement puts forward the idea that recession recovery must accord with the imperatives of sustainable development. Participatory democracy and economic justice are other important objectives. Ekins is a co-founder of the New Economics Foundation in London, and of TOES (The Other Economic Summit), which has accompanied the G-7 summits since 1984.

Erik Dammann created the popular Norwegian Future in Our Hands movement, focusing on social equity and a simpler way of life. His book *Revolution in the Affluent Society* discusses the need for a change of system in the rich world, and argues why it should be non-violent, non-dogmatic and come from below, as an antithesis of what one is struggling to overcome.

He also treats the role of futures studies, wanting them to be linked more directly to people's wishes and expectations. Through surveys, they could arouse an interest in crucial choices about values and social problems among people who otherwise feel that political debate goes over their heads. Reports should be handed over to writers with the literary skill to convey basic ideas in popular books and the mass media. They should stress the main initial consequences that the alternative courses of development will have for various groups.

The main point is the idea of research not as a means of control, but as a means by which the public can consider and participate actively in the formation and development of their own future. Dammann later became a co-founder of the Alternative Future Project.

Robert Jungk and Norbert Müllert's *Futures Workshops* presents another method by which ordinary people can be involved in creating possible and desirable futures. Criticism, fantasy and realization are the main elements in a process where concrete utopias and social inventions are drawn up.

Examples illustrate how participants have changed during the process. Futures workshops can thus be an effective instrument against what Jungk used to call the 'ghost' haunting today's world: the ghost of resignation. The book also demonstrates the kinds of ideas and practical results that can be achieved through this method, which has been especially popular in Germany and Denmark.

The idea of participatory futures studies, involving both academic and less academic circles, is therefore not just a theory. It is possible to put into practice. Robert Jungk, who died in 1994, has probably demonstrated this better than anyone else, not least through his futures workshops. Such approaches are essential for futures studies if they are to democratize, not colonize, the future.

For in the words of the late Nobel Prize winner in physics, Dennis Gabor: 'the future cannot be predicted, but it can be invented'.[5] And since the future belongs to all of us, we all have the right to participate in shaping it.

NOTES

1 Dahle, Kjell, O*n Alternative Ways of Studying the Future. International Institutions, an Annotated Bibliography and a Norwegian Case.* Oslo, Alternative Future Project, 1991, p. 16.
2 From the Futurist Bookstore, World Future Society, 7910 Woodmont Avenue, Suite 450, Bethesda, Maryland 20814, USA.
3 Robert Jungk was also the founder of the International Futures Library, Imbergstrasse 2, 5020 Salzburg, Austria. I have made several visits to this fabulous library, which has been a main resource for my studies of the futures literature.
4 Zacharias, Carna, *Wo liegt Utopia? Nur wer träumt, ist Realist.* Munich, Schönberger, 1985.
5 Gabor, Dennis, *Inventing the Future.* London, Secker & Warburg, 1963; New York, Knopf, 1964.

THE 50 KEY WORKS

Barney, Gerald O. (ed.): *The Global 2000 Report to the President. Entering the 21st Century. A Report Prepared by the Council on Environmental Quality and the Department of State.* Harmondsworth, Penguin, 1982. (First published 1980.)
Bell, Daniel: *The Coming of Post-Industrial Society. A Venture in Social Forecasting.* New York, Basic Books, 1973.
Bestuzhev-Lada, Igor: 'A Short History of Forecasting in the USSR'. Article in *Technological Forecasting and Social Change*, 41:3, May 1992, pp. 341–8.
Blackman, Colin and Olugbenga Adesida (eds): *African Futures.* Special issue of *Futures* (September 1994).
Boutros-Gali, Mirrit: *Tradition for the Future. Human Values and Social Purpose.* Oxford, Alden, 1972.
Brown, Lester R., Hal Kane and David Malin Roodman: *Vital Signs 1994–95. The Trends That Are Shaping Our Future.* New York, Norton; London, Earthscan, 1994.
Brundtland, Gro Harlem (chairman): *Our Common Future.* Oxford and New York, Oxford University Press, 1987.
Cornish, Edward (ed.): *The Study of the Future. An Introduction to the Art and Science of Understanding and Shaping Tomorrow's World.* Bethesda, Maryland, World Future Society, 1977.
Dammann, Erik: *Revolution in the Affluent Society.* London, Heretic, 1984. (Norwegian original: *Revolusjon i velferdssamfunnet*, 1979.)
Ekins, Paul, Mayer Hillman and Robert Hutchison: *Wealth beyond Measure. An Atlas of New Economics.* London, Gaia, 1992. American edition: *The Gaia Atlas of Green Economics.* New York, Anchor Books, 1992.

Flechtheim, Ossip K.: *History and Futurology*. Meisenheim am Glan, Anton Hain, 1966.

Fowles, Jib (ed.): *Handbook of Futures Research*. Connecticut, Greenwood, 1978.

Freeman, Christopher and Marie Jahoda (eds): *World Futures. The Great Debate*. Oxford, Martin Robertson, 1978.

Garrett, Martha J. *et al.*: *Studies for the 21st Century*. Paris, UNESCO, 1991.

Godet, Michel: 'Introduction to La Prospective. Seven Key Ideas and One Scenario Method'. Article in *Futures* 2 (1986), pp. 134–57.

Gore, Al: *Earth in the Balance. Forging a New Common Purpose*. Boston, Houghton; London, Earthscan, 1992.

Group of Lisbon: *Limits to Competition*. Lisbon, Gulbenkian Foundation, 1993.

Harman, Willis W.: *Global Mind Change. The Promise of the Last Years of the Twentieth Century*. Sausalito, Institute for Noetic Sciences, 1988.

Herrera, Amilcar *et al.* (eds): *Catastrophe or New Society? A Latin American World Model*. Ottawa, International Development Center, 1976.

Jantsch, Erich: *Technological Forecasting in Perspective: A Framework for Technological Forecasting, its Techniques and Organization*. Paris, OECD, 1967.

Jouvenel, Bertrand de: *The Art of Conjecture*. New York, Basic Books, 1967. (French original: *L'Art de la conjecture*, 1964.)

Jungk, Robert and Johan Galtung (eds): *Mankind 2000*. Oslo, Universitetsforlaget; London, Allen & Unwin, 1969.

Jungk, Robert and Norbert R. Müllert: *Futures Workshops. How to Create Desirable Futures*. London, Institute for Social Inventions, 1989. (German original: *Zukunftswerkstätten*, 1981.)

Kahn, Herman and Anthony Wiener: *The Year 2000. A Framework for Speculation on the Next Thirty-Three Years*. New York, Macmillan, 1967.

Kennedy, Paul: *Preparing for the Twenty-First Century*. New York, Random House; London, HarperCollins, 1993.

Kothari, Rajni: *Footsteps into the Future. Diagnosis of the Present World and a Design for an Alternative*. New Delhi, Orient Longman; London, The Free Press; Amsterdam, North-Holland, 1974.

Kreibich, Rolf, Weert Canzler and Klaus Burmeister (eds): *Zukunftsforschung und Politik* [Futures Research and Politics]. Weinheim/Basel, Beltz, 1991.

Kumar, Krishan: *Utopia and Anti-Utopia in Modern Times*. Oxford and Cambridge, MA, Blackwell, 1991. (First published 1987.)

Manuel, Frank E. and Fritzie P.: *Utopian Thought in the Western World*. Cambridge, MA and Oxford, Belknap, 1979.

Marien, Michael: 'The Two Visions of Post-industrial Society'. Article in *Futures* May 1977, pp. 415–31.

Marien, Michael and Lane Jennings (eds): *What I Have Learned. Thinking about the Future Then and Now*. New York, Greenwood Press, 1987.

Masini, Eleonora Barbieri (ed.): *Visions of Desirable Societies*. Oxford, Pergamon, 1983.

Masuda, Yoneji: *The Information Society as Post-Industrial Society*. Bethesda, Maryland, World Future Society, 1983. (First published Tokyo 1980.)

Meadows, Donella H., Dennis, L. Meadows, Jørgen Randers and William W. Behrens III: *The Limits to Growth. A Report for the Club of Rome's Project on the Predicament of Mankind*. New York, Universe; London, Earth Island, 1972.

Meadows, Donella H., Dennis L. Meadows and Jørgen Randers: *Beyond the Limits. Confronting Global Collapse. Envisioning a Sustainable Future*. Vermont, Chelsea Green; London, Earthscan, 1992.

Meyer, Niels I., K. Helveg Petersen and Villy Sørensen: *Revolt from the Center*. London, Marion Boyars, 1982. (Danish original: *Oprør fra midten*, 1978.)

Milbrath, Lester W.: *Envisioning a Sustainable Society. Learning Our Way Out*. New York, State University Press, 1989.

Moorcroft, Sheila (ed.): *Visions for the 21st Century*. London, Adamantine, 1992; New York, Praeger, 1993.

Myrdal, Alva (committee chairman): *To Choose a Future. A Basis for Discussion and Deliberations on Futures Studies in Sweden*. Stockholm, Ministry of Foreign Affairs, 1974. (Swedish original: *Att välja framtid*, 1972.)

Naisbitt, John: *Megatrends. The Ten New Directions Directing Our Lives*. New York, Warner, 1982.

Northcott, Jim (ed.): *Britain in 2010. The PSI Report*. London, Policy Studies Institute, 1991.

Polak, Fred: *The Image of the Future*. Amsterdam, London and New York, Elsevier, 1973. (Dutch original: *De toekomst is verleden tijd*, 1968.)

Robertson, James: *The Sane Alternative. A Choice of Futures*. Oxford, 1983 (revised edition).

Sakaiya, Taichi: *The Knowledge-Value Revolution: Or a History of the Future*. Tokyo and New York, Kodansha International, 1991. (Updating of the Japanese original: *Chika kakumei*, 1985.)

Sardar, Ziauddin: 'Colonizing the Future: The Other Dimensions of Futures Studies'. Article in *Futures* 2 (1992), pp. 179–88.

Shakhanazov, Georgi: *Futurology Fiasco. A Critical Study of Non-Marxist Concepts of How Society Develops*. Moscow, Progress, 1982.

Slaughter, Richard: *The Foresight Principle. Cultural Recovery in the 21st Century*. London, Adamantine, 1995.

Sviden, Ove and Britt Aniansson (eds): *Surprising Futures. Notes from an International Workshop on Long-term World Development*. Stockholm, Forskningsrådsnämnden, 1987.

Toffler, Alvin: *Future Shock*. New York, Random House, 1970.

Valaskakis, Kimon, Peter S. Sindell, J. Graham Smith and Iris Fitzpatrick-Martin: *The Conserver Society. A Workable Alternative for the Future*. Toronto, Fitzhenry & Whiteside; New York, Harper & Row, 1979.

Part II

Futures thinking and education

Chapter 4

Futures studies as applied knowledge

James Dator

FUTURES STUDIES AND MODERN ACADEMIC DECISION MAKING

As I will explain a little later, at the present time, futures studies is to modern academia and societal decision making what Science was to academia and societal decision making in the late Middle Ages. Because of this, I am no more likely to get most successful academicians, politicians, and business persons to take futures studies seriously (and thus help them and their organizations to think and act more helpfully about the future), than Copernicus was in getting the powers that were in his time to recognize that the earth isn't the center of the universe, Because futures studies is not like other established fields in academia, it is constantly being misunderstood and misused.

The traditional academic world in the West (as revealed by the organization of its major universities – especially those of the United States) knows of only five kinds of academic pursuits:

First and foremost are the so-called 'natural' sciences (disciplines like physics, astronomy, chemistry, and biology with their necessary handmaiden, mathematics; more recently also earth, atmospheric and marine sciences, and their newer handmaiden, computer and information science). These are the 'real' sciences, based (by and large) on positivistic, reductionistic methods and assumptions. They set the standard for everything else.

Second, and always struggling to return to their medieval place of pride before 'science' marginalized them as the *raison d'être* for the 'liberal (i.e., liberating) arts' – or at least struggling to preserve their rank as number two – are the humanities (history, philosophy, religion, Sanskrit, Chinese, Greek, Latin, and Arabic, and perhaps the literature of and/or in contemporary foreign languages as well as one's own language). These are proudly and defiantly non- – indeed anti- – positivistic disciplines. What is wrong with the world, they might say, is the loss of tradition, discourse, criticism, gentility and mystery in the mad dominance of reductionistic and utilitarian rationalism.

Third (though often considered part of the humanities) are the performing arts: music, drama, painting, sculpture, perhaps now sometimes including film or video as beaux arts (not as a professional career). Here the emphasis is on esthetics, self-awareness, idiosyncratic self-expression, and performance. As a poster my daughter, Tasha, put up in my office long ago says, 'Dance is the only art wherein we ourselves are the stuff of which it is made.'

Fourth, and quite far behind, are the social sciences (sociology, economics, psychology, perhaps anthropology, geography, perhaps even political science). Note that these, too, are 'sciences'. That is what makes them so suspect and yet legitimate. They strive to be scientific (positivistic, reductionistic), but, alas, they cannot quite pull it off and thus are dubbed derisively as 'soft' in contrast to the true 'hard' sciences.

And finally and even farther behind (though in some places, perhaps the real number one) are the various 'applied sciences' and professional schools and disciplines – agriculture, engineering, medicine, architecture, perhaps education, law, urban planning, social work, perhaps even business and all of its subsidiary concerns. These are strictly instrumental, barely scientific, and certainly not critical. But they are very practical, hard-nosed, and successful. To many observers, they appear to be the wave of the future of higher education.

Needless to say, there are many cross-disciplinary combinations of these and the other traditional courses, and even more questionable 'new' courses, though usually they are offered in the mode of one of the five above.

The 'Index of Programs' in the 14th Annual *Directory of Graduate Programs*, published by the Graduate Record Examination Board and the Council of Graduate Schools in the United States, 1991, is nineteen pages long, double column (pp. 425–444). Neither the words 'futures studies', 'futures research', 'future-oriented studies', nor any other similar set or combination of terms appears in the index – even though there are graduate programs in futures studies offered by a few American universities.

Similarly, the two-volume encyclopedia, *International Higher Education*, edited by Philip Altbach (1991), and containing authoritative discussions of higher education for virtually every country in the world, does not show that futures studies, or future-oriented studies, is offered by any university anywhere on the planet. And yet I know it is.

Given the history and curriculum of contemporary higher education, it is not surprising that most people find it difficult to understand what futures studies is, and what it is not. They quite naturally compare it with one of the five conventional streams of academia. Is it a positivistic science which presumes to predict the future? Is it merely some part of the humanities which is interested in utopias and speculative dreaming? Is it a kind of science fiction fit for novels, movies, or television shows? Or is it a profession? Can one learn to become a consulting futurist? More to the point: can one make money as a futurist?

The answer is not clearly yes or no to any of these questions. The answer is, 'Well, it has some of those features, but that really is not the best way to conceive of futures studies. It is indeed something else.'

At the same time, I feel that it is wrong to compare futures studies with Interdisciplinary Studies, Policy Studies, Environmental Studies, Women's Studies, Feminist Studies, Ethnic Studies, Peace Studies, Global Studies, even Sustainability Studies, and all the other '... Studies' which are growing and thriving in the halls of academe these days. These, in spite of what they may claim, are all trying in varying ways to save the old world by reforming it more or less radically. They are all the legitimate sons and daughters of modernity; of Newton and Minerva, you might say.

But futures studies is something else.

SO, WHAT IS FUTURES STUDIES?

That which we call the future – the present at a later time – is not predictable. If any person says to you: 'I know the future. Here it is! Do this!' then run from that person as quickly as possible. The future is not predictable. No one knows with anywhere near sufficient certainty what the future *will be*. Nonetheless the fundamental unpredictability of the future does *not* mean that we should therefore not concern ourselves about the future and merely trust in luck, god, or fate; or else to just prepare ourselves to muddle through when new crises suddenly arise. Rather, it means that we need to take a more appropriate stance towards the future than either a search for predictive certainty, leaving it up to fate, or trying to muddle through.

But what might that 'more appropriate stance' be?

First of all, 'the future' may be considered as emerging from the inter- action of four components: events, trends, images, and actions.

Events

Events are those things which make people doubt the efficacy of thinking about the future at all. Things just seem to happen. What is going to happen next seems to be utterly unknowable. Who knows when the next war, assassination, earthquake, decision by your boss is going to toss society into a completely different direction? For example, for more than forty years, the world was locked into a Cold War which consumed trillions of dollars and gigantic amounts of human resources. Suddenly, and for no clear reason, it was over. The Wall fell. It became time to worry how to spend the Peace Dividend. War was declared obsolete as an instrument of national policy. Only economics was said to matter any more.

Then suddenly some previously unnoticed madman, a new Hitler, was said to have emerged in the body of a former staunch ally in Iraq, and the Persian Gulf was suddenly aflame. Within 45 days, the US declared victory and America's troops returned home in Yellow Ribboned-triumph, virtually untouched. The 'Vietnam Syndrome' was said to be over and with it the American public's concern about military overspending on $1600 screwdrivers vanished as well.

Similarly, for many years, the world eagerly, or fearfully, anticipated the emergence of 'Europe 1992' and an eventually United States of Europe. But as the Wall fell, so also did the dream of a peacefully united, economically-integrated, Europe. Instead militant tribalism of the most disgusting sort has re-emerged from nowhere. Yugoslavia has vanished in flames. Neo-Nazis murder Turks in Germany. The former mighty Soviet Union limps towards bifurcated chaos.

What's next? Who knows? The future has become completely unforeseeable once again. So why even bother? The best we can hope to do is to muddle through, given some preparedness on our part, and much luck.

Trends and emerging issues

On the other hand, many planners believe to the contrary that it is possible to discern the major contours of the future, and to plan effectively for it. They would have us focus on trends in order to anticipate and prepare for the future. But there seem to be at least three types of trends, each requiring different methods of comprehension:

(a) There are trends which are a continuation of the present and the past. In order to understand these trends, we need to understand what is happening now, and what has happened before. Some of that understanding comes from contemplating our own life experiences. Some of it comes from understanding what the natural and social sciences tell us. Some of it may be revealed in historical, philosophical, or religious teachings and traditions. These are the kinds of trends found in most strategic plans.

(b) Other trends are more or less cyclical. They thus are not part of our own personal experience, but they were part of some aspect of the more distant past. Here, the successes or failures of our own lives may mislead us in anticipating the future since we have never personally experienced these trends as we will in the future, or as others experienced them before us. But again, they may be recorded in historical, philosophical, or religious documents or traditions and thus be available to us indirectly through them. Other such trends may require some mathematical technique to discover and understand. Still, because we have not personally experienced the impact of these trends, we will find it very difficult fully to know what to expect from them.

(c) But there may be things in the future which are completely new; which have never before been humanly experienced. These trends might better be called 'emerging issues' because, though potentially looming in the future, they are barely visible in the present, and non-existent in the past. Many futurists would argue that the most important trends of the future are these utterly new emerging issues, and that they are themselves largely the direct or indirect consequence of new technologies which permit humans to do things they could not do before (or, conversely make it difficult for humans to do things that were easy for them to do before) and which also often change the physical environment within which humans live. Methods for determining emerging issues are quite different from the way we can measure and forecast most trends and cycles.

Now, to the extent that our own personal experiences, and the focus of most of the formal educational systems, is only on the first and second trends (and it overwhelmingly is), then most of us may find it very difficult to anticipate the future helpfully – if the futurists are correct who contend – as I certainly do – that the third, 'emerging issue', kind of trend is by far the most important for understanding the next thirty years and beyond. As the Pakistani futurist Sohail Inayatullah says, 'The thing that makes the future interesting is that none of us remember it.'

Actions and images

Now, the third and fourth major factors influencing the future are the images of the future which people hold and the actions which people take on the basis of those images. Some of these actions are taken specifically with the intention of influencing the future. Others are not. But all *do* influence it – though seldom ever as intended!

Thus, one of the things futures studies tries to do is to help people examine and clarify their images of the future – their ideas, fears, hopes, beliefs, concerns about the future – so that they might improve the quality of their decisions which impact it.

Another thing futures studies tries to do is to help people move their images and actions beyond an attempt passively to forecast the future and then to develop plans of action on the basis of the forecasts. That is only the first step in foresight. The next step is to generate positive visions of the future – to create preferred futures – and to base planning and decisions on them. The future-envisioning workshops of the Austrian futurist, Robert Jungk, and of Elise Boulding and many others subsequently, should be mentioned here. Learning to vision, and revision, the future, and then to plan and act in accordance, is at the heart of futures studies and futures research as applied to planning and decision-making (Jungk and Müllert, 1987).

FUTURES STUDIES, DETERMINISM, INCOHERENCE

This is what futures studies and foresight is, I believe. And because it is not something most of us have experienced in our formal education, we either assume that futures studies is impossible (and those who advocate it are frauds or flakes) or else we assume that it is like some academic orientation we *do* understand, such as science, or history, or art, or math. But this also misleads us because futures studies is as different from each of these as science is from art, or history is from math. While futures studies does overlap with each of these traditional academic disciplines, it is not the same as any of them.

For example, as I said earlier, foresight is not 'prediction'. Neither society nor nature is some deterministic machine which can be predicted if we just understand it correctly and collect and analyze the data properly. Rather, we live in a profoundly, and probably increasingly, incoherent society and environment. We need techniques of foresight, planning, and decision-making which acknowledge this. And we need a public (and decision-makers) who understand this, and who permit, indeed demand, the use of techniques which do not assume a deterministic universe. At the present time the public, the electorate, our clients, our boss all generally seem to want predictive certainty about the future, or else they want to hear no information about the future whatsoever. This understandable desire for false assurance is dangerous for the future of democratic society and certainly dangerous for anyone interested in the future of education (Michael, 1989).

What can and should be done, in contrast, is to place foresight, planning, and decision-making within an ongoing, multiple, 'alternative futures' context. This contrasts with the common practice of 'planning' for what is assumed to be the single 'most likely' future or several of its minor variations. To many planners and decision-makers, the most likely future seems to be that which might emerge from the continuation of existing trends. But I have already suggested that events as well as cycles and emerging issues make such an extrapolated, linear future highly unlikely indeed.

Thus plans made on the assumption that 'the present will continue' result in a variety of planning and policy disasters fairly soon, which in turn often discredit the entire attempt at planning and foresight. These failures then encourage people to ignore the future entirely and to hope that we can just muddle through somehow ignorant of things to come.

Likewise, policy made in the name of foresight after a 'one-shot' glance at certain trends, even if the trends be produced by sophisticated computer models and with great mathematical precision, is similarly inadequate and potentially dangerous. Foresight must become a routine continuing process, not a one-time affair. If you are not going to anticipate the future regularly and routinely, I suggest you don't bother to consider it at all. It is a waste of everybody's time – and probably just a whitewash of somebody else's decisions about the future – to make it a one-shot affair.

And finally, foresight that is undertaken as only a technical, scientific, and professional matter is incomplete. Foresight must also and necessarily be a political, ethical, esthetic and very broadly participative project. It must take the form of what Alvin Toffler and Clem Bezold have called, 'Anticipatory Democracy' (Bezold, 1978). It is absolutely essential that all people who have a stake in a future be involved in determining it. Obviously that means that young people – even the youngest of people – should be deeply involved in ways that make sense to them. That also means that not only the elite but all marginalized persons should participate fairly, fully, and frequently. And that is why future-oriented studies must become the heart and soul of all academic endeavors. You can't learn to do useful foresight overnight any more than you can learn to do anything else new instantly and effortlessly. Learning to exercise foresight takes lots of time and practice, with many mistakes and changes of direction.

Most of the organizations I know of which have engaged in future-oriented projects report that a very significant benefit of such activities is that they give themselves, and their constituents, a broad and common sense of what their purpose and mission is, perhaps for the first time. For example, while at one level 'everyone' knows what the purpose of education is, future-visioning processes help everyone reconsider, clarify, and unify that purpose. A secondary benefit groups discover is that people find that after having engaged in a future visioning process they then may have the political and popular support to undertake necessary reforms and thus are able to allocate resources more efficiently and effectively once a common mission has been widely sought and jointly identified. And then, to the extent envisioning and scanning the future become a normal part of the organization's activities, these benefits become also more routine and more widespread – the community becomes truly 'sustainable'. To the extent a true cross-section of the relevant public participates genuinely in these futures activities and the subsequent reforms, this public's sense of efficacy and support of sustainable community development grows.

And, if futures activities are found to be beneficial for one community, then other communities, presently unfamiliar with or suspicious of foresight, may be inspired to become more future-oriented themselves, and the future of society as a whole may become more secure and sustainable, and less chaotic and drifting.

ATTRIBUTES OF A FUTURIST

I was recently asked to describe the attributes of a futurist, or what I thought was necessary if one wanted to become a good student and practitioner of futures studies. This was my response:

To be a good futurist, you need the:

widest possible knowledge of the history and present condition of as many cultures and civilizations as possible; knowledge of more than one culture, and thus more than one language, intimately;

widest possible knowledge of all aspects of all the social sciences;

widest possible knowledge of current and emerging developments in the natural sciences, and their emerging subdisciplines and transdisciplines, for example, evolutionary systems theory, chaos theory, and brain science;

widest possible familiarity with developments in engineering (especially electronics and genetics), architecture, and space sciences;

widest possible familiarity with philosophy, ethics, morals, and religions, and certainly the ethical discourse of as many different traditions as possible;

widest possible familiarity with law and planning;

an active awareness of esthetics and the esthetic element in all aspects of life. A continuing experience of esthetic expression in some, or preferably many, modes;

creativity, imagination, the willingness to think new thoughts, to make unmade connections, to be ridiculed, laughed at, and to laugh at yourself;

ability to synthesize, combine, invent, create;

willingness to be politically active, to test out new ideas on yourself first and while trying actually to create a better world, or some portion of it;

ability to try to anticipate the consequences of actions before you act, but also the willingness to risk failure and to learn from mistakes and criticism – indeed to seek out and provoke criticism – but to keep trying to do better, and constantly to relearn what 'better' might be;

insatiable curiosity, unbounded compassion, incurable optimism, and an unquenchable sense of humor and delight in the absurd.

All of this can be described in one word – 'Aiglatson' which is 'Nostalgia' spelled backwards: the yearning for things to come; the remembering the future; without being disrespectful to the past (remembering that once it was all that was humanly possible), preferring the dreams of the future to the experiences of the past; always desiring to try something new; to go where no one has ever gone before in all areas of human – and non-human, and, soon, post-human – experience.

Is it possible for anyone to do that? Is it possible for anyone, given our current systems of education?

THE FUTURE OF HIGHER EDUCATION

So far I have said nothing about the future of education, and hence of the structure or process within which I envision futures studies to be embedded, or 'delivered', in the future. Let me just say that while I would be delighted to see the current campus-based higher education system continue forever, I do not expect it to survive even the 1990s, and certainly not much beyond. I agree that the future of education is a network, and not a place. Also I (regrettably) do not expect to see the continuation, much less expansion, of the unified, publicly-financed educational system into the future. Education will no longer be the single-worldview-producing machine it was, and was intended to be, in the nineteenth and twentieth centuries. Instead, there will be many competing, conflicting networks, many claiming monopoly on Truth but none having it.

FUTURES STUDIES SHOULD BE USEFUL

The development of futures studies as I understand it was very strongly influenced by attempts to apply it in real, practical grassroots situations. That specifically in my case means the old Hawaii 2000 experience of the 1960s–70s (Chaplin and Paige, 1973), and everything that flowed from it, including the establishment by the Hawaii State Legislature, in 1971, of the Hawaii Research Center for Futures Studies. Also, one of the reasons the Alternative Futures Option was created in the mid-1970s by the Department of Political Science of the University of Hawaii, with a strong intern component, was to satisfy a demand for people to be able to 'do' futures research for various governmental, commercial, civic, non-profit and other groups and individuals (Dator, 1986).

Similarly, my involvement in the creation and subsequent work of the Institute for Alternative Futures in Washington, DC, and the need thus to provide useful information about the future to its political, commercial, civic, non-profit and other clients, greatly influenced the shape and content of my understanding of futures studies. Futures studies has never been a strictly educational or theoretical enterprise to me. It has always been driven by the need to be useful both to ordinary people and to elite decision-makers without giving in to their desire to have The Wondrous Things To Come Foretold by Ye Ole Mystic Soothsayer. My understanding of futures studies has been strongly influenced (and leavened) by my experiences with the needs and ideas of these people. I suspect the same is true of many other people in the field and thus of the field itself. I am sure that everyone learns much from such a practical, local interchange of visions, fears, plans, hopes, and actions.

FUTURES STUDIES IS LOCAL *AND* GLOBAL

At the same time, my involvement in futures studies has been from the very beginning not only at a local academic and community level, nor even only at a national level. Rather, through my early and continuing involvement in the World Futures Studies Federation, futures studies has also been for me, and for many others, a global and globalizing exercise. This, too, I think makes futures studies quite different from most past and present academic orientations, and itself a harbinger of the global future common for all humankind. I hope that futures studies is given the opportunity to grow and thrive. That is my challenge to each reader of these words.

REFERENCES

P. Altbach ed. *International Higher Education*, New York and London: Garland Publishing (1991).
Clem Bezold, ed., *Anticipatory democracy*. New York: Random House, 1978.
George Chaplin and Glenn Paige, eds, *Hawaii 2000. Continuing experiments in anticipatory democracy*. Honolulu: University Press of Hawaii, 1973.
James A. Dator, 1986 'The Futures of Futures Studies: A View from Hawaii', *Futures* 18,3: 440–445.
Graduate Record Examinations Board and the Council of Graduate Schools in the United States, 1991 *Directory of Graduate Programs*, 14th edn, Princeton, New Jersey: Educational Testing Service: pp. 425–444.
Robert Jungk and Norbert Müllert, *Futures workshops: how to create a desirable futures*. London: Institute for Social Inventions, 1987.
Donald Michael, 'Forecasting and planning in an incoherent context', *Technological forecasting and social change*, pp. 79–87, 1989.

FURTHER REFERENCES

Kjell Dahle, *On alternative ways of studying the future*. Oslo: Alternative future project, 1991
James A. Dator and Sharon Rodgers, *Alternative futures for the state courts of 2020*. Chicago: American Judicature Society, 1991.
Michel Godet, *Scenarios and strategic management*. London: Butterworths, 1987.
Michel Godet, *From anticipation to action: a handbook of strategic prospective*. Paris: Unesco Future-oriented Studies, 1991.
Michael Marien and Lane Jennings, eds, *What I have learned: thinking about the future then and now*. New York: Greenwood, 1987.
Eleonora Barbieri Masini, *Why futures studies?* London: Gray Seal, 1993.
Peter Schwartz, *The art of the long view*. New York: Doubleday, 1991.
Richard Slaughter, *Futures concepts and powerful ideas*. University of Melbourne (Australia): Futures Study Centre, 1991.

Richard Slaughter, ed., *Futures studies and higher education*. Articles by Martha Rogers, Christopher Jones, Allyson Holbrook, Wendy Schultz, Richard Slaughter and Kjell Dahle. *Futures research quarterly*. Winter 1992.

Richard Slaughter, ed., *Teaching about the future*. Proceedings of the seminar organized jointly by Unesco and the Canadian Commission for Unesco, Vancouver, 21–23 July 1992. Essays by Howard Didsbury, Wendy Schultz, Martha Rogers, Richard Slaughter, Allen Tough, Kaoru Yamaguchi, Tony Stevenson and Pierre Weiss.

World Futures Studies Federation, *et al.*, eds, *Reclaiming the future: a manual of futures studies for African planners*. New York: Taylor & Francis, 1986.

Chapter 5

The Institute for Social Inventions, London

Nicholas Albery

The late Dr Robert Jungk used to warn that 'at present, the future is colonized by a tiny group of people, with citizens moving into a future shaped by this elite. I believe we should not go blindly into this future.' When, with a group of friends, I founded the Institute for Social Inventions in London in 1985, as an educational charity, Jungk seemed to us the natural person to invite to become President – given that our primary aim was to encourage so-called 'ordinary' people to take a part in designing imaginative ideas and projects that could improve the quality of life for people in the future. The colleagues who accepted our invitation to join us in this new adventure included imaginative writers such as Fay Weldon, Ken Campbell and Colin Wilson, mould-breaking business people such as Anita Roddick, Ernest Hall and Sir Peter Parker, and thinkers and management consultants such as Edward de Bono, Tony Buzan, Professor Charles Beer and Professor Charles Handy.

As for the title for our organization, we could equally have used the term 'social innovations' rather than 'inventions' since we were excluding anything to do with products or patentable devices or processes. Instead our focus was to be on ideas for new organizations, new social services, new electoral systems and new ways for people to relate. The kind of schemes we were looking for were exemplified for us by the lifetime's work of one of the Institute's associates, Michael Young (Lord Young of Dartington), possibly Britain's most prolific social inventor: he drafted the ambitious Labour Party manifesto for 1945; he helped found the Consumers Association and its magazine *Which?*; he originated the concept that was to become the Open University; he coined the term 'Meritocracy' with his book of the same name; and he founded a range of small organizations ranging from Brain Trains (study clubs on trains for bored commuters) to the Family Covenant Association (which encourages the formal expression of commitments to new-born babies as an alternative to religious baptism).

The term 'social inventions' has interesting antecedents, particularly in North America, first appearing in the literature in the 1920s. One of the theoreticians of social inventions has been George Fairweather, who in his book *Social Change: the Challenge to Survival*, prescribed social inventions as a positive alternative to revolution. Revolutions, in his view, produce a new crop of leaders who become paranoid about protecting their precious revolution, tending to become as oppressive as those they have replaced. As Yeats put it:

Hurrah for revolution and more cannon-shot!
A beggar upon horseback lashes a beggar on foot.
Hurrah for revolution and cannon come again!
The beggars have changed places but the lash goes on.

Fairweather pointed out that our survival on earth was threatened as never before and that revolution and non-violent protest were unlikely to bring about the social transformations required. What was needed, according to him, were organizations that could promote, not continuous revolution, but continuous evolution, continuous problem-solving social change – identifying problems, finding possible solutions, setting up trial projects, evaluating and disseminating the results. It was as if he had been drawing up a blueprint for our Institute, although in fact we had not heard of his work before the launch.

Another North American social inventions pioneer has been Stuart Conger with his book *Social Inventions*. He has traced the history of social inventions since prehistoric times – noting that marriage, money, laws and schools were all social inventions once upon a time:

'In fields of medical research or electronics or chemistry, governments recognize the need for, and give support to, research laboratories,' writes Conger. 'But the equivalent resources for research and experimentation are not put into helping resolve social problems such as poverty, unemployment, inter-racial conflict, drug addiction, crime, mental illness, labour disputes, poor education and family breakdown. Part of the difficulty is that social scientists are wary of creating social inventions, preferring a passive and analytic role.'

Another flaw, he points out, is that government agencies do not share the business world's seductive approach and its love for the new – social services need to turn aside from their puritanical, impersonal and punitive style, and to adopt the car maker's welcoming attitude to obsolescence, with regular 'improved' models.

Conger thus identified two of the major obstacles facing organizations such as our Institute for Social Inventions: lack of funding and the rejection of new ideas by the powers-that-be – for just as a body rejects a transplant, so these government bodies routinely reject anything 'not invented here'.

The Institute's way of surmounting these obstacles has been to focus initially not on persuading governments to take up suggestions, but on more modest schemes at a neighbourhood level; and to pare down administration costs so that minimum funding is required whilst looking out for the one-in-a-thousand social invention that could make money so as to support the others that can't (one of our directors has now set up a desktop publishing 'launderette' in London, where you can come in and use a machine or get a 'service wash' of individual help and attention; a proportion of the profits have been used to support the Institute).

The neighbourhood approach fits the Institute's ideology, which is summed up in the slogan 'For small nations, small communities and the human scale'. The Institute has developed the line of thinking first adumbrated by Professor Leopold Kohr in his book *The Breakdown of Nations*. He pointed out that the main concern today should be not pollution, resource depletion, over-population, the nuclear threat, poverty, unemployment or crime, but rather the scale on which these problems are occurring. Everything in our mass societies is heading for explosive breakdown, the inevitable natural consequence of a structure grossly exceeding its optimum scale. Consequently, none of our social problems will be soluble until the scale of our societies is reduced, with the ideal model (at least politically, if not economically) being Switzerland – a small population, a federal or confederal structure (with not even a minister for education, this being left to the regions), and with villages within cantons, both enjoying a degree of autonomy through decision-making by referenda. But even if this reduction in size takes place, there is no guarantee that social problems will be tackled successfully – there are, as is only too apparent, several recent examples of small human-scale nations with particularly vicious infighting and atrocities – but a small scale does at least allow the possibility of a solution, does mean that 'ordinary' human beings can begin to feel empowered, and able to exert noticeable influence through their individual leverage. Many people's helplessness concerning the future stems from their feeling overwhelmed by the problems surrounding them, and by the feeling that any contribution they could make would be too trifling to make a difference. Whereas in a human-scale society, any two or three people of goodwill, energy and perseverance, gathered together, can begin to feel that they could move at least small mountains. The Institute certainly sees itself as being in this mountain-moving business.

For the first few years, the Institute focused on gathering ideas from around the world and on publishing the best of these. Each year, the Institute runs a competition, with people from around the world encouraged to send in up to one thousand words about their ideas and projects for social improvements; and with our international network of members also sending in details of schemes that have caught their eye in their local media. The Institute then gives awards, money prizes and publicity to the best ideas, using as criteria, where relevant, the following questions: 'Is the scheme new, imaginative and feasible? Are there signs of progress? Could it act as a model for other schemes elsewhere? Is it community-based? Will a large number of people be affected? Will its effects be long-term?'

This idea-gathering has culminated in our Global Ideas Bank, an International Suggestion Box, which has been available on the Internet from July 1995 (at the address <http://www.newciv.org/worldtrans/GIB/> and which anyone can submit ideas to. It is built on the Institute's past paper-based publications, including several editions of an *Encyclopaedia of Social Innovations* – the size of a large telephone book, entitled *The Book of Visions* in its latest incarnation, followed by annual supplements since (the latest a 280-page affair called *Re-Inventing Society*). Over 2,000 best ideas are described in these volumes, along with the addresses and contact details of their originators. A few of the ideas merited manuals or booklets of their own, and the Institute has published some thirty of these, for example one on how to establish a forest garden (an all-food, minimal maintenance, three-layer garden, with fruit and nut trees above shade-tolerant bushes, vegetables and herbs); and one on how to set up a computer-based neighbourhood multi-barter system (going beyond the present LETS schemes).

In recent years, however, whilst maintaining the competition and the publishing programme, the Institute has moved more into developing some of the best ideas from these publications as actual projects. The Institute tries to launch four major projects a year, with the directors choosing ideas whose time they feel has come. It is then a matter of raising the funds for these new offspring from foundations and of recruiting people to run them (often the hardest part), and then looking after the project (tweaking the idea into shape, providing ideas and back-up, office space, DTP and accounting services, etc.) until the project is able to stand on its own feet as an independent entity. The following are examples of some of my favourite schemes that have been helped in this way.

ON THE EDUCATIONAL FRONT: SOCIAL INVENTIONS WORKSHOPS IN SCHOOLS

This was in fact our first project and is the subject of a manual on how to run such sessions in schools (entitled *Social Invention Workshops*). Over 4,000 social inventions workshop sessions have been run to date, mainly in state schools in the London area. The pupils are encouraged to look at problems in their home lives, their neighbourhoods and within their schools, and to pick one problem to tackle for the term. They are then taught brainstorming as a method and are encouraged to come up with the wildest, zaniest scheme they can think of that will be of assistance. It should be one that is at least imaginative enough to be featured in the local media, as this gives the pupils an extra thrill and an extra motivation to persevere. At which point the pupils draw up a more sober action plan, one that includes their own list of questions for evaluating at the end of term their degree of success or failure. The rest of the term is spent carrying out the project, with a performance or exhibition as appropriate in the final school assembly, where individual 'Certificates of Applied Creativity' are awarded.

Thus 11-year-olds in the Paddington area of London chose as their problem the fact that pavements were fouled by dogs' mess. Their response was to set up a Pooper Scooper Action Squad, using their seaside spades to clear the streets around the school, followed by placard demonstrations and pressure on the council; leading to the first import to the UK of a motorbike from Paris that goes up on the pavement to hoover up the dogs' mess.

Another example: 14-year-old 'under-achievers' at a school in East London chose trouble with the police as their problem, and ended up making a video for showing at local schools about shoplifting, complete with police van and flashing lights, arrest, and film taken in the police cells and the magistrates' court. They reported back with a new level of self-esteem as a result of this work and a new feeling of co-operation with the police, stemming from the latter's assistance with the filming.

ON THE POLITICAL FRONT: THE EAST EUROPE CONSTITUTION DESIGN FORUM

Years before the collapse of the Soviet Union, we were running seminars on the theme of the break-up of the Soviet Union and how best to cope with this inevitable occurrence. And years before the troubles in Bosnia the Institute was concerning itself with the inevitability of civil war in the Balkans. In 1990 we finally persuaded the Swiss government to host a seminar in Lausanne for key politicians and academics from throughout Central and Eastern Europe on the theme of innovative designs for constitutions and electoral systems that could help avert ethnic turmoil. Later the same year we persuaded the government of Malta and the Council of Europe to co-host a follow-up conference on this theme, attended by high-powered politicians and others. This was the first occasion at which delegations from emerging nations such as Estonia and Slovenia had received recognition at an official international gathering, and the discussions, particularly concerning Swiss-style decentralist safeguards as a form of protection for ethnic minorities, certainly influenced the delegates, many of whom were in the throes of designing their constitutions and electoral systems. The conference saw the launch of the East Europe Constitution Design Forum, whereby Western and Eastern experts gathered together in a network to give each other advice and help. This has since also launched the Democracy Design Forum, based in Suffolk, UK, which offers the same sort of advice for countries elsewhere, with electoral systems tailored to the needs of Northern Ireland, South Africa and other potential trouble spots. It has also resulted in three key books by the Democracy Design Forum director, Dr David Chapman, published by the Institute, entitled *Instant Democracy*, *Can Civil Wars Be Avoided?*, and *Re-Inventing Democracy*.

ON THE WELFARE FRONT: THE NATURAL DEATH CENTRE

At least in the UK, there seems to be a superstition that by avoiding the subject of one's own mortality (as opposed to fascination with multiple deaths in the media) one will somehow live longer. Two-thirds of people do not even take the basic first step of writing a will. And the Sainsbury's Homebase DIY store that a colleague approached with the proposition that they should stock flat-pack coffins, wrote in reply that they would not sell coffins, as their 'Homebase' stores were intended for family shopping 'based on the future and therefore not associated with death', whereas of course death in the future is one certainty that every family faces!

To confront such taboos, the Institute founded the Natural Death Centre, primarily to support families looking after a dying person at home. Nowadays, with the disappearance of the extended family and the loss of a sense of neighbourhood, it is increasingly difficult for people to be able to die at home, despite the fact that the majority in surveys express a wish to do so. The Centre trains volunteers to go into people's homes to give carers a break. But their secondary role is as important: they press doctors and priests to recreate an informal neighbourhood care network for their areas; urging these key local leaders to use their influence as opinion leaders to recruit residents prepared to look after those who are critically ill.

The Natural Death Centre is an example of the need for extreme adaptability in 'earthing' a vision. You have a vision. But yours then rubs up against other people's visions, needs and desires. The outcome, if you remain flexible, is often a very new creature altogether. Thus the Centre discovered that families looking after a dying person at home did not then want to hand over to strangers in suits after the death, but wanted to organize the funeral themselves. Now the Centre, which had no intention of dealing with funerals, finds itself answering up to 500 letters a week from families enquiring about DIY funerals, and has had to develop a wide range of expertise on back garden burial, woodland burial, burial at sea, cardboard coffins, etc. It has responded by publishing two books, *The Natural Death Handbook* and *Green Burial – The DIY Guide to Law and Practice*, and by giving awards to the most helpful funeral directors, cemeteries, crematoria and funeral suppliers. It has also set up an Association of Nature Reserve Burial Grounds, which persuades farmers and local authorities to use set-aside land for burial grounds, where a tree is planted for each grave, instead of having a headstone (thus dealing with the problem of overcrowded cemeteries and reducing the need for air-polluting crematoria). Families are also enabled to manage without funeral directors, as each burial ground has to make available cardboard and regular coffins or shrouds to the general public.

ON THE SPECIFICALLY FUTURES-ORIENTED FRONT: THE COUNCIL FOR POSTERITY

This was an idea from Professor Richard Scorer, a mathematician at Imperial College, which won the Institute's main award for 1990. Richard Scorer was in no position to launch such an organization himself and was suggesting that it required hundreds of thousands of pounds of government money. The Institute decided to launch it on minimal funding and to see where it led.

The aim of the Council is to act in an advocacy role for future generations. As Scorer put it:

> The Council for Posterity must take on the role of Counsel for Posterity. It must consist of people who can devote their deepest thoughts on the theme and muster all the arguments to call the present generation away from its myopic trends. ... It must concern itself with the prospect of the widespread dearth of resources, starvation, and the present uncontrollable growth of human numbers and its incompatibility with the hope of future freedom.

This advocacy for posterity could include lawyers who would represent future generations at planning enquiries into developments with potentially awesome long-term consequences. It was for this reason that two lawyers were included amongst the fifteen council members. The others were all chosen as being nationally respected elders, for instance the novelists Doris Lessing and Sir William Golding, the science fiction writer Brian Aldiss, the self-sufficiency expert John Seymour and the ecologist Teddy Goldsmith.

The Council's activities to date have been as modest as its budget. It has acted as the UK National Liaison Unit for the Malta-based Global Network on Responsibilities Towards Future Generations, distributing the *Future Generations* journal in Britain. It has generated papers by Herbert Girardet and others on future-related themes, including organizing an Academic Inn dinner discussion on this topic for a hundred people in London. Its members have represented the UK at international futures-related conferences. And, with financial assistance from the Calouste Gulbenkian Foundation, the Council has launched Adopt-a-Planet in UK schools, details of which have been circulated to 33,000 schools.

Adopt-a-Planet involves encouraging a class in a school to adopt, on a permanent basis, a derelict or vandalized piece of land in the vicinity of the school. The pupils are asked to visualize themselves as Planetary Guardians, somewhat in the style of the Guardian Angels in New York with their anti-mugger project on the underground. The Adopt-a-Planet pupils design uniforms or T-shirts or badges for themselves. They dream up imaginative ways of improving their adopted territory. And the Council for Posterity gives prizes to the best schemes.

The idea behind Adopt-a-Planet is that we are all at this stage desperately needed as caretakers for our home neighbourhoods, and that the appropriate time to inculcate such feelings is pre-puberty. If it is possible to give young people a feeling that they can have a creative and positive effect on their local environment, they are less likely to go around smashing things up post-puberty, once under the influence of their hormones and the gang spirit. Indeed one of the recent prize-winners had their renovated area destroyed by older children. They renovated it anew but this time took the precaution of touring the secondary schools with a presentation about their project, telling how they were caretaking their particular spot and had become very attached to it, and warning off the older pupils.

The Council for Posterity's most ambitious scheme to date has been to help with the import to the UK of the Swedish Natural Step programme. This is a project started by a cancer specialist, Dr Karl-Henrik Robert. He gathered together all the most respected scientists in Sweden, who drew up a consensus document on environmental problems and on the most critical avenues for action. This was then backed by the King of Sweden, by key industrialists and by the media, and was circulated to every household in Sweden. It has led to the greening of big international firms like IKEA, to papers on energy policy and other topics being distributed to MPs, and to an environmental youth parliament. In the UK the main backer to date has been the industrialist John Pontin but it is still early days, and it remains to be seen if the project will take root.

The Council for Posterity has also participated in drawing up Declarations of the Rights of Future Generations. Its own legally worded version contributed towards Malta's efforts in this direction. But it was also felt that there was a need for a more poetic version that a person on the Clapham omnibus could relate to. The following Declaration was the result:

A Declaration of the Rights of Future Generations

Those who live after us have no voice amongst us

We therefore declare and determine their right
to inherit a planet which has been treated by us
with respect for its richness, its beauty and its diversity

a planet
whose atmosphere is life-giving and good, and can
remain so for aeons to come

a planet
whose resources have been carefully maintained and
whose forms of life retain their diversity

a planet
whose soil has been preserved from erosion
with both soil and water unpoisoned
by the waste of our living

a planet
whose people apply their technologies cautiously
with consideration for the long-term consequences

a planet
whose people live in human-scale societies
unravaged by population excess

a planet
whose future generations have interests
which are represented and protected
in the decision-making councils of those alive today.

There are sometimes those whose first scornful reaction to the Council is, 'What has posterity ever done for me?' To these the Council answers: 'It offers you an altruistic aim independent of age, sex, family, creed or nationality; that is, a life with added meaning.'

The above is a brief taster of some of the Institute for Social Inventions' activities. There are many more that I am extremely proud of – the Global Suggestions Box, to be available via Internet, where participants can rate the ideas, so that newcomers can access the *crème de la crème* without drowning in a sea of information; the Hippocratic Oath for Scientists, Engineers and Chief Executives, signed by 35 Nobel Prize Winners and used in some university graduation ceremonies; the Apprentice–Master Alliance, that links school leavers and new graduates on a long-term basis with a one-person business person with real skills to teach; not to mention our Adventure and Romance Agency, which pairs people off for risky holidays on the basis of research which indicates that romance happens most readily in adventurous settings (the female researcher handed out her card to men on a rope bridge and to men on a normal bridge. Many more men from the rope bridge contacted her).

People sometimes ask the Institute how to become a social inventor. My answer is, not only to look for ideas that inspire you or that have a certain magic to them, but also to consider every problem in life as an opportunity for a social invention. At the Institute we always ask ourselves: 'How could we tackle this personal problem in such a way as to help solve similar problems for other people in future?' For instance, we knew a number of women in their thirties without partners as a result of concentrating too hard on their careers. Hence the Adventure and Romance Agency. We knew a number of spirited and deserving teenagers without jobs. Hence the Apprentice–Master Alliance. We knew of deaths at home where the families had lacked information and support. Hence the Natural Death Centre.

There are now Institutes for Social Inventions modelled on ours in Sweden, Russia, Germany and Holland*. If there is not something similar already happening in your country, please consider starting your own institute. All it takes is a few like-minded friends. I sometimes feel a bit like a recruiting poster: 'Your country (whichever country it may be) needs you and your ideas!' And so do future generations.

* For more information contact The Institute for Social Inventions, 20 Heber Road, London NW2 6AA, UK (tel 44 181 208 2853; fax 44 181 452 6434).

REFERENCES

Albery, Nicholas (1986) *Social Invention Workshops*, London: Institute for Social Inventions.

Albery, Nicholas (1992) *The Book of Visions*, London: Virgin Books.

Albery, Nicholas and Mezey, Matthew (1994) *Re-Inventing Society*, London: Institute for Social Inventions.

Albery, Nicholas *et al.* (1993) *The Natural Death Handbook*, London: Virgin Books.

Bradfield, John (1994) *Green Burial – The DIY Guide to Law and Practice*, London: The Natural Death Centre.

Chapman, Dr David (1990) *Instant Democracy – Constitutional Proposals for Emerging Democracies*, London: Institute for Social Inventions.

Chapman, Dr David (1991) *Can Civil Wars Be Avoided?*, London: Institute for Social Inventions.

Chapman, Dr David (1995) *Re-Inventing Democracy*, London: Institute for Social Inventions.

Conger, Stuart (1974) *Social Inventions*, Ottawa: Information Canada, p. 9ff.

Fairweather, George (1974) *Social Change: the Challenge to Survival*, Moristown, New Jersey: General Learning Press.

Jungk, Dr Robert (1987) *Future Workshops*, London: Institute for Social Inventions.

Kohr, Professor Leopold (1986) *The Breakdown of Nations*, London: Routledge and Kegan Paul.

Yeats, W. B. (1965) *The Collected Poems of W. B. Yeats*, London: Macmillan; p. 358: 'The Great Day'.

Chapter 6

Education systems as agents of change: an overview of futures education

Jane Page

WHY APPLY FUTURES CONCERNS IN EDUCATIONAL SETTINGS?

There can be no more eloquent testimonial for the need for futures education than the growing body of international research on youths' attitudes to the future.[1] This research consistently underlines the extent to which young people experience difficulty coming to terms with the future, which they generally view with trepidation and ambivalence. Youths fear the consequences of change, the threats of war and technological innovation and environmental destruction. Their expressions of what the world will be like in the future indicate their sense of alienation from their understanding of the global future, which they perceive in consistently negative terms.

This sense of disconnection is evident as much in the imagery drawn upon by the youths as it is in the messages of alienation relayed to the interviewers. Recurrent within the interviews are images of increasing automation, computers, robots, nuclear weaponry and scientists controlling the future:

> I saw a science and technology based planet where robots and machines are taking over. Life will be all mechanical. . . . That is computer operated machines will dominate. . . . The environment will be mainly demolished and many animals will be extinct. . . . Wars will be very common. . . . What I saw seemed to me like one of those science-fiction movies.[2]

Such negative descriptions draw heavily upon conventional, often stereotypical, science fiction imagery of the future. The picture of the global future built up by the youths thus represents an alien world which has been formed for them by conventionalized cultural values. By focusing on the fantastic and technological aspects of the future, youths commonly leave themselves out of the equation of what the future will be like:[3]

I fear the world in the twenty-first century will be much like a comic book science fiction story. Especially one like 'Judge Dredd' will become reality. If we don't attempt to bring these thoughts to the surface now, then the Earth will become a vast waste dump.[4]

The blame for the creation of such patterns of thinking should not be laid solely on the mechanisms of popular culture and the mass media. Culturally generated stereotypes fill a vacuum of understanding about the future. Youths draw upon dystopian imagery in the absence of any alternative philosophical and methodological frameworks with which to understand their place within the future. What is needed, therefore, is an alternative framework for understanding the future and an alternative forum in which to develop it.

There can be no doubting the potential effectiveness of education as a forum in which to address these issues. In the case of Australia, for example, education is the largest national industry, servicing over three million pupils.[5] It is, therefore, a fundamentally important means of transmitting social and cultural attitudes. Pre-school to secondary education is, moreover, inherently futures oriented since its function is to provide children with the knowledge and skills to participate effectively in society now and in the future. Children spend a significant amount of their time in educational settings and their outlooks, attitudes and ability to address issues related to the future will be directly influenced by their learning experiences in educational contexts.

FUTURES STUDIES AND THE EDUCATION SYSTEM

The education system has not, to date, responded well to the challenge of applying futures issues in pre-school to secondary educational curricula. This is partly attributable to the lack of an awareness on the part of most educators of the methodologies and philosophical orientations of futures studies. As a result of this gap in the educational knowledge base, the majority of educators do not possess the critical frameworks necessary to analyse their understandings of the future relevance of education and to convert futures concerns into practical learning experiences. In order to remedy this situation, futures researchers will need to continue the long-term objective of disseminating information about the discipline of futures studies across educational settings.

But while still allowing for this lack of knowledge, the criticism can justly be made that the education system has not adequately addressed its mission to provide children with the knowledge and skills to participate effectively in society now and in the future. In Australia, the education system has been criticized for its lack of an adequate commitment to its future component. Gough has drawn attention to the manner in which educational researchers and policy makers frequently pay lip service to the importance of preparing students for the future without, however, seriously addressing this as an objective in their curricula and in their methodologies.[6] According to Gough, the education system is characterized by a largely superficial understanding of futures issues. When addressed, the future is generally considered according to three sets of assumptions: the first, where futures are addressed tacitly in educational statements but not discussed in direct terms; the second, where a token reference to futures issues is used solely for rhetorical purposes; and the third, where taken-for-granted futures apply a predetermined version of the future as a basis for decision making.[7] The conclusion that educational discourse relies too heavily on past and present analysis of issues has been strongly argued by Richard Slaughter and Headley Beare, who have warned of the consequences of an education system which replicates educative frameworks which are rooted in a sense of the past.[8] Slaughter cautions that 'If education stays stubbornly locked into outdated paradigms and past perceptions of problems it becomes a *source* of social rigidity, not a remedy for it.'[9]

Critical theorists stress the importance of educational institutions as transmitters of the dominant culture of society.[10] The educational curriculum should, therefore, be ranked alongside television and other forms of mass media as a fundamentally influential forum for the forma-tion of youth attitudes to the future. Any deficiencies in its approach to the future will, accordingly, have a potentially significant, negative impact on youth perceptions of the future. As an illustration of this concern, we would cite the criticism of the *Social Education Survey*, which examined the presentation of the future in Australian year ten secondary school texts. In these texts, the future was found to have been addressed according to a consistently negative framework which stressed social, economic and environmental problems without making allowance for the potential of future generations to contribute energetically and creatively to solving problems.[11] Through the use of dystopian images of the future, these texts are thus perpetuating the previously articulated problem of youths' attitudes to the future, rather than helping to alleviate it.

The failings of this approach to education are rendered more apparent by the research undertaken in the 1970s which highlights the importance of students developing a positive and active approach to the future. An American study concluded in 1977, for example, posited a correlation between an active orientation towards the future and higher levels of self-esteem and social responsibility.[12] This research follows studies under-taken in the 1940s, 1950s and early 1960s which found a correlation to exist between high academic achievers, optimistic attitudes and a greater concern for future goals or a future time perspective.[13]

Some of these studies place special emphasis on the importance of an understanding of the future for an individual's development. Stinchcombe, for example, identifies an awareness of the future as the major factor distinguishing high school achievers from under-achievers.[14] Benjamin Singer similarly emphazises the importance of future role images for youths' social and educational development.[15] Bell and Mau postulate that a futures-focused image forms the basis upon which to achieve social change.[16] While these latter studies may run the risk of underestimating the formative influence of social and economic backgrounds, there can be no doubting their conclusion that students who do not believe that the future will bring them anything will inevitably regard education as boring and irrelevant.[17]

That students might themselves wish for a fuller exploration of futures issues in their curricula was highlighted in a study undertaken in New Jersey in 1978.[18] Over 75 percent of the 2,400 students interviewed identified the future as one of the main subjects requiring their study.[19] The students' desire for a new curriculum perspective may, in part, be attributable to their dissatisfaction with the concerns of the traditional educational curriculum.[20] In this context, Allen and Plante and Hutchinson have all underlined the extent to which secondary school students frequently find the curriculum restrictive and irrelevant to their concerns.[21] The exploration of futures issues can offer students a means of exploring their hopes and fears in a more flexible and personally relevant manner than many of the traditional subjects which make up educational curricula.

There can be no doubting the real need which exists for the incorporation of futures-based components in educational curricula. The studies of youth attitudes towards the future, of the importance of a positive sense of the future, and of the failings of the educational system as a whole to address these issues, renders this conclusion clear. But how are these issues to be addressed? What should the objectives of such a curriculum be and how should they be framed? To answer these questions we need to examine more closely the principles of futures studies as they are applied in educational contexts.

This task is rendered difficult by the fact that the study of futures in education remains a developing and relatively under-researched area. As Slaughter has underlined, little synthesis and comparative evaluation of futures in education has taken place.[22] This is particularly true of the futures educational initiatives which have occurred outside primary, secondary and tertiary educational contexts, such as in the work of non-government organizations, conferences, symposia, special courses and futures workshops.[23] The following discussion will build upon the growing body of research and literature concerning futures education which seeks to draw together, from a disparate range of sources and initiatives, the underlying tenets of futures studies as they are applied in education.

PRINCIPLES OF FUTURES EDUCATION

The curriculum is the fundamental means by which the objectives of futures education will be transmitted and realized. The concept of curriculum renewal, accordingly, informs the objectives of all futures educators. Futures educators emphasize the importance of an integrated curriculum, seeking to move beyond the discrete, discipline-oriented system of traditional curricula to a broader, inter-disciplinary approach.[24] A curriculum of this kind, they suggest, would stress the links between different aspects of the curriculum and recognize the complex range of factors influencing every element of the curriculum. The traditional educational discipline, which commonly claims possession of a single, unitary meaning by excluding divergent or opposing viewpoints and methodologies, is countered in this model by a more open-ended set of teaching and learning strategies. The emphasis in the futures-based curriculum is not so much on the learning of facts as on the process of learning how to learn, nor so much on the acquisition of absolute knowledge as on the development of varying skills and attitudes towards learning.[25]

The more open-ended curriculum well prepares students for adulthood since it reflects more accurately the dynamism which characterizes contemporary society and the lack of certainty which exists about the future. It is also more flexible and responsive to the continuing learning processes of individuals.[26] The futures-oriented curriculum would allow many points of entry for students' differing needs and interests and would adopt appropriately varied methods of instruction and options of instructional objectives.[27]

This principle of flexibility provides students with a heightened awareness of the importance of their own roles in shaping the curriculum. A flexible curriculum would enable students to perceive the extent to which learning grows out of a process of collaboration between students and the educator. They would, in this manner, be encouraged to view themselves as pro-active and in control of setting the agenda for the curriculum. One of the advantages of this approach is that it would render the curriculum more personally meaningful to the students.[28]

The students' sense of control of the curriculum would also reinforce their understanding of one of the key principles of futures studies: that individuals should develop skills to enable them actively to control their destinies rather than passively to accept them.[29] This emphasis, futures educators would argue, demonstrates the degree to which the objectives of futures education are already consonant with the central principles of traditional educational approaches. The futures-oriented curriculum shares with the traditional curriculum the fundamental goal of providing students with the means to exercise participation and choice in their present and future lives.[30] The main distinction between the traditional curriculum and the futures-oriented curriculum, in this respect, is that the latter seeks to go beyond the rhetoric which frequently characterizes the former and to address this goal directly and systematically.

The previous discussion should already have highlighted the emphasis, in futures education, on the development of a strong self-concept. An active, participatory approach to education places the individual's sense of self at the forefront of change. For Kauffman, the cultivation of a sense of self is particularly important for contemporary education. A strong self-concept can constitute an internal anchor for individuals seeking to function successfully in a dynamic and changing world.[31] It also encourages the development of the students' sense of self-motivation, so that they can assume responsibility for propelling themselves through life.[32]

The combination of flexibility and self-motivation in the futures-oriented curriculum encourages students to consider, more broadly, ways in which they can counter the narrowly defined roles often assigned to them by society with new roles and concepts.[33] The futures-oriented curriculum would facilitate the development of the students' ability to renew their thinking by continually re-assessing and, where necessary, modifying their understanding of concepts against their changing experiences. Students would, in this manner, be encouraged to accept and enjoy the challenge of living with ambiguities and differing alternatives rather than with a closed sense of meaning which is achieved only through a reductive denial of the diversity of experience.[34]

It would be misleading to conclude from this analysis that futures educators espouse a purely relativist approach to education. The literature sometimes includes reference to the recently defined condition of post-modernity,[35] and futures educators would certainly share the concerns of these commentators to reveal the basis of knowledge in ideology and power relations. But the vast majority of futures educators would not seek to construct curricula based around the anti-humanist critiques of much post-structuralist critical theory. Futures education is, instead, characterized by a consistently strong ethical and philosophical orientation which seeks to instil in students a sense of their place in what has recently been described as 'a truly global web of social and ecological relationships'.[36]

This philosophical orientation is in accordance with the objective of futures studies to facilitate students' recognition of their connections with the outside world of culture, society and the environment. The holistic, global perspective results in an emphasis upon students developing qualities of tolerance and empathy,[37] an appreciation of diversity and difference,[38] and a strong sense of justice and equality.[39] The stress upon students reaching out beyond their immediate concerns also commonly results in a link being established between futures education and environmental awareness, a connection which is evident, for example, in the publications on futures education sponsored by the World Wide Fund for

Nature.[40] This emphasis enhances the students' awareness of the extent to which each individual forms part of a broader, interconnected network of relationships, an understanding which is generally absent from the previously cited youth attitudes to the future.

There is an idealism inherent in much of this thinking, and futures educators occasionally refer directly to the utopian tradition from which they derive some of their fundamental perspectives.[41] But most futures educators temper the idealism of their beliefs with an equally strong emphasis upon sustained critical thinking and questioning of the taken-for-granted truths of society. For Slaughter, the ability to 'probe beneath the surface' of accepted norms and conventions constitutes one of the key strategies of futures education. An enterprise of this kind, he suggests, will not result in a deconstruction of the frameworks of meaning. It will rather heighten the quality of meaning that students can derive from the curriculum since it will encourage them to perceive the much wider range of present and future options which exists for them.[42]

The emphasis on critical thinking lies behind the frequent reference in futures educational studies to the development of such thinking skills as flexibility, curiosity, inventiveness and imagination and the ability to deal with surprise, conflict and irresolution.[43] The re-assessment and re-definition of fundamental meanings and assumptions involved in critical thinking will further assist students to view themselves as creators of change, rather than passive recipients of the future, and to contemplate a range of options for the future rather than a fixed, singular ideal.[44] As Slaughter has noted, 'individuals who know that they stand at the centre of their own history as agents rather than spectators are well placed to negotiate conceptions and images of futures worth living in'.[45]

One way of framing this process is to develop concepts of probable, possible and preferable options for the future. The usefulness of a framework of this kind lies in the manner in which it encourages individuals to develop an awareness of how to act on issues. Time lines and futures wheels have also been used as a means of diagrammatically conceptualizing and exploring future options.

Futures education is thus concerned with understanding the processes of change and developing the ability within individuals to control and direct their futures. It encourages individuals not to fear change but, rather, to feel that they can manipulate and influence events directly. Futures education, in short, empowers individuals to bring about change rather than suffer it. It also stresses the individual's links with the outside world, encouraging them to recognize the extent to which we are all bound together in the common project of forming the future. The relevance of the development of these skills for the present should be immediately obvious. They are of fundamental significance on the deepest and most pervasive level of human development as they encourage a positive self-concept and a sense of bonding with the outside world, an outlook which stands in stark contrast to the youth attitudes which began the discussion.

When viewed as a whole, futures initiatives group themselves into a global enterprise aimed at reinvigorating educational practice and research. This global perspective will be difficult to achieve, however, while the discipline still lacks a co-ordinated network of educational bodies, non-government organizations and individuals who might exchange ideas, evaluate initiatives and learn from each other's work in the area. The significant potential of futures education to effect a quantum shift in the way we perceive education should, nonetheless, remain clear. Futures education provides the frameworks, the tools and the methodologies to facilitate social change in a manner which encourages individuals to regain a sense of control over their future lives. It has the potential to reinvigorate existing educational frameworks with a new sense of purpose while also enabling educators to address seriously and systematically their charter to lay significant foundations for future lives.

NOTES

1 F.P. Hutchinson, 'Educating beyond Fatalism and Impoverished Social Imagination: Are we Actively Listening to Young People's Voices on the Future?', Ph.D. thesis, Department of Asian Languages and Societies and Department of Sociology, University of New England, 1993; R. Eckersley, *Australian Attitudes to Science and Technology and the Future: A Report to the Commission for the Future*, Canberra, Australian Government Publishing for Commission for the Future, 1988; R. Eckersley, *Casualties of Change, The Predicament of Youth in Australia: A Report on the Social and Psychological Problems Faced by Young People in Australia*, Canberra, Australian Government Printing Service for Australia, 1988; R. Eckersley, *Apocalypse? No! Youth and the Challenge to Change: Bringing Youth, Science and Society Together in the New Millennium*, Melbourne, Commission for the Future, 1992; P. McGregor, 'Visions of the Future', in R. A. Slaughter (ed.), *Studying the Future: An Introductory Reader*, Melbourne, Commission for the Future and the Australian Bicentennial Authority, 1989, pp. 30–35; N. Wilson, 'The State of the Planet and Young Children's Minds', in R. A. Slaughter (ed.), *Studying the Future*, pp. 36–41; D. Hicks, *Exploring Alternative Futures: A Teacher's Interim Guide*, London, Global Futures Project, Institute of Education, University of London, 1991, pp. 6–7; D. Hicks (ed.) *Education for Peace: Issues, Principles, and Practice in the Classroom*, London, Routledge, 1988, pp. 3–5; P. M. Wagschal and L. Johnson, 'Children's Views of the Future: Innocence Almost Lost', *Phi Delta Kappan*, 1986, vol. 67/9, pp. 666–69.
2 Mohamed, a year eleven student, in Hutchinson, 'Educating beyond Fatalism', p. 9.
3 A point also made by Wagschal and Johnson, 'Children's Views', p. 668.
4 Chris, a seventeen-year-old student, in Hutchinson, 'Educating beyond Fatalism', p. 11.

5 B. O. Jones, 'Carnivores, Vegetarians and Beef Consommé', in P. Noyce (ed.), *Futures in Education: The Report*, Melbourne, Commission for the Future and Hawthorn Institute's Centre for Curriculum, 1986, p. 29; I. Castles, *Australian Statistics Yearbook, 1994*, Canberra, Australian Bureau of Statistics, 1993, p. 126.
6 N. Gough, 'Tacit, Token and Taken for Granted', *Futures*, April 1990, p. 299.
7 N. Gough, 'Futures Education – For Whose Future?', *Primary Education*, 25/5, 1994, p. 11; Gough, 'Tacit Token', pp. 301–7.
8 H. Beare and R. A. Slaughter, *Education for the Twenty-First Century*, London, Routledge, 1993, p. 102.
9 R. A. Slaughter, 'Futures in Education: A Human Agenda', in Noyce (ed.), *Futures in Education*, p. 18.
10 J. Germov, 'What To Do with the Working Class? Towards a Cultural Critique of the Curriculum', *Curriculum Perspectives*, vol. 14/1, 1994, p. 2.
11 McGregor, 'Visions of the Future', pp. 31–32.
12 J. Plante, 'A Study of Future Time Perspective and its Relationship to the Self Esteem and Social Responsibility of High School Students', Ph.D. dissertation, 1977, cited in D. W. Allen and J. Plante, 'Looking at the Future of Education', in L. Jennings and S. Cornish (eds), *Education and the Future*, Bethesda, World Future Society, 1980, p. 113.
13 J. E. Teahan, 'Future Time Perspective, Optimism, and Academic Achievement', *Journal of Abnormal and Social Psychology*, vol. 57, 1958, pp. 379–80.
14 W. Bell and J. A. Mau, cited in A. Stinchcombe, 'Images of the Future: Theory and Research Strategies', in W. Bell and J. A. Mau (eds), *The Sociology of the Future*, New York, Russell Sage Foundation, 1971, p. 33.
15 B. Singer, 'The Future-Focused Role Image', in A. Toffler (ed.), *Learning for Tomorrow: The Role of the Future in Education*, New York, Random House, 1974, pp. 19–32.
16 Bell and Mau, *Sociology of the Future*, p. 35.
17 D. L. Kauffman, *Futurism and Future Studies*, Washington, National Education Association, 1980, p. 44.
18 Allen and Plante, 'Looking at the Future', pp. 111–12.
19 Ibid., p. 111.
20 N. Wilson, 'State of the Planet', p. 39.
21 Allen and Plante, 'Looking at the Future', pp. 111–12; Hutchinson, 'Educating beyond Fatalism', p. 22.
22 R. A. Slaughter, 'What is Futures Education?', in R. A. Slaughter (ed.), *Studying the Future*, pp. 16–17; R. A. Slaughter, *An International Overview of Futures Education: A Report for Unesco's Clearinghouse for the Future*, Melbourne, 1991, pp. 14–15.
23 Slaughter, *International Overview*, pp. 4, 10–14.
24 United Nations Education, Scientific and Cultural Organization, *The World by the Year 2000*, Paris, Unesco, 1987, p. 10; S. Benjamin, 'An Ideascape for Education: What Futurists Recommend', *Educational Leadership*, vol. 7/1, 1989, p. 10.
25 D. van Avery, in D. van Avery *et al.*, *Futuristics and Education: An ASCD Task Force Report*, Alexandria, Association for Supervision and Curriculum Development, 1979, p. 10; Kauffman, *Futurism*, p. 47; N. Postman and C. Weingartner, *Teaching as a Subversive Activity*, New York, Dell Publishing, 1969, p. 172.
26 C. Sachs, 'Exploring the Human Dimensions of Development: A Review of the Literature', Paris, Unesco, Bureau of Studies and Programming Major

Programme 1, *Reflection on World Problems and Future-Oriented Studies, Studies and Documents*, 1990, p. 17.

27 R. G. Glaser, 'The School of the Future: Adaptive Environments for Learning', in L. Rubin (ed.), *The Future of Education: Perspectives on Tomorrow's Schooling*, Boston, Allyn and Bacon, 1975, p. 131; Kauffman, *Futurism*, p. 47.

28 J. Cumming, 'Educating Young Adolescents: Targets and Strategies for the 1990s', *Curriculum Perspectives*, vol. 14/3, 1994, p. 42; Australian Curriculum Studies Association, 'A Vision for Australian Schooling', *Curriculum Perspectives*, vol. 13/2, 1993, p. 43.

29 R. A. Slaughter, *What Do We Do Now the Future is Here? Essays on: Futures, Education and the Speculative Imagination*, Lancaster, University of Lancaster, Department of Educational Research, 1985, p. 5.

30 H. Beare cited in A. Crawford, 'Painting a New Picture', *21.C*, vol. 8, Summer 1992, p. 81.

31 Kauffman, *Futurism*, p. 45.

32 R. E. Barnes, 'An Educator Looks Back from 1996', *The Futurist*, vol. 12/2, 1978, p. 123.

33 R. A. Slaughter, *From Fatalism to Foresight, Educating for the Early 21st Century: A Framework for Considering Young People's Needs over the Next 20 Years*, Melbourne, Australian Council for Educational Administration, 1994, p. 41; A. W. Combs, 'What the Future Demands of Education', *Phi Delta Kappan*, January 1981, p. 370.

34 D. van Avery, 'Futuristics and Education', *Educational Leadership*, February 1980, p. 442.

35 W. E. Doll 'Foundations for a Post-Modern Curriculum', *Journal of Curriculum Studies*, vol. 21/3, 1989, pp. 243–53; R. A. Slaughter, 'Cultural Reconstruction in the Post-Modern World', *Journal of Curriculum Studies*, vol. 21/3, 1989, pp. 255–70.

36 Slaughter, *International Overview*, p. 41.

37 P. E. Griffin, 'Educational Futures: An Issue to be Considered Now', *Curriculum and Research Bulletin*, vol. 20/2, 1985, p. 23; H. Beare, 'Education and the Post-Industrial State', *Unicorn*, vol. 10/2, 1984, p. 130; Combs, 'What the Future Demands', p. 372.

38 Allen and Plante, 'Looking at the Future', p. 115.

39 B. Wilson, 'Social Outcomes, Power and Education', *Curriculum Perspectives*, vol. 10/2, 1990, p. 6.

40 See S. Greig *et al.*, *Earthrights: Education as if the Planet Really Mattered*, London, Kogan Page and the World Wildlife Fund, 1987; R. Lorenzo, *Some Ideas and Goals for Environmental Education*, Milan, Associazione Italiana World Wildlife Fund, Settore Educazione, 1986 (and subsequent publications); S. Fountain, *Learning Together: Global Education 4–7*, Leckhampton, Stanley Thornes and the World Wide Fund for Nature, Centre for Global Education, 1990; J. Smart (ed.), *My World: Exploring the Future*, Godalming, Scholastic Publications, on behalf of the World Wide Fund for Nature, 1991; H. B. Joicey, *An Eye on the Environment: An Art Education Project*, London, Unwin Hyman and the World Wide Fund for Nature, 1986.

41 D. Hicks, 'Preparing for the Millennium: Reflections on the Need for Futures Education', *Futures*, July–August, 1991, p. 634.

42 R. A. Slaughter, *Futures Concepts and Powerful Ideas*, Melbourne, Futures Study Centre, 1991, p. 34.

43 J. I. Goodlad, 'A Concept of School in 2000 AD', in R. W. Hostrop (ed.), *Foundations of Futurology in Education*, Homewood, Etc. Publications, 1973, p. 220; D. E. Tinkler, 'Change and Choices for Education: Learning and

Teaching for the Future', paper presented at the Australian Education Conference, Wesley College, Perth, 29 September 1987, p. 4.

44 Beare and Slaughter, *Education*, pp. 114–15.
45 R. A. Slaughter, *Recovering the Future*, Melbourne, Monash University, School of Environmental Science, 1989, p. 149.

Chapter 7

Critical futures study as an educational strategy

Richard A. Slaughter

This chapter has three main purposes. The first is to clarify the relationship between critical futures studies and critical futures research. The second is to show how each has been implemented in post-graduate courses at the University of Melbourne. The third and major purpose is to draw out some implications of this approach as an educational strategy.

For some years I pursued the development of critical futures studies as a particular approach to futures work. For reasons explained elsewhere, and outlined below, a critical approach seems highly productive and the term 'studies' appeared at first to characterize what was being attempted.[1] But increasingly I became aware that the sustained pursuit of such studies led on to a more substantive research orientation. The relationship between study and research therefore needed to be articulated. For example, beginning students should be expected to engage in futures studies but, initially at least, not research. The former necessarily involves an induction into the area, the latter assumes it.

Such distinctions are important for the development of futures work. Recognition and support depends upon playing the game according to accepted standards. On the other hand, I am aware that some study *is* research; that the two are not entirely separate or distinct. None the less, this is a secondary point. We must know what we mean by 'study' and 'research' in relation to critical futures work. Most beginning students will start with the former and may reasonably expect to move on to the latter at a later stage.

I taught futures studies at the University of Lancaster for some years, and then again at the University of Melbourne. Both had Departments of History, yet neither had one of Foresight or Futures Studies. In education the past is evidently of much greater interest than the future. This 'temporal chauvinism' is a long-standing concern. H.G. Wells commented upon it in the 1930s in a paper called 'Wanted: Professors of Foresight'.[2] In the absence of a Department of Futures, the courses described in this chapter were offered from within an Education faculty. While this was not an ideal arrangement, it did mean that the articulation between futures concerns and educational ones was plain to see. Over a period of about ten years the appeal of futures studies to students also became clear. While it still may be 'early days' in this context, the evaluations were unambiguous: futures studies clearly provides a valuable component in training and professional development at the post-graduate level.

What is it that futures studies provides, that other disciplinary foci do not? I have seen successive cohorts of students go through broadly the same process: early difficulty with new concepts, challenging language, new methodologies, soon followed by deepening insight and elation at new perspectives.[3] Consequently I became convinced that such studies accomplished at least three things.

First, they allowed people to 'put things together' in new ways. That is to re-frame many conventional ideas about the world (including the move away from a 'default', taken-for-granted, static frame to a critical, dynamic and proactive one). Second, by understanding what has gone wrong in human affairs *and* the associated processes of cultural innovation and renewal, they provided individuals with the chance to achieve their own personal recovery of vision and purpose. Third, they made available the powerful symbolic resources of the futures field: concepts, language, ideas, methodologies, networks, projects, etc. These are vital because they facilitate the emergence of *a futures discourse*. To my mind it is this above all that can support the shifts of understanding, perception and policy, upon which our collective future depends.

So far as I am concerned, futures studies has already won many of the important arguments about legitimacy, applicability and relevance in educational settings. But it remains caught up in two kinds of lags. One is institutional. The universities are full of rhetoric about strategic planning, being proactive and serving their communities. Yet there is a cultural gulf between their outlook and one that takes the future as a substantive concern. Many have planning and administrative arrangements that fail to incorporate standard futures tools and methods. As noted, there are still too few Departments of Futures. On the whole, universities remain preoccupied with conservative forms of knowledge and enquiry. Admitting futures studies into the approved map of knowledge involves shifts of understanding and perception that many powerful decision-makers have yet to achieve. The second lag is related to this.

I have come to realize that there is a very considerable, but *latent*, demand for futures work both in schools and in higher education. That is, once people understand what it is, how it contributes, most find it valuable. But to reach this stage they must first know it exists, have some prior knowledge or intuition of what it provides and, finally, find a way of tapping these resources. These are demanding conditions and, naturally enough, they are not fulfilled in many places. But they will be. Long before the twenty-first century arrives there will be futures courses, debates, resources of many kinds available on the Internet.

WHAT IS CRITICAL FUTURES STUDY?

The term 'critical' is often misunderstood, particularly in the USA. However, it does not simply mean 'to criticize'. Nor does it signify a negative or derivative stance. It is not threatening and should not be construed as such. Rather, it signifies a range of methods and tools through which we may look 'beneath the surface' of social reality in order to realize the full potential of futures work.[4] Critical futures study does recognize the *partiality* of traditions, cognitive frameworks and ways of knowing. It is therefore possible to *problematize* aspects of the existing social and economic order and to explore some of their contradictions. Why is this a constructive enterprise?

An unproblematic status quo is one which is accepted without question; one which embodies certain quasi-transcendental goals which are to be progressively realized now and in the future. Such goals could include 'health, wealth and prosperity for all humankind'. Others might be 'racial equality', 'steady growth of GNP' and 'peaceful international relations'. These all sound highly attractive. But, given the real substantive character of ideologies, assumptions, systems of exploitation, repression and destruction now in place, they may not be realizable. Like the advertisements for women's fashions or impossibly perfect holidays they have little substance.

I take the view that regardless of its very many impressive technical achievements, late industrial culture is the most rapacious, self-centred, humanly and environmentally destructive system yet seen upon the earth. It presides over numerous wars, the repressive exploitation of many Third World populations (and their underprivileged equivalents in Western countries) and the implacable destruction of the world's life-support systems. Given this context, conventional sanguine views of the future have a flat, unconvincing and, indeed, blatantly spurious quality. The standard Western worldview, far from leading to universal peace and prosperity, actually leads directly toward the abyss. It holds out no possibility whatsoever of sustainable human futures. Hence, in the extraordinary conditions of the late twentieth century, business-as-usual outlooks are positively dangerous. These uncomfortable facts tend to be missed by conventional educational discourses and practices, many of which are locked into short-term thinking and remain preoccupied with questions of status, power and control.

Hence there is value in looking in depth at this culture and asking some penetrating questions. This is exactly what critical futures study attempts to do. Calling the bluff of anodyne views of futures (or overly negative ones) helps us to isolate aspects of our present culture and way of life which urgently require critical attention. No one should doubt that this is a responsible and constructive task.

If it were *not* possible to interrogate the received wisdom of industrialized cultures, then we would most certainly be set on an irreversible path toward global catastrophe. If we were *not* able to understand our situation and act with informed foresight to avert the worst dangers, we would be committed to social learning by the crudest of experiences. We would have to experience catastrophe in order to prevent it! This is clearly unacceptable. The price of crisis learning becomes too great in an over-stressed and endangered world.[5] Critical futures study therefore aligns with other critical/interpretive initiatives to explore the possibility of productive discourse about the character, assumptions and likely directions embedded within the dominant culture, as well as some lying beyond it.[6] Some key propositions of this approach are given below.

1 Discourse is not neutral. It is grounded in particular traditions and speech communities which cannot, by definition, be 'objective'. Intersubjectivity is only partly rational.
2 It is helpful to adopt a reflexive posture; that is, one in which the observer does not simply observe (speak, act, etc.) but is aware of the active, shaping character of these processes.
3 A presumption is made in favour of what Habermas called 'the human emancipatory interest'; or, simply, the fundamental interest of all persons in freedom, self-constitution and unconstrained conditions of life.
4 It is suggested that 'progress' is no longer a term which can be used without irony. It has much less to do with tools, techniques and the external conditions of life than with (a) understanding the breakdown of a cultural synthesis at the epistemological level and (b) recovering the ability to discern a basis for qualitatively different futures.
5 Technologies are not regarded merely as neutral tools but as cultural processes embodying specific ideological and social interests. The most notable features of technologies are often invisible and intangible (which is why they are overlooked by empiricist approaches).
6 Stories are regarded as powerful explanatory devices. They are not 'mere fiction' because they model human reality in novel and useful ways. They can therefore be used to explore some aspects of human futures in ways not accessible to reason, analysis or the techniques of futures research (such as forecasting).
7 There is an explicit focus on *the negotiation of meanings* (such as work, leisure, defence, health). This gives access to some of the most important shaping processes involved in social and cultural change, including those associated with cultural editing.[7]

The origins of these propositions lie in a number of related fields. They include the following:

- the interpretative perspective, itself emerging from critical practice, hermeneutics, the analysis of discourse and semiotics;
- the sociology of science and technology: science as a social product, technology as cultural text;
- the critical theory of society: cognitive interests, Habermas' theory of communicative action, etc. Foucault's analysis of power;
- speculative writing: stories which comment with awareness on past, present and a wide range of futures;
- environmental scanning and strategic planning: techniques of futures research applied in organizations.

The careful use of these cultural and symbolic resources provides futures study and research with some powerful metatheoretical tools.

TEACHING CRITICAL FUTURES STUDY

Critical futures study can be defined as *the application of critical futures concepts, ideas, theories to futures problems.* Teaching it is first and foremost a matter of providing an induction into the conceptual and methodological aspects of a futures discourse. It is about learning the language, engaging with the literature, clarifying understandings and joining a global conversation with peers. An outline syllabus for an introductory postgraduate course on critical futures studies could include such elements as: an introduction to the futures field, building blocks of the approach, case studies, analysis of the industrial worldview, cultural innovation and the recovery of meaning, imaging futures, and futures study in education.

Specific foci for critical futures study may include:

- critical analysis of discourse and ideological interests;
- the critique of worldview assumptions and practices;
- the reconceptualization of 'world problems';
- analysis of person/person, person/nature and person/machine relations;
- dealing with fears and concerns about futures; and
- the design and implementation of futures curricula.

From this outline, critical futures study is seen as *a scholarly and applied activity.* It is not a science and it does not search for laws. It is certainly not concerned with prediction, nor even forecasting (though it may use, or refer to, forecasts, trends and the like). It has nothing to do with the so-called 'futures market', and nothing whatsoever to do with crystal balls and the latest commentaries on Nostradamus. Such activities belong to vastly different traditions of enquiry and action.

Rather, critical futures study seeks to provide a critical purchase on our historical predicament. It attempts to develop and refine tools of understanding that, on the one hand, reveal processes of cultural formation, cultural editing and, on the other, reveal options for intervention and choice. It seems to me that when this work is successful it has a number of outcomes: a new (or renewed) ability to diagnose 'where we are', to clarify what is at stake, to reconceptualize 'the problem' and to re-direct human effort through self-constitution and cultural innovation. In educational terms these outcomes mean that teaching and learning can be re-connected to 'the big picture', the wider world.

Critical futures study is therefore not social science, though again, it may *use* some of the tools of the latter. It is not 'owned' by a professional elite, though it is certainly aided by practitioners and futures organizations. It is, perhaps, as much *a cultural formation* as an academic discipline, in part because it incorporates some elements of the futures-related social innovation movements. However, an academic 'backbone' is essential. Critical futures study flourishes where it has access to the skills and other resources available through scholarship. It also requires political and organizational skill and a range of humanistic competencies. The latter are expressed in futures workshops and other facilitative milieux where people are actively engaged in futures visioning, design and implementation.[8]

In summary, critical futures study combines rational intelligence with intuitive and visionary abilities to provide a forward-looking context in which some of the 'big questions' can be posed and answered. 'Where are we going? How do we get there? What problems need to be solved? And why take this path rather than another?' Such questions are too central to be overlooked. Yet they go well beyond those that tend to be asked in related fields such as critical theory and cultural studies.

CRITICAL FUTURES RESEARCH

Critical futures research emerges from the above. A working definition would perhaps see it as *the attempt to generate new knowledge about the constitution of human futures.* Obviously, such knowledge cannot be limited to particular domains. It will routinely cross existing disciplinary boundaries and often challenge settled norms and procedures. Like critical futures studies, this approach to research differs from futures research *per se* in that it is not primarily concerned with using and applying the standard methodologies (such as scenarios, matrices, Delphi and the like). Rather, these are utilized sparingly and more commonly seen as part of the subject matter. Critical futures research has a number of characteristic foci which include the following:

- research into the social construction of temporality;
- the formation, negotiation and significance of images of futures;
- the clarification of social learning processes and the application of social inventions;

- the evolution of post-modern outlooks and worldviews;
- the re-formulation and re-presentation of knowledge for global and futures-oriented uses;
- the development of an ethical basis for acknowledging our responsibilities to future generations; and
- the study and implementation of foresight.

While, as noted, critical futures studies and research cannot be completely separated, it can be seen that the latter assumes a mastery of the former and is applied to more extended and demanding areas. It may be used to create and refine knowledge that will help to focus and implement futures initiatives or projects. For example, while critical futures studies may merely survey and/or critique young people's fears about futures, critical futures research would move on to consider the grounds of systemic solutions within a renewed worldview and culture.

The methodologies involved in critical futures research are derived from the critical/hermeneutic skills and metatheoretical perspectives outlined above.[9] They include the study of different types of futures discourses, of paradigm phenomena, of foresight contexts and the conscious design of post-modern worldviews.[10] An example of a post-graduate research course is discussed below.

AN OUTLINE OF THREE COURSES

Three futures courses were offered at Melbourne. One was a strand of a Diploma in Education course for post-graduate students who would normally proceed to teach after the diploma year. It was basically an introductory course organized around the theme of: *Social Change: Problems and Prospects.* This title deliberately played down the futures component. The course was interactive and formal lecturing was held to a minimum. The emphasis was on group processes such as critical reading, reporting, discussion, workshops, negotiation and role-play.

The course was spread over two semesters, interrupted by three rounds of teaching practice. In the first ten or so sessions the students were introduced to a number of introductory themes such as: young people's views of futures, dealing with fears, futures in the media, origins and development of futures education, concepts and principles of teaching futures. Each two-hour session was different, but always included one practical futures teaching tool or technique per week. This served to build up a professionally useful repertoire from the start.

The second series of meetings in semester two looked at aspects of the 'idea base' of critical futures work. Session themes included: understanding the present cultural transition, the foresight principle and the grounds of (socio-cultural) recovery. The aim here was to open up a couple of intellectual perspectives on the field and, most importantly, to show students that there are many sources of insight, empowerment and creativity which can be drawn on by teachers and students. Overall, the Dip. Ed. course served as a mainly practical introduction to futures studies in education.

Two Master's courses were also offered. The first was a Master's qualifying year 5 course (or year 1). The second was a Master's year 6 (or year 2) offering. The former was originally entitled: *Futures Study and Curriculum Innovation* but was later re-named *Education for the 21st Century*, partly to tie in with the book of that title.[11] It was intended to be a foundation course in the application of critical futures methods to curriculum issues and problems. The aims of the course were as follows:

- to introduce students to the futures field and a range of educationally relevant concepts and methodologies;
- to show how critical futures methods can be applied to curriculum problems;
- to provide a framework for the analysis of the global problematique and its pedagogic implications;
- to examine the nature of the transition from industrialism in the context of Australian history and culture;
- to consider the role of Australian education in (a) exploring solutions to global problems and (b) supporting shifts toward more sustainable ways of life.

The course began with an overview of the futures field and used case studies to explore a range of concerns. These included: the nature of the industrial worldview; the transition from industrialism; technology and cultural texts; responding to uncertainty; and curriculum responses to structural change. The latter part of the course re-interpreted the curriculum in the light of the above and showed how such concepts and methods can be employed in explicitly forward-looking curriculum innovation.

The rationale for the course was based on the fact that the global transition from industrialism has rendered many assumptions, meanings and practices obsolete. Given its innate conservatism, this was (and remains) perhaps even more true in education than elsewhere. There is an urgent need to move away from crisis management, short-termism and merely coping with change. Developing a more active and strategic stance must be much more than rhetoric. It requires practical competencies such as reading signals from the environment, interpreting their significance and developing appropriate responses. All educational processes require a forward-looking or prospective view and effective means of responding to change.

The course rationale also suggested that critical futures methods provide a means of understanding our cultural transition and reflecting upon the shifts of value and meaning which may underpin forward-looking curriculum innovation. This explains why the course drew on sources *outside* education: the sociology of science and of knowledge, hermeneutics, critical practice, speculative writing, futures workshop techniques and the futures field *per se*. In summary, the course provided an introduction to critical futures study and its utilization for the design, implementation and assessment of school curricula. It provided a foundation for curriculum innovation in a range of subject areas, and opportunities to review educational policy and practice in relation to wider structural shifts in society and culture.

The Master's year 6 course (M6) had a complementary, but different orientation. *Education, Foresight and Cultural Change* was a more advanced course in the application of critical futures methods to research problems and implementation issues. All those taking the course participated in continuing research and carried out their own small-scale studies. Students were required to carry out a research project involving the study of foresight in an organization. This involved asking questions like, how does the organization scan its environment; look ahead; make decisions; pursue strategies? In this context, examples of good practice provided models for emulation, while poor practice provided opportunities to consider improvements.

The taught components of the course covered topics such as: the epistemology of futures scanning, implementing foresight, foresight and national policy, foresight through art and literature, and foresight and cultural change. Methodologies were taught in a workshop format and covered such topics as: environmental scanning skills, team-building and the use of the Futurescan technique. All gained an extra dimension by being explored through a *critical* futures framework. The course led on to a range of further options, including a PhD thesis and doctoral seminars.

It quickly became evident that foresight provides an ideal focus for post-graduate work. It is a significant human capacity at the individual level, but its implementation at the organizational and social levels is less common. It is used by some large organizations for strategic planning purposes. A foresight tradition is developing at the state and federal level in the USA and elsewhere. Yet in spite of the undermining of traditional structures and expectations by a range of powerful change processes, foresight work in the public interest remains rare.[12]

The course objectives reflected this concern. On completing the subject students were expected to be able to:

- critically evaluate educational processes in terms of underlying cultural commitments, assumptions and temporal orientations;
- demonstrate their understanding of the principles and practice of foresight methods and approaches through critical/empirical research work;

- participate in the study of foresight contexts, and
- contribute original thinking/research to the field.

Overall, the M6 course provided a range of opportunities to move beyond the induction and familiarization process toward research and the implementation of foresight in various contexts.

Evaluation and outcomes

The Master's courses outlined here were offered annually, sometimes in an intensive summer school format. Unfortunately evaluation has sometimes been a weak point in the field, so particular care was needed. All were evaluated by student questionnaires, interviews or structured group discussion. This was necessary for legitimation purposes as well as for developmental ones.

General tone of the evaluations

It is clear from the responses that these were successful courses. While they certainly challenged the participants, the latter obviously enjoyed them and gained a lot from them. Some factors mentioned were: insight, empowerment, new perspectives, hope, courage, an extra dimension and making greater sense of existing ideas. Positive comments were also made about: use of media, the sense of collaboration and community-building, the refreshing character of original and stimulating material from sources outside education and the value of maintaining current links with international colleagues and organizations.

Areas of difficulty

A number of respondents mentioned problems with some terminology, reading and unfamiliar concepts. It was acknowledged that these do present difficulties for those who begin such courses without prior knowledge of futures studies. However, it is also significant that one person noted: 'after a while it all comes together'. So, while steps can be taken to ease the transition, it seems clear that time for reading, reflecting, clarifying, discussing ideas, etc., is necessary for all students. People who *actively engage with the material* normally experience this movement toward clarity and integration after a few weeks. Tools such as annotated bibliographies and futures glossaries can also be a great help.[13]

At the M6 level, and in summer school format, the problems of running such courses for mixed groups with, and without, prior knowledge of the area sometimes created real difficulties. Those who had done the earlier course possessed an extensive understanding of the conceptual structures of futures study and therefore moved easily on to more demanding, research-oriented work. One way to address this problem was to require prerequisites of new students; for example, in-depth reviews of two books from a core list. However, not all students actually completed the reading in time.

Areas for improvement

Several areas for improvement were mentioned. One was the need for more structured discussion times. I tried to avoid imposing too much structure on discussions because I preferred a collegial approach which gives people sufficient time/space to draw on experience and make comment. However, since some time-wasting was noted on occasions, strategies were also needed for reducing it.

A second area was the relative lack of local content. This was a valid criticism. I had taken some trouble to scan local publications and media for material, but this was not always easy to find in Australia. Another option was to use local people and organizations whenever possible.

Thirdly, more explicit links between theory and practice were requested. This, again, became a developmental task. My first concern in setting up new courses had been to provide an appropriate framework – including the nature of the conceptual outline, teaching sequence, materials and access to literature. However, as time went by and the framework became established, attention turned to exemplifying some of the theory by developing clearer links with concrete practices, for example curriculum planning, environmental scanning, forecasting, creative and business enterprises. This was achieved through case studies, visiting speakers and appropriate use of local media.

Areas for development

Surprisingly (at least to me) the main area suggested for further development was methodology. A number of people felt that a separate course was desirable, and in principle it was possible. However, as a single member of staff with sole responsibility for a rapidly growing area like futures it was beyond my ability to provide it.

In conclusion, the evaluations provided firm evidence that the courses worked out pretty much as intended. However, the points outlined above show that there was certainly room for improvement. Some responses could be made at the individual and institutional level, while others required wider co-operation and support. But as futures educators well know, these are not always available. Despite clear academic standing and strong student approval, the hierarchies of universities often overlook futures studies altogether. Why is this?

CHALLENGES FOR FUTURES EDUCATORS

The above suggests that futures studies can be successfully integrated into the post-graduate programme of a major university department such as an Institute of Education. However, there are clearly difficulties to overcome before such work becomes commonplace. Teaching futures at the tertiary level is an idea which has made steady progress over the last quarter-century, but its time is yet to come: it still has some way to go before it is universally regarded as a legitimate part of the intellectual mainstream. On the other hand, the potential of educational futures has been appreciated for well over twenty years.[14] So it is essential to try to understand the gap between aspiration and reality. Michael Marien has suggested four factors which may help explain this gap.

1 Academic institutions favour vertical depth over horizontal breadth, retain ancient boundaries and have few resources for experimentation.
2 Futures organizations have declined in membership, or simply failed to grow. Organizations like the Club of Rome have lost visibility and impact.
3 The future can seem too difficult to study and there is evidence that time-horizons are shrinking.
4 The above factors are exacerbated by 'infoglut'; i.e. information overload and the fragmentation it encourages.[15]

To this can be added the following.

The US model of futures studies at the school level did not travel well. While many practical teaching tools and innovations were successfully developed in US schools, colleges and some universities, implementation tended to be of a higher quality than accounts written of it. It was therefore possible for the 'intellectual gatekeepers' in universities and elsewhere to sideline these innovations and to miss their significance.

Some of the early futures literature became a liability because its repetitious description of 'world problems' and 'solutions' missed the point in certain ways. When a deeper analysis is overlooked, the prescriptions of futurists can be readily dismissed. It is therefore unsurprising that futurists were not particularly welcome when they tried to penetrate the advanced and interrogative discourses of higher learning.

Those who begin to teach futures studies in isolation tend to use what they find to hand. However, often this turns out to involve *extrapolating* from the present. An issues-based 'future of ...' approach tends to enlarge or exaggerate aspects of the present world. In many cases an underlying assumption remains that of *a basically static frame of reference.* While exploring some superficial changes, an extrapolative approach also assumes that present ways of life possess more strength and durability than, in fact, they have. It is a mistake to overlook deeper shifts and phenomena.

A close look at futures modules, curricula and projects suggests that in many cases inadequate attention was paid to evaluation. This means that futures studies may be seen as purely 'inspirational' and marginalized on spurious grounds. But *why* should they be marginalized?

It is clear that critical futures studies and research do not automatically align with the dominant norms of growth-oriented, resource-intensive and habitually short-termist societies. On balance, and the corporate sector notwithstanding, there tends to be a hidden opposition of interests between the best futures work and much of the underlying 'software' of Western societies. This hidden opposition of interests and agendas is, perhaps, the basic reason why futures studies have not yet entered the intellectual mainstream. The former have confronted powerfully embedded cultural and economic forces but, in lacking critical, countervailing power, they have engaged in a very unequal struggle.

If this analysis is correct, futures studies and research will find it hard to achieve their full potential until they become securely grounded in more durable, penetrating methods and approaches. At minimum this may involve: providing a penetrating critique/diagnosis of industrial era psychology, epistemology and worldviews; utilizing critical futures tools for re-negotiating deeply embedded cultural values and assumptions; and making the role of futures clearer to many more people than at present. Since these are by no means easy tasks, it follows that futures study and research will take longer to become fully established than many would wish.

In the meantime, innovators can certainly take heart: the underlying impulses driving futures work are strengthening, as is the *structural* need for quality, well-founded futures work. The structural imperative arises from fundamentally changing conditions of life: the need to manage the biosphere and reduce the threat of war, the challenge of powerful new technologies and the need to reduce the escalating costs of social learning by crude experience.

WIDER IMPLICATIONS

It is clear from the above that critical futures study and research have grown out of a critique of the dominant empirical/rational tradition of futures research and the development and use of new intellectual and methodological tools. They address futures concerns at a deeper level than can normally be accessed by empirical/rational approaches. They operate at the level of constitutive understandings about social and cultural life. Such work typically involves comparative analysis of assumptions, presuppositions, paradigms, ways of knowing, interests, power relationships and different cultural traditions. Why is this approach fruitful?

Much of the early futures literature considered 'world problems' and proffered a variety of 'solutions'. But the fact is that very *many 'problems' have no solution at the level upon which they are first experienced or described*. This has frequently been overlooked in fields which are over-reliant upon empiricist assumptions and methods (measuring, calculating, instrumental reasoning). In this context the partiality of cultural traditions, of disciplinary paradigms and ways of knowing has been largely over-looked. Similarly, the role of language in actively shaping perception and mediating views of the world was often missed. Hence 'problems' tended to be described in superficial, culturally specific and taken-for-granted ways. This led to the familiar 'litany' of global concerns and a number of repetitious books, many of which ended up saying much the same thing.

By contrast, *a critical futures approach reveals the embedded systems which lie behind everyday experience*. In one dimension these spread through space and time and, in another, they extend throughout the socio-cultural matrix in the form of ideologies (e.g. planned obsolescence) and cultural assumptions (e.g. we are separate from nature and can therefore abuse it). Few individuals could be expected to unravel these relation-ships on their own. So it is important to establish a method for dealing with them.

One place to start is with what I term the 'architectural metaphor'. This draws a parallel between physical architecture and social architecture. While the former is built upon a physical substructure and foundation, the latter is founded upon a structure of norms, assumptions, etc. and also upon a worldview or paradigm. The worldview contains a number of key assumptions: about the nature of reality, of nature, human nature, time, meaning, purpose and so on. Critical futures work suggests that many of the problems we face in the everyday world arguably have their origin (and their possible resolutions) at one or more of these deeper levels.

It follows that *futures work which misses the shaping significance of socio-cultural foundations will increasingly be seen as naive and superfi-cial*. This is so because it misses the richest opportunities for problem-solving, re-conceptualization and cultural renewal. The latter cannot be identified merely with changes in surface structures. We have to deal in depth with the problematics of cultures in stress and in transition. So it is useful to recognize distinct levels in futures work. Four possibilities are given in Table 7.1. *Pop futurism* tends to be technophilic, conservative and diversionary. It thrives in mass market TV programmes and in the popular press. It can be marketed. *Problem-focused futures study* is often earnest and well-meaning, but its prescriptions lack credibility for the reasons given above. *Critical futures study and research* is still fairly uncommon, but some of the best futures work available draws upon critical sources and traditions of enquiry. Finally, *epistemological futures study* provides the necessary depth.

Table 7.1 Levels of futures work

---

1 POP FUTURISM: takes existing social relations as given; ideologically naive; provides unconscious support for status quo; futures constructed externally via science and technology. EG. *Future Shock* (Toffler 1970).

2 PROBLEM-FOCUSED FUTURES STUDY: identifies problems and seeks to explore solutions at a superficial, taken-for-granted level. EG. *The Limits to Growth* (Meadows 1972).

3 CRITICAL FUTURES STUDY: comparative analysis of assumptions, pre-suppositions, paradigms; actively considers the influence of different cultural orientations and traditions of enquiry. EG. *The Politics of the Solar Age* (Henderson 1988).

4 EPISTEMOLOGICAL FUTURES STUDY: locates and problematizes sources of 'problems' in worldviews and ways of knowing; sees 'solutions' as arising from deep-seated and unpredictable shifts at this level. EG. *The Reenchantment of the World* (Berman 1981) and *Eye to Eye: The Quest for the New Paradigm* (Wilber 1990).[16]

As one moves from level 1 to level 4, an increasingly rich array of options present themselves. At the most superficial level one remains imprisoned by unregarded 'givens' and unstated assumptions. It is true that the deeper one goes, the more demanding the work. But, equally, greater scope exists to look freshly upon assumptions and meanings which have come to seem natural and inevitable, but are in fact not so. At the epistemological level futures work merges imperceptibly into the kind of fundamental re-thinking which is clearly philosophical in character and orientation. Here is one of the key bridges between futures work and the older, better-established disciplines.

These are welcome developments. For it is here in the foundations of culture that all 'world problems' have their origins. Equally, 'solutions' will not emerge from ill-founded analysis or superficial tinkering. They will not grow from media hype or pop futurism. They will not result from empirical/analytic work which ignores the foundations of the social order. *Effective solutions will involve deep-seated shifts of perception, value and understanding at the deeper levels.* This means that work at the tertiary level will always remain vital. It also suggests that futures workers in different traditions, as well as futurists and educators, should all work much more closely together.

CONCLUSION: CRITICAL FUTURES STUDY AS AN EDUCATIONAL STRATEGY

This chapter has outlined some propositions about critical futures study and research in higher education. It has discussed how they have been implemented at the tertiary level over the course of a decade. I have concentrated on this level because it has great symbolic power and performs a wide range of servicing and gatekeeping roles for other educational levels. However, I want to affirm that over the last quarter-century much good work has also been done at primary and secondary levels.[17] (See Chapters 6 and 8 by Page and Hutchinson respectively).

I conclude that besides being an appropriate focus of disciplined enquiry in tertiary contexts, futures study is indeed a core dimension of education at all levels. While it can be, and often is, successfully introduced as a secondary subject,[18] it is not *merely* another subject entering into competition with others in an overcrowded curriculum. Even at this relatively early stage it can be regarded as a true metaperspective grounded in the coherent body of theory and practice which I have tried to sketch in here. Equally, we should not forget that a very substantial part of such work is not owned by futurists at all. I refer to the standard skills of scholarship: clear expression, careful argument, fit with the evidence, and so on. These are common starting points for advanced enquiry and this is also where students and teachers of futures must begin.

The justification for regarding critical futures study as an educational strategy is that it brings two vital gifts that are all too rare in other contexts. One is the gift of a futures perspective, with its advanced discourse, methods and literature. The other is the rich insights it provides into the constitution of viable human futures. By carefully questioning what is frequently taken for granted (such as continuous economic growth, ethnocentricity or the marketing imperative) it is possible to distinguish new personal and social options. *This 'unfreezing' of the status quo has powerful implications: it provides us with new (or renewed) sources of freedom. It also permits a much wider variety of alternatives to be imagined and explored than are conceivable from within a dominant, catastrophe-prone paradigm.* It is for such reasons that critical futures study can contribute toward a re-invigorated educational enterprise. We should also expect an increase in strategic thinking, constructive, empowering attitudes and, overall, an enhanced 'steering capacity' for individuals, groups, organizations and the wider society. Together these provide an enhanced ability to engage in the critical and practical tasks of moving away from unproductive, destructive and chronically short-sighted ways of life toward new stages of personal and cultural development.

Those who are now in the teaching force and who are being prepared for it are frequently told that they hold 'the future' in their hands. They are also told that the young people they are dealing with are 'the citizens of the twenty-first century'. However, the vast majority of education systems throughout the world lack anything approaching a substantive futures perspective. So the deliberate introduction of futures studies (critical or otherwise) as a foundation discipline of education is long overdue. As the twenty-first century approaches, schools, colleges and universities that attempt to make the shift into a new millennium without some of the tools and understandings outlined here will find themselves backing into an increasingly tight corner. Those who do take them up will discover many new personal and professional options. Futures studies have a vital role to play in all the key areas of educational practice, including curriculum innovation, teacher preparation, professional development and the training and support of principals.[19]

At the end of the day it is really very straightforward: all teaching, learning and research is *from* the past and *for* the future. The latter is the primary focus for all education because *education is an inherently forward-looking enterprise* and the future looks increasingly different to the past. The prospect may be daunting, but there are undoubtedly grounds for informed optimism and many paths beyond every imaginable disaster.[20]

There are few really substantial barriers to prevent the expansion of futures studies and research in education. It remains basically a question of picking up the available tools, adapting them and using them for a range of purposes.[21]

REFERENCES

1 Slaughter, R. A. 'Towards a Critical Futurism', *World Future Society Bulletin* 18, 4, 19–25 and 18, 5, 11–21, 1985.
2 Wells, H. G. 'Wanted Professors of Foresight', reprinted in *Futures Research Quarterly*, 3, 1, 89–91, 1987.
3 Rogers, M. and Tough, A. 'What Happens When Students Face the Future?' *Futures Research Quarterly* 8, 4, 9–18, 1992.
4 Slaughter, R. 'Probing beneath the Surface: review of a decade's futures work', *Futures* 22, 5, 447–465, 1989.
5 Milbrath, L. *Envisioning a Sustainable Society,* New York, SUNY Press, 1989.
6 Macy, J. *World as Lover, World as Self,* Berkeley, California, Parallax Press, 1991.
7 Many of the ideas in this chapter and the two courses mentioned are explored in Slaughter, R. A. *Futures Concepts and Powerful Ideas,* Futures Study Centre/DDM Media, Melbourne, 1995, second edition.
8 For an introduction see Zieglar, W. 'Envisioning the Future', *Futures* 23, 5, 516–527, 1991.
9 Belsey, C. *Critical Practice*, London, Methuen, 1980 and Slaughter, R. 'Probing beneath the Surface'.
10 Slaughter, R. *The Foresight Principle: cultural recovery in the 21st century*, Praeger (USA), Adamantine (UK), 1995.
11 Beare, H. and Slaughter, R. *Education for the 21st Century*, London, Routledge, 1992, 1993.
12 See Slaughter, R. A., op. cit. Note 7.
13 Marien, M. *Future Survey* (series) World Future Society, Washington DC. Also the *Annotated Futures Bibliography* (series) Futures Study Centre/DDM Media, 117 Church Street, Hawthorn 3122, Melbourne, Australia.

14 Marien, M. and Ziegler, W. (eds) *The Potential of Educational Futures*, Washington, Charles A. Jones, 1972.

15 Marien, M. *Prep 21 Bulletins*, World Future Society, Washington DC, 1988–90.

16 Toffler, A. *Future Shock*, London, The Bodley Head, 1970. Meadows, D. *The Limits to Growth*, New York, Universe Books, 1972. Henderson, H. *The Politics of the Solar Age*, Indianapolis, Knowledge Systems Inc., 1988. Berman, M. *The Reenchantment of the World*, Cornell, Cornell University Press, 1981. Wilber, K. *Eye to Eye: The Quest for the New Paradigm*, Boston and London, Shambhala.

17 Hicks, D. *Educating for the Future: A Practical Classroom Guide*, WWF, Godalming, Surrey, 1994.

18 The Board of Senior Secondary School Studies in Brisbane, Queensland, is trialling a new year 10 & 11 course called *Futures: Personal, Social, Global* for introduction into all secondary schools. This initiative is outlined in Hicks, D. and Holden, C. *Visions of the Future: Why We Need to Teach for Tomorrow*, London, Trentham Books, 1995, Chapter 7.

19 Slaughter, R., *et al. Strategic Leadership in Victoria's 'Schools of the Future'* (Research Report), Institute of Education, University of Melbourne, 1995.

20 Slaughter, R. 'Changing Images of Futures in the 20th Century', *Futures* 23, 5, 499–515, 1991. Also Zieglar, *Ways of Enspiriting*, FIA International, Denver, 1995.

21 Slaughter, *Futures Concepts*, and *Futures Tools and Techniques*, Futures Study Centre/DDM Media, Melbourne, 1995, second edition.

Chapter 8

Educating beyond violent futures in children's media

Francis P. Hutchinson

Study of cultural artefacts has been very much part of the traditional tools of trade of anthropologists and, more particularly, archaeologists. Such study has sought to illuminate aspects of the development of particular societies and cultures. Yet, the cultural lens has tended to be on the origins of Western civilization and on past and present times in so-called less developed societies of Asia, Latin America and Africa. There has been a relative neglect of critical studies of cultural artefacts in contemporary Western industrialized societies.[1] In this chapter an exploratory sampling is made of a number of broad categories of young people's media arte-facts in Australian society (see Table 8.1) and of what epistemological assumptions they may reveal about 'the future'.

Guiding imagery of the future may be explicit or, more commonly, implicit. In the case of the latter, there may be silence or near silence about alternative knowledge traditions on resolving conflicts non-violently and living in peace with the Earth. From a futures-oriented peace study per-

Table 8.1 Studying cultural artefacts as aspects of child and adolescent socialization about 'reality' and 'potential reality': some major analytical categories and examples

Play media	Print media	Electronic media	Expressive art media
War toys	Newspapers	Television news	
Gendered game materials	School texts	Television science and technology programmes	Sculpture
	Teen magazines		Paintings
	Comic books		Musical recordings
	Science fiction stories	Television drama	
		Science fiction movies	
		War movies	
		Computer games	
		New multi-media 'virtual reality' software	

spective, the challenge for teachers is not, for example, to employ Socratic techniques of dialogue in the classroom to reach some 'correct' bedrock understanding of how 'the reality' of such silence restricts anticipations of the future but to encourage critical and imaginative readings in which teachers and students are co-learners in negotiating preferable futures. The challenge is more than a matter of learning how cultural violence, as mediated in many contemporary Western artefacts, defuturizes social alternatives, fragments non-mainstream knowledge traditions and marginalizes human agency. It is an invitation to teachers and students to start new journeys in the present, that seek to move beyond hatred, hopelessness or even passive hope, through developing classroom milieux congenial to cooperative learning, divergent thinking and pro-social skills.[2]

Almost twenty-five years ago Lewis Mumford claimed that many aspects of young people's media in Western industrialized societies such as the USA were 'increasingly committed to enactments of cold-blooded brutality and physical violence: pedagogical preparations for the practical use of homicide and genocide'.[3] To diagnose possible aspects of cultural violence in young people's media artefacts is an important but insufficient task, pedagogically.[4] Such an approach on its own may unwittingly make 'necessity' and despair convincing rather than hope practical. Arguably a crucial part of the task is to broaden dialogue on future alternatives by seeking to demystify and problematize colonizing traces of selective traditions in school textbooks and other young people's media artefacts.

PLAY MEDIA ARTEFACTS

Important connections probably exist between the selective processes of childhood political socialization, on the one hand, and restricted consciousness of alternatives to sexist, militarist and technocratic futures on the other. If there are strongly selective traditions that condone or legitimize certain behaviour as 'normal' or 'inevitable' and marginalize others, then taken-for-granted views about the future are likely to be powerfully propagated. In such a cultural context, arguably significant traces of colonizing images of the future may be discernible, for example in childhood play artefacts.

A steady diet of gendered toys, gendered games and other gendered forms of media such as televised violence, in which male role-models handle conflict situations aggressively and often with hi-tech firepower, is likely to have a cumulatively disabling effect on whether a boy grows up with pro-social skills such as conflict resolution literacy.[5] It is a serious challenge for parents, teachers and schools in a late industrial society such as Australia that among the most common images marketed to boys by toy manufacturers and distributors are the violent, imitative and colonizing. Complex interrelations probably exist among such images, a lack of conflict resolution skills and image illiteracy of social alternatives to contemporary patterns of gender stratification. Whilst any simple reflectionist explanation is far from adequate, such violence-condoning images for males may contribute to various types of aggressive behaviour, including bullying in the playground when a child and, perhaps, sexual harassment and domestic violence when an adult.

Many toys are unconducive to creative play, cooperative learning and social imagination. The marketing trends in recent years have tended to become more insidiously exploitative of insecurities, with toys presented as part of a 'lifestyle' package. Especially since the futuristic toy arms bazaars that accompanied the cinema release of *Star Wars* in the late 1970s, there has been a major thrust to integrated forms of marketing.

The Teenage Mutant Ninja Turtles 'craze' of 1990–91 provides a case in point of why it is important for children to be encouraged to be critical consumers. Here the commercialization of violence extended beyond the television set and the cinema. Combined with the television release of the *Teenage Mutant Ninja Turtles* series was a range of companion product lines that included not only plastic toys but other items such as home computer games, T-shirts, shampoos, school lunch boxes and even toothbrushes. Market penetration was further enhanced by product visibility not only in traditional toy outlets but also in supermarket chains, local pharmacies and home video hire outlets.

Already, a new merchandising blitz for the boys' toy market segment is starting in Australia with the release on commercial television of *The Toxic Crusaders*, a hit US cartoon series in which 'an environmentally informed and hideously deformed' band fight 'the evil pollutant mutant' Dr Killemoff. Children's insecurities and fears about an environmentally degraded future are exploited for commercial ends. Feelings of helplessness and needs deprivation are played on, in a variation on Nietzschean themes, when 'hideously deformed creatures of superhuman size and strength' come to the rescue and engage in combat to resist Dr Killemoff's efforts to pollute the local environment. As with other similar toy lines, such as the integrated marketing artefacts associated with the films *Jurassic Park* (1993) and *Judge Dredd* (1995) and the *Mighty Morphin Power Rangers* television series, manufacturers and merchandisers commonly rationalize restricted offerings for imaginative play as 'meeting market demand'.

There is evidence to suggest impoverished assumptions about future gender relations in the sexual division of play in the marketing of many toy lines to children. This may be seen, for example, in the emphasis in the Barbie doll series on stereotypic female behaviour compared with the macho images of a Major Bludd in the *GI Joe* series or a Kelly Nightwing 'Nitro Blast' in the *Multinational Police against Crime and Turmoil* series. With the former, there are images of passivity, preoccupation with looks and saccharine sweetness. With the latter, there are images of hi-tech weaponry and gung-ho aggression that are reinforced by simulated battle sounds and voice commands such as 'Destroy it!' Many of these war toys are mass-produced for transnational corporations under licence in low-income countries, such as China and the Philippines, often using child labour. There is a coalition of interests between such transnational toy manufacturers and the aerospace defence and arms trade industries.

Such evidence of restricted 'texts' on the future in toy media artefacts, however, should not mean uncritical acceptance of the fallacy of restricted alternatives. It implies invariance neither in gender role expectations nor in the transmission of selective traditions on armaments, technology and the conquest of nature. There are practical ways both within the formal educational sector and outside for resisting violence-condoning imagery in war toys and gendered toys in general. These include the introduction of gender equity and peer mediation programmes in schools and the development of opportunities for imaginative play and cooperative learning. It is important to encourage in both boys and girls a sense of empowerment in their lives through learning socially imaginative and pro-active skills:

> children need to know that they can make a difference in their world and they need to learn how to do it. . . . Providing interesting materials for dramatic play is a key to helping children get beyond the narrow and limiting war play which can result from too many single-purpose toys and violent TV cartoons.[6]

Experience with professional development programmes in primary schools that use creative futures work to deconstruct gendered toys and hi-tech war play, also suggests constructive possibilities. Especially if workshop participants are encouraged to be co-investigators, it is possible to raise constructive dialogue on both cultural violence and alternative social futures. This is not to say that such work offers easy answers. After all, the negotiation of futures in schools is a long-term rather than short-term project.[7]

PRINT MEDIA ARTEFACTS

School textbooks

If play media artefacts offer important insights on the need to problematize colonizing images of the future, so too do school textbooks and other print media artefacts. In considering critical issues in futures in education, the print media artefacts examined in this subsection may be interpreted as being on a continuum from the formal to the informal curriculum. They range from school texts, through newspapers-in-the-classroom to adolescent comic books. In 'decoding' what image statements

there may be about the future in this sample of print media cultural artefacts, a number of 'key problems of humanity' are taken as a useful bench-
mark. These global futures problems have been the subject of extensive
discourses by United Nations agencies, such as UNESCO, UNICEF and
UNEP, and by international non-governmental organizations (INGOs)
during the past two decades.

As still the most widely used teaching resource in Australian classrooms,
how do school textbooks treat these 'key problems of humanity' as identified in UN and INGO discourses? Here a number of general observations
may be made in the context of an analysis of a representative sample of
commonly used textbooks in upper secondary classes in Australian
schools. First, the strength of selective traditions on war and conflict resolution, gender relations, humanity's relations to other species, and science,
technology and human development are much in evidence. With rare
exceptions, this is most discernible for school textbooks in the physical
sciences and in those social sciences, such as economics, with particular
pretensions to 'exact science' status.

The Cartesian selective tradition on science, with its myth of dualism
between 'facts' and 'values', remains very strong. Even though, according
to UN estimates, some 40–50 per cent of scientific R&D since 1945 has
been directed to military-related objectives, this reality is 'hidden' in high
school physical science and economics textbooks. The problematique of
social responsibility in science and technology and the opportunity costs
of military-related R&D for civil development and environmental security
are ignored or almost entirely neglected.

In physics and chemistry school textbooks, it is rare, indeed, for instance,
for discussion of nuclear physics to include any mention of the connections
between the civil and military nuclear industries, let alone invite dialogue
on the moral dimension of scientific knowledge harnessed for hi-tech
weaponry. Similarly, moral dilemmas, such as those concerned with the
human genome project and hi-tech medical futures, the genetic engineering industry and agribusiness, and the perpetuation of biological
determinist myths that underpin sexist, racist and militarist assumptions
about potential reality, remain invisible or unscrutinized in widely used
biology texts in Australian schools. Such cultural artefact evidence underlines the importance of contemporary efforts at reconceptualizing
gendered, mechanized and linear guiding imagery of science and technology education.

The vast diversion of economic resources to militarism from civilian
reconstruction and global ecological security receives scant, if any, treatment in widely used upper secondary economics texts. There is an evident
lag in terms of any greening of school economics textbooks in ways that
question conventional assumptions about resourcism, and that open up
dialogue on issues of intergenerational equity and the negotiation of

sustainable futures. With the current generation of school economics texts, even Keynesian economic theory barely rates a mention; the language of economic orthodoxy is technocratic and predominantly economic rationalist in its depiction of present reality and extrapolated reality.

There are, moreover, important pedagogical challenges suggested from this, particularly in the context of related evidence from recent social survey research in Australian schools. The data show that over 40 per cent of the student respondents were in agreement with the statement, 'generally school texts are very objective sources of facts about the world, especially in science and social science'. Less than 20 per cent were in disagreement.[8]

A second major observation about Australian school textbooks in upper secondary classes is that even when they contain diagnoses of particular problems of humanity identified as important in UN/INGO discourses, they rarely combine the language of critique with the language of active hope. This underlines the need to develop more holistic literacies that not only deconstruct colonizing imagery but facilitate democratic dialogue and non-violent action in relation to negotiating preferable futures.

Where a combination of critique and a sense of active hope occurs in these artefacts, it is usually in subject areas in which there are greater contemporary responses to cross-disciplinary influences and to 'vanguard' educational movements such as global education, peace education, development education and environmental education. There is evidence of this in some of the textbook materials for the new Geography, Society and Culture, General Studies, and Science and Life courses. However, more typically, as is the case with several of the most widely used English and History textbooks, there is a propagation of problem-laden imagery. There may be diagnosis but seldom is this combined in these texts with the language of creative prognosis concerning people and planet.

In upper secondary history texts, evidence of this is given by the treatment of war as a seemingly inevitable or normal part of human society and culture *ad infinitum*. There is invisibility or near invisibility of alternative knowledge traditions on peace making and peace building that may help to question such *ex cathedra* assumptions about trends in violence and the institution of war. There is, for example, scant if any discussion of the gendered nature of much violence and of the histories of resistance by feminist, anti-war and other movements of non-violent social change.

Such evidence provides further substantiation for the point that schools need to encourage holistic forms of literacy. As Fran Peavey comments:

> One's changeview is deeply influenced by the interpretation of history one accepts. In school, my history books implied that national change

was a function of war: which wars a country won and which it lost. It's taken me a long time and a lot of reading and thinking, to come to a new, more complex analysis – one which includes the possibility of large-scale change without war.[9]

There are opportunities for choice and engagement about how school texts are treated in the classroom. Are they treated as putatively neutral sources of facts? Or are they read as cultural artefacts with traces of selective traditions on what has been, what is and what might be? With the latter reconceptualization, it becomes important to problematize guiding images of reality and potential reality in textbook accounts. Experience with school-based professional development programmes offers some practical insights on how creative futures work on textbooks and other print media may help to develop multi-media literacy. Time-capsule activities using school textbooks or other media artefacts to challenge taken-for-granted 'truths' in times past, times present and times future provide one useful technique for broadened literacy.[10]

Newspapers-in-the-classroom

For the scanning of contemporary trends in young people's media arte-facts, analysis of press classroom resources has been limited to the *Sydney Morning Herald*. This leading Australian metropolitan newspaper produces a series of topic booklets and has a cuttings service for schools. These resources are widely used in English and social science classes in New South Wales.

Among the regularly updated press cuttings is a topic file titled 'The Future'. It is mostly used in English classes in the senior secondary school, where there is a major study topic of the same name. The same topic file is used also in many General Studies and Society and Culture classrooms. The core books for this topic area are Huxley's *Brave New World* (1932), Bradbury's *Fahrenheit 451* (1953) and Carson's *Silent Spring* (1962).

In attempting the topic 'The Future' in English classes, students are required to do 'supplementary material research' from the print and electronic media. For example, one widely used commercial study guide cites *The Day After* (1983), a film about nuclear holocaust; the film version of Orwell's dystopian fable, *Nineteen Eighty-four* (1949); and *Blade Runner* (1982), another dystopian film on a violent future, as important for illuminating this study area.[11] Of course, none of this genre of media materials is *per se* disempowering if its imagery of the future is prob-lematized rather than regarded as unilinear necessity. If handled critically in the classroom, and if students are given opportunities to generate imagery of alternative social futures and to engage in action planning, there is a good prospect of quality responses to a feared future.

If, however, the pedagogical approach is mainly to pile up selective imagery of the future that seemingly confirms dystopian interpretations, then there may be a real risk of reinforcing feelings of impotence. Arguably there is such a risk with the *Herald*-in-the-classroom materials in reinforcing *fait accompli* assumptions about the future. With media artefacts of this kind, a strong case may be made for the need to encourage forms of media literacy that go beyond dogmatic closure in epistemological thinking about present choices and future alternatives.

A critical reading of the clippings file items reveals predominant imagery of direct violence, environmental destruction and an inexorable technological ontology. There is a pervasive sense of the penetration of technological determinist epistemological assumptions in the restricted symbolic forms given to what is real and what is potential reality. It is a mindscape of the future that is inhabited by robotics, computerization and structural unemployment, technocities, nuclear accidents, toxic gas emissions and ecological catastrophe, macho hi-tech weaponry, gene shears, hi-tech medicine and anti-cancer 'super pills', cryonics, and multi-media virtual reality. The imagery conveyed is much more than reactive technophobia. Science and technology tend to emerge in more ambiguous and Faustian terms, as offering both threat and possible salvation, but in ways that marginalize human agency. Such narrowed imagery is well illustrated in the following extract from 'The Future' file. It comes from an article entitled, 'As smart as the human brain':

> Japan plans to create computers made in the image of the human mind. In a major presentation, Japanese and foreign scientists outlined their ideas for a government-funded international research project that would propel computer science into the 21st century.... The new machines will be like HAL, the computer in the movie '2001: A Space Odyssey' – capable of talking, thinking and learning. They will be indispensable in a world burdened by an avalanche of information and by threats of ecological disaster.[12]

In such narratives, there is largely a silence on alternative social futures. Silence of this kind may convey fatalism. In so doing, there is a denial or marginalization of alternative knowledge traditions that affirm a partnership model of potential reality.[13] There is a reassertion of taken-for-granted ways of thinking of a dominator model.[14] Figure 8.1 provides a simplified diagrammatic representation of the treatment of several global futures matters in these classroom resources.

Evidence such as this about implicit and explicit imagery of the future in the *Herald*-in-the-classroom materials underlines the importance of creative futures work in the school curriculum on the mass media. This point is further emphasized in the findings on ageism and bias in a major survey of the Australian print media over the period 1988 to 1992:

whether in newspaper or magazine reporting, the cultural message about young people is that they are a trouble-stricken, undifferentiated group characterized by moral illness, irresponsibility and powerlessness. The media constantly sets up problems, yet rarely resolves them. Clearly, there is a need to expose these journalistic practices to rigorous scrutiny, and to develop means by which established methods of news reporting no longer remain unchallenged.[15]

A gardening metaphor may be helpful here. What this kind of evidence from print media artefacts suggests is the need to cultivate in schools a 'sense of humus' about imaginatively parched and infertile images of the future. From a critical futurist perspective, an important pedagogical task is to work with young people in 'composting' or reconceptualizing such monocultural imagery. This in turn may help diverse seeds of peace, sustainability and practical Earth-caring to germinate.

Comics for adolescents

In reading adolescent comics from a peace research and critical futurist perspective, a number of observations may be made about the current situation. First, in terms of possible enculturative influences, it is important to note that the readership of these print media artefacts is mostly adolescent males. The materials are pitched at the same market segment

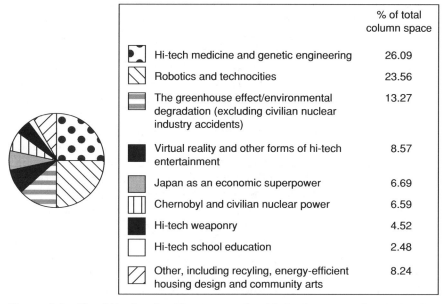

		% of total column space
	Hi-tech medicine and genetic engineering	26.09
	Robotics and technocities	23.56
	The greenhouse effect/environmental degradation (excluding civilian nuclear industry accidents)	13.27
	Virtual reality and other forms of hi-tech entertainment	8.57
	Japan as an economic superpower	6.69
	Chernobyl and civilian nuclear power	6.59
	Hi-tech weaponry	4.52
	Hi-tech school education	2.48
	Other, including recyling, energy-efficient housing design and community arts	8.24

Figure 8.1 Herald-in-the-classroom treatment of 'the future': a diagnosis of major themes as a proportion of the total column space for the period June 1990 to August 1991.

that is now increasingly taking up so-called interactive computer game artefacts or electronic variants of the traditional comic book. Whilst there remains something of a cult following for such titles as *The Phantom* and *Superman* among older male readers, the biggest individual sellers in recent years among adolescent Australian males are the *2000AD* and *Judge Dredd* series brought out by the now-under-siege Maxwell multinational publishing empire. Other titles with a significant combined market share among 15- to 18-year-old males are the Marvel formula comic series, such as *X-Men* and its colonizing theme of 'the extinction agenda', *Iron Man*, *The Spectacular Spider Man*, and *GI Joe*, vintage in social relations but now armed with 'state-of-the-art' weaponry.

Second, in all these titles, there is a strong tendency to foreclosure of the future. There are recurring ideological themes of militarism, sexism and technocratism. It is overwhelmingly a threat-filled and crisis-ridden mindscape of the future but one in which present feelings of alienation, powerlessness and relentless change may be compensated for through hi-tech 'answers' and Nietzschean, superhero violence. Figure 8.2 helps to exemplify these points.[16]

One of these examples of cartoon comic book content is taken from the *Judge Dredd* series. Judge Dredd's new world order is situated in Mega-City-One, a vast metropolis of the twenty-second century. Its guiding imagery both harks back to the American gunslinging narratives of the Wild West and to more recent Cold War apocalyptism, but also projects forward to a hi-tech, fascist world order in which a warrior caste of lawmen fight alien forces with the help of 'state-of-the-art' weapons.

The other example deals with a comic book character called Rogue Trooper who is a major figure in the *2000AD* series. Here the worldview is masculinist and mechanistic. It is a companionless world in which humanity survives in a neo-Social-Darwinist landscape as a fighting machine. It is a futuristic world in which there is a constant round of threat, crisis and competitive struggle that the superhero meets through his man-machine, genetically engineered combat capacity and 'intelligent', hi-tech weaponry. Image themes of might-is-right, fascism and military technofixes for conflicts are infused throughout this series. As in a contemporary genre of books, such as John Wiseman's *The Australian Urban Survival Handbook*, there is a climate of fear in which frequent feelings of individual helplessness or powerlessness are given limited and mostly authoritarian forms of survivalist release.

For teachers, a practical classroom response to such comic book artefacts is neither to ignore them nor to attempt to censor them. It is far better to invite dialogue on them in English, Media Studies or Social Science classes. It is also important to encourage extension of this dialogue through alternative resources that offer images of less deterministic and violent futures. One such example is the *Streetwize* comic series, a human

Figure 8.2   Mechanized and macho mayhem: example images of violent futures in comic book artefacts.

rights literacy project for adolescents funded by the Legal Aid Commission of New South Wales.

Unlike the *Judge Dredd* series, *Streetwize* takes generally a proactive approach. Problems are not ignored but the fallacy that 'trend is destiny' is challenged. Proactive skills are emphasized rather than a propagation of masculinized and mechanized reactions to 'the future'. With *Streetwize*, there is a move away from dogmatic closure in epistemological thinking about what the future holds. In this there are echoes, in some ways, of the comments by Kenneth Boulding about personal choice and social responsibility:

> At every present moment the future stretches out before us like a giant fan, each fold of which is a possible future. We can range these from total catastrophe on one side to the fulfilment of human potential on the other. To each segment we can assign a rough probability . . .
>
> For some of us the range of decision is very small; for the prisoner in jail who has not served his term tomorrow will be very much like today – there is not much choice. For all of us, however, there is some choice and we cannot escape a moral responsibility to choose. . . . Every decision that any human being makes, changes, however infinitesimally, the probability of catastrophe . . . or betterment.[17]

ELECTRONIC MEDIA ARTEFACTS

Computer games

In a large number of cases, computer games, like adolescent comic books, show a poverty of imagination about social alternatives. There are good exceptions such as *Sim City*, an educational software package that invites student lateral thinking from the perspective of systems philosophy and cybernetic feedback loops, but much of the current offerings are linear-mode. Future worlds tend to be strongly tunnel-visioned. Culturally violent imagery is propagated that addresses feelings of powerlessness among many young people by normalizing seeming psychological and societal invari-ances, such as the institution of war and a 'future shock' technological trajectory, through individuated and atomistic flight-or-fight responses.

The cultural messages are not in terms of democratic participation and non-violent group action but rather the flight of escapism or the fight of macho violence and machine-dependency in an insecure, fragmenting and crisis-filled mindscape of what might be. In many ways, it is a mindscape in which nature has been de-sacralized and a Faustian bargain of short-term salvic grace is offered by 'state-of-the-art' violent technology. Just as with the toy artefacts for younger children, there tends to be a strong gender division of play with these adolescent computer games. Table 8.2 helps to further elucidate these points.

Table 8.2 Adolescent computer games: a sample of leading titles on sale or hire through Australian software retailers and home video chains (1993–95)

Formal education: example artefacts	Informal education: example artefacts
Social studies curriculum (K-1 2)	*Arcade games*
Sim City (LV)	Teenage Mutant Turtles (HV)
Sim Earth (LV)	The Punisher (HV)
Where in the World Is Carmen Sandiego? (LV)	Tunnels of Armageddon (HV)
	The Terminator (HV)
Where in Time is Carmen Sandiego? (LV)	The Terminator II (HV)
	The Plague (HV)
Flowers of Crystal (LV)	Dr Chaos (HV)
	Matrix Marauders (HV)
	Autoduel (HV)
	Fantasy/Adventure/Horror
	2400AD (HV)
	Escape from the Planet of the Robot Monsters (HV)
	If It Moves Shoot It (HV)
	Ninja 3 (HV)
	The Punisher and other Marvel comic games (HV)
	Ultima V: Warriors of Destiny (HV)
	Robo Cop II (HV)
	Advanced Dungeons and Dragons (HV)
	The Pirates of Pestulon (HV)
	Night Trap (HV)
	Jurassic Park (HV)
	Space wars/Combat simulation
	Wing Commander (HV)
	Gulf Strike (HV)
	F16 Combat Pilot (HV)
	F29 Retaliator (HV)
	Star Wars (HV)
	Street Fighter II (HV)
	Mortal Kombat (HV)

HV = Imagery with predominantly high violent content; recurring themes of direct violence and macho machines as normal and natural ways to handle conflict, needs deprivation or feelings of helplessness. Leading software artefacts available in the entertainment or informal educational category are mostly HV. Sega, Nintendo and Atari are industry leaders in the production of these kinds of media artefacts for shopping mall arcades and the home.
LV = Imagery with comparatively low violent content.

In critically studying computerized violence, one important epistemological and pedagogical assumption that needs to be questioned is the neo-Pavlovian, behaviourist myths about children. Behaviourist child psychology bears the imprint of the Newtonian selective tradition with its doctrines of materialism and the clockwork universe.[18] According to these myths, children and adolescents may be likened to a highly impressionable *tabula rasa* on which, for example, images of computerized violence are assiduously copied to become conditioned responses for dealing with conflicts in a mean world. However, just as it is a 'neglect-of-alternatives' fallacy to typecast teachers as 'structural dopes' mindlessly reproducing the status quo, it is inadequate to picture young people narrowly through the mechanistic lens of victimology. To assume reflectionism is to deny young people as beings of praxis who in varying degrees may accept or resist the authoritativeness of the selective traditions on peace, sustainability and development in computer games, television programmes, school texts and other student cultural artefacts.

Beyond 2000 television series

As with adolescent computer games, the long-running television series *Beyond 2000* is an important one for critical classroom study. It is a major source of informal scientific education in Australia, with young males outnumbering young females in the audience mix. Transmitted weekly on numerous city and non-metropolitan commercial stations, it has a much wider audience than comparable programmes on Australian non-commercial television such as *Quantum* and *A Question of Survival*. Worldwide it is now screened in nearly a hundred countries.

The approach of this series is anything but a systems philosophy one. It provides a segmented treatment of issues of science and technology. Generally, interconnections with various forms of violence, both direct and indirect, are denied or taken as normal and natural. Publicized as offering 'a journey to the future', there are underlying epistemological assumptions of one true world of development. There is foreclosure on social alternatives.

More holistic scientific and technological literacies are circumscribed. Throughout this series, there is evidence of the penetration of consciousness-limiting imagery of what is and what might be. Anthropologically speaking, a kind of technological cargo-cultism is proffered in meeting the needs deprivation and feelings of helplessness of many in a seemingly bizarre and bewildering world of 'future shock' and 'incredible machines'. Guiding imagery of science and technology is of the techno-wizardry and techno-fix variety. Major contemporary trends in micromechanics and nanotechnology, for example, are presented uncritically as inexorable progress rather than as important matters for foresight and negotiation over the terms of the introduction of new technologies.

The tenor of many narratives in this series is clearly shown in the extract below. Techno-hype is developed to a considerable art form as illustrated in this prefatory quotation from one of several book adaptations:

A holiday on Mars? Animals that not only talk but sing? Insights into the bizarre and everchanging world of science and technology have been captured by the Beyond 2000 team in this third book based on the popular *Beyond 2000* television program.

Diverse, enlightening and definitely unusual stories have been selected. From energy to entertainment, sport to space, aviation to architecture, the settings are as different as the subjects. Photographs and state-of-the-art graphics illuminate these stories, providing a window to the future.[19]

The content analysis of a sample episode, summarized in Figure 8.3, helps, furthermore, to illustrate another aspect of the need for encouraging a futures dimension in both the formal and informal school curriculum. Too often in schools today holistic forms of electronic media literacy are

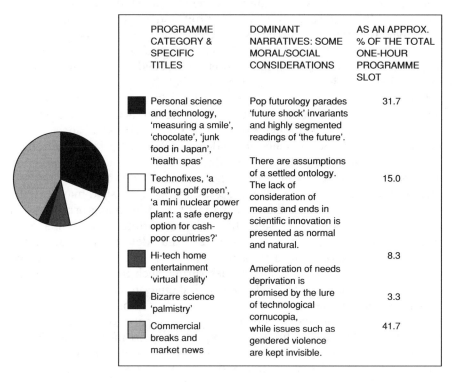

PROGRAMME CATEGORY & SPECIFIC TITLES	DOMINANT NARRATIVES: SOME MORAL/SOCIAL CONSIDERATIONS	AS AN APPROX. % OF THE TOTAL ONE-HOUR PROGRAMME SLOT
■ Personal science and technology, 'measuring a smile', 'chocolate', 'junk food in Japan', 'health spas'	Pop futurology parades 'future shock' invariants and highly segmented readings of 'the future'.	31.7
□ Technofixes, 'a floating golf green', 'a mini nuclear power plant: a safe energy option for cash-poor countries?'	There are assumptions of a settled ontology. The lack of consideration of means and ends in scientific innovation is presented as normal and natural.	15.0
■ Hi-tech home entertainment 'virtual reality'	Amelioration of needs deprivation is	8.3
■ Bizarre science 'palmistry'	promised by the lure of technological cornucopia,	3.3
▨ Commercial breaks and market news	while issues such as gendered violence are kept invisible.	41.7

Figure 8.3 A content analysis of a sample *Beyond 2000* episode. First transmitted on non-metropolitan TV stations in Australia on 17 September 1991.

neglected. Although this may be seen as indicative of the strength of the causal flow of selective traditions as mediated by institutions such as schools, the situation, as argued above, is far from unproblematic in terms of site-specific cultural politics. The latter may be more or less conducive to colonization of the future. Depending in part on building peer support networks among other teachers and on endeavours to create more cooperative learning environments, pop-futurological assumptions about technological determinism of the kind propagated by the *Beyond 2000* series may be problematized through creative futures work in the classroom.

STUDENT EXPRESSIVE ART MEDIA ARTEFACTS

The evidence presented here adds weight to the importance of developing multi-media literacy in schools. From a reading of several hundred student expressive art media artefacts, coupled in some cases with small-group interviews with student artists, important questions may be raised about the influence of the mass media on students' perceptions of reality and potential reality. Notwithstanding the point that students are far from passive in their interpretations of the print and electronic media, major narratives revealed in their art work convey a sense, in many cases, of narrowed vision about future alternatives and present choices. As suggested above, arguably in this restriction of social imagination, the mass media plays a major if not unambiguous role.

One major narrative in the student art works studied related to feelings of powerlessness, the futility of non-violent action and a loss of meaning or purpose. Although examples of this cut across all social strata, it was particularly in evidence in student expressive art media artefacts from low-income areas. In these works, the future looks bleak or grim, and there is little if anything that one can do to improve the situation. Such imagery of the future, whether it is explicit or implicit, may take the form of schools and other major social institutions as being prison-like in character. There are, at the same time, in these artefacts often images of forced personal trajectories in which external determinants are overwhelmingly decisive as to a person's fate. There may be a sense of no escape. At their most poignant and despairing, such images may take the form of completely shattered dreams and alienation, ending in death.

Another major narrative relates to images of violence and machine culture. In this grouping of student art works, largely gone is the myth of the mechanical paradise that was so important in art movements, such as Futurism and Constructivism, in the early part of the twentieth century. This myth was to remain influential in modernist art over several decades.[20] With the approach of the new millennium, there is a deep sense of the dystopian character of modern technology and pathos about the de-sacralization of nature reflected in many Australian student art works.

Although the technological cornucopian dream remains for some, many of the art works suggest a movement beyond the glib, technocratic promises of pop-futurological television series such as *Beyond 2000*. There is implied in a significant proportion of the sampled art works a strong sense of existential crisis about violent science and technology and their impact on nature. Sometimes this takes ironical forms as in send-ups of genetic engineering. At other times, it is more grimly predictive in images of the 'death of nature'.

With the latter artefacts, there are attenuated images of the future that convey a deep sense of technological determinism but with technoscience as enslaver rather than rescuer. Imagination of social alternatives seems pointless in the face of the relentless ontology of a greedy machine culture. In cultural politics, the metaphors remain those of the Newtonian clock-work universe rather than the Tao of the new physics (see Figures 8.4 and 8.5).[21]

Among the more positive contemporary images of a sustainable world are those from some Koori art students and non-Koori students influenced by renewed interest in less epistemologically reductionist ways of seeing reality and potential reality. Often these art works contain not only critical comments on the marginalization of indigenous Aboriginal culture and the destructive aspects of the Western industrial paradigm of development but a dignified and organic sense of time and place. There are creative expressions of 'we have survived' that affirm the longevity of each student's indigenous cultural roots, draw on alternative knowledge traditions about the Dreamtime and sustainability over millennia, and invite dialogue on building bridges of understanding for a better society. Such expressions are part of the contemporary renaissance in Koori painting, music and film which has grown since the 1960s with the civil rights movement and, more recently, the land rights movement (see Figure 8.6).

The growth of the environmental movement, particularly over the past decade, may help to explain the beginnings of another student expressive art genre concerned with images of greening the planet. Although for many there remains a sense of relentless progression to an ecologically disastrous future, this is not the whole story. Likewise, those works of art which have a predominant mood of nostalgia, with appeals to the security of a long-lost Arcadia in a dangerously insecure world, provide only a partial account of present trends in student expressive art media artefacts. A reading of some student art works suggests a movement beyond either fatalism or romanticism. Foresight is combined with a growing sense of the importance of making quality responses to disturbing empirical trends (see Figure 8.7).

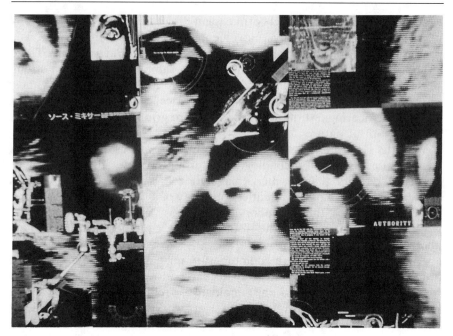

Figure 8.4 'Virtual reality' – technoscience as enslaver (Jamie Stevens, 1991)

Figure 8.5 'La Gourmandise' – a greedy machine culture (Ika Newman, 1991)

Figure 8.6 'My heritage in time' – alternative knowledge tradition about sustainability (Brett Clarke, 1990)

Figure 8.7 'This world we share' – making quality responses (collaborative classroom artwork, 1991)

CONCLUSION

Major aspects of cultural violence have been discerned in the frequently attenuated forms of imagery of the future in a range of cultural artefacts from gendered toys through school textbooks to aspects of the informal curriculum such as comic books and computer games. Such trends, it has been argued, however, are not destiny. No crudely reflectionist assumptions are made about the processes of childhood and adolescent enculturation.

This point is well illustrated in the young people's creative art media artefacts where certain trends are discernible but are far from universal. Reality and potential reality are much more complex than any reductively reflectionist or extrapolative lens on these artefacts might imply. What is suggested as important is the development of applied foresight in schools about such trends in young people's media.[22]

Arguably, teachers may play a vital part not only in helping to problematize violence-condoning images of the future but in facilitating social imagination of alternatives and in developing skills of conflict resolution and active citizenship. If forms of non-violent resistance to colonizing imagery of the future are to be more rather than less effective, there are crucial choices to be made. It is important to recognize that our anticipations of the future rebound on what we do or do not do in the present. Quality responses by schools and by teachers imply the encouragement of forms of multi-media literacy that challenge assumptions about foreclosed futures.[23]

NOTES

1 For examples of recent attempts to broaden this cultural lens, see R. Slaughter, 'The machine at the heart of the world: technology, violence and futures in young people's media', *Papers: Explorations into Children's Literature*, 2(1), 1991, pages 3–23 and P. Regan, 'War toys, war movies, and the militarization of the United States, 1900–85', *Journal of Peace Research*, 31(1), 1994, pages 45–58.

2 These issues are explored in more detail in F. Hutchinson, 'Futures consciousness and the school: explorations of broad and narrow literacies for the twenty-first century with particular reference to Australian young people', PhD thesis, University of New England, 1992.

3 Lewis Mumford, *Interpretations and Forecasts* (New York, Harcourt Brace Jovanovich, 1973), page 384.

4 This broadening of the concept of violence to include 'cultural violence' is indebted to the peace researcher and critical futurist Johan Galtung. He comments: 'one way cultural violence works is by changing the moral color of an act from red/wrong to green/right or at least yellow/acceptable; an example being "murder on behalf of the country as right, on behalf of oneself wrong". Another way is by making reality opaque, so that we do not see the violent act or fact, or at least not as violent.' Johan Galtung, 'Cultural violence', *Journal of Peace Research*, 27(3), 1990, page 292.

5 For a further discussion of these issues, see, for example, W. Belson, *Television, Violence and the Adolescent Boy* (Farnborough, UK, Saxon House, 1979); L. Vriens, 'Peace education and children: a structural dialogue about global responsibility', *WCCI Forum*, 3(2), 1989, pages 48–67; A. Takala, 'Feminist perspectives on peace education', *Journal of Peace Research*, 28(2), 1991, pages 231–235; E. Boulding (editor), *New Agendas for Peace Research: Conflict and Security Reexamined* (Boulder, CO, Lynne Rienner, in association with the International Peace Research Association, 1992), pages 6 and 172–174; and M. Miedzian, *Boys Will Be Boys: Breaking the Link between Masculinity and Violence* (London, Virago, 1992).

6 N. Carlsson-Paige and D. E. Levin, *Who's Calling the Shots? How to Respond Effectively to Children's Fascination with War Play and War Toys* (Philadelphia, PA, New Society, 1990), pages 123 and 137.

7 For further discussion, see R. Lacey, C. Heffernan and F. Hutchinson, *Education for Peace: Explorations and Proposals* (Canberra, Commonwealth Schools Commission, in association with the Catholic Education Office and New South Wales Department of Education, 1986); E. Boulding, *Building a Global Civic Culture: Education for an Interdependent World* (New York, Teachers College Press, Columbia University, 1988); R. Howitt and F. Hutchinson, *Educating for Peace in Primary Schools* (Sydney, NSW Department of Education, 1988); D. Hicks, *Exploring Alternative Futures: A Teacher's Interim Guide* (London, Global Futures Project, Institute of Education, University of London, 1991); A. Tough, *Crucial Questions about the Future* (Lanham, University Press of America, 1991); and H. Beare and R. Slaughter, *Education for the Twenty-first Century* (London, Routledge, 1993).

8 Hutchinson, 'Futures consciousness', page 225.

9 F. Peavey, *Heart Politics* (New Society, Philadelphia, 1986), page 165.

10 Hutchinson, 'Futures consciousness', pages 351–355.

11 S. Gazis and S. Thomas, *The Future* (Melbourne, Longman Cheshire, 1990).

12 John Fairfax Education Unit (editors), *The Future* (Sydney, *Herald*-in-the classroom series, 1991), page 5.

13 See J. Burger, *The Gaia Atlas of First Peoples* (Harmondsworth, Penguin, 1990).

14 R. Eisler, *The Chalice and the Blade: Our History, Our Future* (London, Mandala/Unwin, 1993), *passim*. Also see F. Hutchinson, 'Making peace with people and planet: some important lessons from the Gandhian tradition in educating for the twenty-first century', *Peace, Education and Environment*, 3(2), 1992, pages 3–14.

15 Australian Centre for Independent Journalism, *Youth and the Media* (Sydney, University of Technology, 1992), page 46.

16 These examples are from 'Rogue Trooper: you only die twice', *The Best of 2000AD Monthly*, February 1991; and 'Death aid', *Judge Dredd*, January 1991, page 1.

17 Kenneth Boulding, *Human Betterment* (Beverly Hills, CA, Sage, 1985), pages 214–215.

18 Carl Rogers, *Carl Rogers on Personal Power* (London, Constable, 1978), pages 18–19 and 69–74.

19 See J. Fairall, S. Glover and C. Renouf, *Beyond 2000*, Vol. 3 (Richmond, Victoria, Heinemann Australia, 1989), for an example of technocratic narrative.

20 For a discussion on Futurism, see R. Hughes, *The Shock of the New: Art and the Century of Change* (2nd edition, London, Thames and Hudson, 1991), *passim*.

21 Necessarily the young people's expressive art media artefacts illustrated in this chapter are a limited sample from the many studied. Further examples are given in Hutchinson, 'Futures consciousness', pages 299–310. The latter contains specific acknowledgements and other details as to source. For the sharing and displaying of their works publicly, many thanks are due to these creative artists.

22 R. Slaughter, 'The foresight principle', *Futures*, 22(8), 1990, pages 801–819.

23 For further discussion on crucial issues of choice and engagement in schools, see F. Hutchinson and L. Waddell, *People, Problems and Planet Earth* (2nd edition, Melbourne, Macmillan, 1986); L. Waddell and F. Hutchinson, *Learning for a Fairer Future: Classroom Activities on Global Trade and Social Justice Issues* (Sydney, Geography Teachers' Association, in association with the World Development Tea Cooperative, 1988); F. Hutchinson, C. Talbot and L. Brown, *Our Planet and its People* (Melbourne, Macmillan, 1992); and F. Hutchinson, 'Educating beyond fatalism and impoverished social imagination: are we actively listening to young people's voices on the future?' *Peace, Environment and Education*, 4, Winter 1993, pages 36–57.

Part III

Social learning for a new millennium

Chapter 9

Ways to develop the knowledge base of futures studies

Allen Tough

How can we get from here to a satisfactory future? Several steps will be necessary. Clearly one of those steps is the rapid development of highly relevant knowledge, understanding, wisdom, ideas, images, and insights.

Humanity could benefit greatly if our generation were to increase at least threefold the creative thinking, disciplined inquiry, theory-building, basic research, profound books, doctoral theses, and cutting-edge conference sessions devoted to the future. The long-term benefits of this increase would far outweigh the costs. Even a tenfold increase might not be extravagant compared to the payoff. We cannot be sure of the optimum level of spending for developing the future-relevant knowledge base, but we are sure that the gap between that optimum level and our current level is huge, bizarre, poignant, and foolish.

World problems are outstripping our knowledge of how to deal with them. We will have to run much faster than now simply to catch up. Then we will probably find that the problems, too, are speeding up. To develop the knowledge to outrun the world's problems, we will need to speed up our efforts even further. We certainly have the potential to win the race, but not by coasting along at our present level of effort.

In addition to applied knowledge, it is important to develop sophisticated conceptual frameworks and a scientific knowledge base about the future. 'Scientific' here means using the best social science approaches, most of which do not resemble the approaches in the physical sciences. Lengyel (1987) has pointed out that all the social sciences, especially at the international level and within international organizations and meetings, are placing too much emphasis on application and not enough on theory-building. To put it bluntly, we need to do plenty of social *science* before emphasizing applications. In addition, there is a great need for wisdom, for a broad long-term perspective, for seeing the big picture, and for profound thinking about the most important questions of all.

It is also important to support and attract people with especially lively and penetrating minds to contribute ideas and knowledge about the future. An innovative use of $2 million would be to scour the world for the twelve best thinkers about the future and then offer each of them one-twelfth of this amount to write a thoughtful comprehensive book relevant to the future.

SEVEN DIRECTIONS

As we vigorously move ahead to develop the future-relevant knowledge base, what particular directions are most likely to benefit the next few generations? In order to stimulate further thought and discussion, let me suggest seven possibilities. These seven directions seem to me most likely to pay off well for future generations.

Conceptual organization of existing knowledge

First, we need to pay much more conceptual and theoretical attention to the knowledge base that we already have. We need to step back in order to reflect on better ways to organize it conceptually. For instance, we need meta-analyses, reflection on our current conceptual frameworks and paradigms, and critical paring and organization of our knowledge base. Futurists such as Richard Slaughter, James Dator, Donella Meadows, Michael Marien, and Warren Wagar have contributed interesting categories and frameworks to the literature, but few people critique or build on their thinking. My intention in writing *Crucial Questions about the Future* (Tough, 1991) was to provide a set of key questions and provisional answers on which others could build; I am disappointed that so far no one has pursued such building. In the field of futures studies, we need to increase our intellectual interaction in order to move the knowledge base forward, instead of operating in intellectual isolation and constantly reinventing the wheel.

Turning now to university courses about the future, the dearth of significant, deep powerful frameworks and syntheses is a serious problem that inhibits further growth of courses. When asked how to get more universities to provide quality courses and programs relevant to the future, many people say that we should use our political skills with university presidents and deans. Others say that we need better teaching methods or more money. In addition, though, it is important to develop the knowledge base. Futures education will be much more attractive to the rest of the university if its ideas, concepts, and theories are profound and well organized.

Cutting-edge ideas at conferences

The key futures organizations could do much more to stimulate, foster, and disseminate cutting-edge intellectual contributions at their conferences.

Compared to other fields of knowledge, conferences in the field of futures studies provide few forums for face-to-face discussion of the latest theory-building efforts. I sometimes feel that such conferences are anti-intellectual or at least non-conceptual. Certainly my own experience is that futures conference sessions are not usually the best place to seek cutting-edge ideas relevant to the future.

Thesis students should be enabled to attend and present their research, and even participate in a student caucus. In addition, one of the futures periodicals could assist by publishing an annual list of recently completed theses and thesis research in progress.

Social change and governance

We need to know far more about potential future scenarios, policy development and effective governance. We need to study the causes and possible consequences of various world problems, along with practical solutions. We need much better understanding of common beliefs that threaten our future, of why so much human behavior undermines our chances of a flourishing future, and of the appropriate actions that we need to take in order to achieve social change. To work on almost any global problem, as Richardson (1987) has pointed out, we need to understand individual values and goals, social and political will, why people behave as they do, and how such things can be changed.

What fosters appropriate and sufficiently rapid social change, and what blocks it? What role is played by powerful ideas, images, world views, and cultural beliefs? How can we profoundly influence the extent to which people care about future generations – the extent to which they gain meaning and purpose from efforts to enhance the well-being of people not yet born? We need to study why people, even when informed and convinced about the dangers, act in ways that produce not only short-term benefits but also undue long-term costs and risks.

We need vigorous thinking and research about the arrangements and institutions that are most likely to produce individual and group behavior in the long-term interests of human civilization (Firey, 1967; Hardin, 1981; Sorokin, 1954; Stern, 1978). We need greater sophistication concerning the likely outcomes of various paths and strategies: successfully fostering good outcomes and avoiding negative outcomes can be an incredibly difficult and subtle process. We need strong creative efforts to understand how to offset the natural tendency for things to go from bad to worse (Boulding, 1985; Meadows *et al.*, 1992). The study of human history, too, can illuminate the future even though no cycles or theories of the historical past can be guaranteed to apply to our future.

How can we increase the extent to which the actual decisions and behavior of citizens, organizations, and governments enhance our chances for a reasonably positive future? In short, how can we get humanity to take its own future seriously?

Education. learning, and individual change

Most futurists agree that any path to a successful future will require deep changes in individual perspectives, values, and behavior. But this phenomenon is neglected by futures researchers. What fosters and hinders people from learning about global issues and potential futures, and then clarifying their emotional reactions and the implications for their own lives? What resources, advice, and skills will people of all ages need most over the next ten years for this sort of learning and change? What strategies will result in people caring so much about the continued flourishing of human civilization that they will make deep adjustments? Research along these lines to extend the work of Roger Walsh, Duane Elgin, Joanna Macy, and Martha Rogers could yield valuable insights. Rogers (1994) found that learning about the future not only involved cognitive and emotional struggles: it also plunged some adult learners into questions about the meaning and purpose of life, and what they should do with the rest of their life in order to make a difference. Research on education for the future could range from studies of the individual through to studies of the school and university curriculum (Tough, 1979, 1982; 1991: 54–58). The place in education of making a pledge to future generations could also be further explored (Tough, 1993a).

Guardians for future generations

The need for a spokesperson, representative, or guardian for future generations – a designated person to speak in various legislative bodies on behalf of the needs and future well-being of those not yet born – has been emphasized by several authors (summarized in Tough, 1993b). Several years ago, the Future Generations Program based in Malta began discussing this concept and seeking ways to implement it through international law and organizations. More recently, the Future Generations Alliance Foundation based in Kyoto has sponsored various seminars and books. What now needs to be done is some actual experiments with a designated Guardian in a few diverse decision-making situations. As we see what works, what does not, and why, we will then be able to move ahead with wider use of ombudsmen or spokespersons for future generations.

Cosmic evolution

Within the field of astronomy, it is now commonly accepted that we are not alone in the cosmos. Although no scientific evidence has yet been found for the actual existence of other intelligent species and civilizations in our galaxy, astronomers and other scientists are vigorously pursuing several approaches to finding such evidence. If we eventually detect an encyclopedic message sent to us from another star system, or make contact in some other way, the long-term impact on humanity will be profound. Even before such an event, however, the cosmic perspective is already having a powerful influence on individual perspectives, understanding, values, meaning and purpose in life, and spirituality.

Creative yet disciplined exploration of this situation can probably produce some fundamental implications for the knowledge base in futures studies. Indeed, as more and more people view their lives and our planet within the context of cosmic evolution, the development of new core values and a new global ethic becomes imperative. Who are we as an intelligent species in the universe, who else lives in our galaxy, and where are we all heading? These questions may well rise higher on the futurists' agenda as we realize that the cosmic perspective can fundamentally change our self-image about who we are and our place in the universe, our caring about humanity and future generations, and our commitment to a global ethic.

Finding a path to a positive future

Finding a path that can actually lead to a satisfactory future is surely one of the central tasks of research and inquiry in futures studies. There is an urgent need for in-depth studies of the *résolutique* – the total approach needed to cope successfully with the problematique. In order for citizens and political leaders to create a path leading to a satisfactory long-term future, researchers and thinkers/philosophers need to study several questions in particular. Why do we act in ways that hurt future generations? Why do we put immediate narrow concerns ahead of humanity's flourishing over the next few decades? What higher priority is there for people than maintaining human culture and avoiding massive deterioration? How can we get people to change fast enough in the necessary directions? What are the long-term costs and benefits of our present path, even with slight improvements over the next few years, compared to dramatically different paths? Within the various agendas and lists of priorities in the futures literature, what are the most promising directions of all and how can these be conceptually organized?

REFERENCES

Boulding, Kenneth E. (1985) *Human Betterment*. Beverly Hills: Sage.
Firey, Walter (1967) 'Conditions for the realization of values remote in time', in E. A. Tiryakian (ed.) *Sociological Theory, Values, and Sociocultural Change: Essays in Honor of Pitrim A Sorokin*. New York: Harper.

Hardin, Garrett (1981) 'Who cares for posterity?', in Ernest Partridge (ed.) *Responsibilities to Future Generations*. Buffalo: Prometheus.

Lengyel, Peter (1987) 'The future of international organizations', in Ray C. Rist (ed.) *Policy Studies Review Annual*, vol. 8. New Brunswick, NJ: Transaction Books.

Meadows, Donella, Meadows, Dennis, and Randers, Jorgen (1992) *Beyond the Limits: Confronting Global Collapse, Envisioning a Sustainable Future*. Post Mills, Vermont: Chelsea Green Publishing.

Richardson, John M. (1987) 'Global modeling: A retrospective', *Futures Research Quarterly* 3 (1): 5–25.

Rogers, Martha Elizabeth (1994) 'Learning about global futures: An exploration of learning processes and changes in adults', Doctoral dissertation, Graduate Department of Education, University of Toronto.

Sorokin, Pitrim A. (1954) *The Ways and Power of Love: Types, Factors, and Techniques of Moral Transformation*. Boston: Beacon.

Stern, Paul C. (1978) 'When do people act to maintain common resources? A reformulated psychological question for our times', *International Journal of Psychology* 13 (2): 149–158.

Tough, Allen (1979) *The Adult's Learning Projects: A Fresh Approach to Theory and Practice in Adult Learning*. 2nd edition. Toronto: OISE Press. (Now available from the author.)

—— (1982) *Intentional Changes: A Fresh Approach to Helping People Change*. Chicago: Follett. (Now available from the author.)

—— (1991) *Crucial Questions about the Future*. Lanham, Maryland: University Press of America and London: Adamantine Press.

—— (1993a) 'Making a pledge to future generations', *Futures* 25 (1): 90–92.

—— (1993b) 'What future generations need from us', *Futures* 25 (10): 1041–1050.

Chapter 10

Envisioning a sustainable society

Lester W. Milbrath

In my judgment, *the most important reality in today's world is that modern industrial civilization cannot be sustained.* Even though many world leaders do not recognize this fact, it is nevertheless true.

Recently I spent three months in Southern California, teaching at the University of California at Irvine. I shocked my students when I made the point that North America has the two most unsustainable societies on the planet (Canada and the USA) and that Southern California is the most unsustainable part of North America. The southern Californians have erected a huge metropolitan area with nearly 20 million inhabitants on a terrain of mountains and valleys that is essentially a desert and highly susceptible to earthquakes. The city must import all its water, energy, and food from elsewhere. Its transportation system depends overwhelmingly on heavy, fast, automobiles that travel on multi-lane freeways that criss-cross the area. If Southern Californians had intentionally set out to design an unsustainable society, they could hardly have exceeded the reality of today's LA area.

On January 17, 1994, a moderate earthquake struck the northern part of the metro area and reminded its inhabitants how vulnerable they are to the disruption of their imported services. Two hundred years ago that earthquake would have barely been noticed in the area. Today, water, energy, and transportation links were broken in addition to the loss of life and buildings. One might have thought that people would see the folly of their situation and abandon the area but almost none did. The possibility of not rebuilding the freeways never came up for public discussion; there was no public awareness of the unsustainability of the city. The people in the area took for normal that which is entirely unnatural, and hastily set about rebuilding that which had failed them.

The most important problem faced by mankind is *how do we transform an unsustainable society into one that is sustainable*? That question raises a series of additional questions: how did we get into this predicament? Why is modern society unsustainable? What happens if we do not change? What must be changed if human society is to survive? What can we do to bring about the requisite changes? I will discuss all of those questions but I cannot promise to have all the needed solutions.

HOW DID WE GET INTO THIS PREDICAMENT?

We did so by becoming too successful. It did not occur to people in the LA area to abandon the city because it is, for them, successful. They assume it will continue to be successful indefinitely. Our vision is blinded by *the tragic success of the human species. Homo sapiens* have lived for only a tiny fraction of the time our planet has existed. If the time of the earth's existence (4.6 billion years) were compressed into one calendar year, human existence would extend for only eleven minutes; civilization would have lasted only one minute; modern industrial society would have lasted only two seconds. Nearly all of the changes that threaten the existence of our civilization transpired in the last two seconds. We are now so powerful that by using science and technology we can move mountains, slash down forests, fly to the moon, and destroy all life – even our own.

Nowadays we often hear that we face an environmental crisis. But do we properly understand our predicament? Is this an environmental crisis? Try this thought experiment: imagine that suddenly, poof, all the humans disappear but leave behind the buildings, roads, shopping malls, stadiums, factories, skyscrapers, automobiles, ships, planes and so forth. Now imagine that three or four centuries pass. What will have happened? Nature will have swiftly taken over; buildings will have crumbled; vehicles will have rusted and fallen apart; plants will have grown into and broken up roads and parking lots; much of the land will have been recolonized by forests. Water, air, and soil will have gradually been cleansed by nature; most endangered species will once more flourish. Nature, you see, would thrive splendidly without us.

That experiment makes it clear that we do not have an environmental crisis; we have a crisis of the human species. More accurately, we have a crisis of human civilization. It was not until humans became civilized and took more and more of the biosphere to serve our exclusive needs that we began to reproduce at epidemic rates. Just in this century, human numbers will have doubled twice, from 1.5 billion, to 3 billion, to 6 billion. Population will double again within the next fifty years, bringing us to 11 or 12 billion. Still another doubling would carry us beyond 20 billion. Allowing that to happen would be total folly. If reproductive success is the sign of a successful species, we have become tragically successful.

WHY IS MODERN SOCIETY UNSUSTAINABLE?

Our use of resources and discharge of wastes more than doubles with each doubling of the human population. Those growth rates cannot help but force a great transformation. Growth simply cannot continue for two reasons: first, more than half the resources in the earth's crust have been consumed and scattered; there simply will not be sufficient resources for all those new humans, even at present consumption rates.

Even more importantly, the emission of the greenhouse gases (carbon dioxide, methane, nitrous oxides, and chlorofluorocarbons) is beginning to change the way the biosphere works. Scientists estimate that the earth will warm 3 to 5 degrees Celsius in the next seven decades; perhaps sooner. That will be sufficient to change climate patterns. We cannot be sure that the climate will change gradually and then settle down into a new pattern; it is likely to oscillate unpredictably and bring unexpected catastrophe. You have probably read predictions of good farm land turning to desert, devastating floods, rising sea levels, killer hurricanes. Climate change and loss of the ozone layer will injure ecosystems all over the planet and reduce their productivity at the very time all those new humans will be looking for sustenance.

Equally devastating, climatic instability would destroy the confidence people need in order to invest. People will not be sure that they could ever live in the house they would like to build. Entrepreneurs would have little confidence that their business could get supplies or that their goods would have a market. Investors would fear that their stocks, bonds, and loans would become worthless. Young people would not know how to plan for a career. If the climate oscillates unpredictably, we will become victims of our own success. Be forewarned: chaos in climate patterns means economic catastrophe.

By just doing what we have been doing every day, we are unintentionally conducting a giant planetary experiment to see how far we can perturb biospheric systems before they change their patterns and drastically change everything about our lives. *By being singlemindedly successful at doing what society expects of us, we have created a civilization that is headed for breakdown.* We are facing a massive transformation of modern society that we cannot avoid. We should change the direction of our society now before we find out the answer to that unintended experiment. In 'earth time' we have less than one second to make the necessary changes. Either we learn to control our growth in population and in economic activity or nature will control it for us. Remember, *nature's solution is death.*

WHAT HAPPENS IF WE DO NOT CHANGE?

If we persist on our current trajectory we can expect, as already mentioned, that we will double human population within fifty years. We will treble or quadruple world economic output. That will lead to swift depletion of the world's resources as well as to the emission of such a torrent of pollutants that the planet's ecosystems cannot assimilate them. Most seriously, we are likely to change the pattern of the planet's biogeochemical systems with all of the terrible consequences that I have already mentioned. We are likely to seek technological solutions to those problems but it is my considered opinion that trying to solve societal problems with more and better technology will fail. We will belatedly and painfully learn that most socio-economic-political problems are not amenable to a technological fix.

Not only has modern industrial society created this crisis, but, in my judgment, it is not capable of producing a solution. It is blinded to the existence of the crisis and disabled in trying to avoid it by the values it pursues. Think of the values upheld as good in contemporary political discourse: economic growth, consumption, efficiency, productivity, jobs, competitiveness, taking risks, power, winning. Societies pursuing those goals cannot avoid depleting their resources, cannot avoid degrading nature, cannot avoid poisoning life with wastes, and cannot avoid upsetting biospheric systems. Will we thoughtfully transform our society to a sustainable mode, or will we stubbornly refuse to change and have change forced upon us by the collapse of society's fundamental underpinnings? *Resisting change will make us victims of change. I repeat for emphasis, resisting change will make us victims of change.*

WHAT MUST BE CHANGED IF HUMAN SOCIETY IS TO SURVIVE?

How do we transform from our present unsustainable society to a new sustainable society? We all know that both societies and people resist change. Achieving change is not as easy as giving an order; even the most powerful dictators must persuade the people that they will be better off if they change. My answer, I believe it is the only answer, is that we must *learn* our way to a new society. The key aspect of our relearning is to transform the way we think. *It is absolutely essential to change the way we think.* All other attempts at change will fail if we do not transform our thinking. If we can make the right changes in our thinking, the necessary changes in society will follow.

Can we learn in time? We all know that most social learning is slow and painful, but not always; sometimes we cross a threshold and learning comes about astonishingly swiftly. Who among us would have predicted the sweeping changes that occurred in Eastern Europe in the fall of 1989? How many foresaw that the Soviet Union would disintegrate with hardly a shot fired? When people changed their thinking, the old order simply disappeared. When a society has no other choice than to change, we get little guidance from the past; we cannot predict the future from the past in those circumstances.

Can we manage to look ahead and make careful plans to bring about the changes that we know must come or will we resist change and have it painfully forced upon us? Either way, our only option is to relearn; nature, and the imperatives of its laws, will be our most powerful teacher as we learn our way to a new society.

I characterize the new society that we must create as sustainable; but, what do I mean by sustainable? A sustainable society does something more than keep people alive; living is more than merely not dying. In a sustainable society, people conduct their lives so that nature can cleanse itself and living creatures can flourish. People living sustainably husband nature and resources so that future generations of people, and other creatures, can enjoy a life of decent quality.

The values appropriate to a sustainable society are displayed in Figure 10.1.

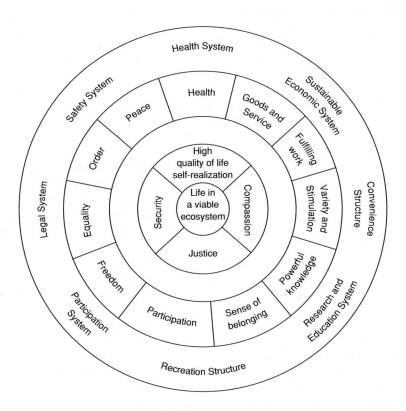

Figure 10.1   A proposed value structure for a sustainable society

CONTRASTING VALUES AND GOALS BETWEEN SUSTAINABLE AND MODERN SOCIETIES

Life in a viable ecosystem must be the core value of a sustainable society. Viable ecosystems nurture all life, not just human life. Ecosystems function splendidly without humans but human society would die out without a viable ecosystem. Individuals seeking quality of life require a well-functioning society that must be supported by a well-functioning ecosystem. If we follow the logic of those statements, we must give *top priority to the good functioning of our ecosystem, second priority to the good functioning of our society*; only when the viability of both systems is assured is it permissible to seek quality of life in any way we choose.

But do we live according to the priority of those values? Obviously not! Leaders in modern society equate material consumption with quality of life. They urge us to swiftly exploit resources to maximize economic output without careful forethought about future consequences. By placing top priority on economic values, they sacrifice the good functioning of vital life systems, making it unlikely that those systems can support the huge increase in human population that is coming. At the very time when all the capabilities of life systems will be needed, our lack of foresight will have greatly weakened them.

A sustainable society affirms *love* as a core value. It extends love and compassion not only to those near and dear but to people in other lands, future generations, and other species. It recognizes the intricate web of relationships that bind all living creatures into a common destiny. Life is not mainly conflict and competition between creatures; rather, a sustainable society emphasizes partnership rather than domination; cooperation more than competition; love more than power.

In contrast, modern society rewards power, competitiveness, and domination over others. In America, especially, people surround themselves with a luxuriant array of private goods that tend to isolate people from each other. Each household attempts to fulfill its needs using money alone. There is little sense of a common destiny; little bonding with each other or with nature.

A sustainable society affirms *justice and security* as other core values. Those are core values in every society but the way they are realized differs from society to society. A modern industrial society that emphasizes wealth, power, competition, and domination generates great differences in status that seem inherently unjust to those of lower status. Individuals often resort to crime and violence to improve their situation. The values of justice and security are continually under assault in such a society. A sustainable society that emphasizes love, partnership, compassion and cooperation can more easily provide justice and security.

A sustainable society would encourage *self-realization* as the key to a fulfilling life. A sustainable society would help persons become all they are capable of being whether they possess a talent that is highly valued in the labor marketplace or not. Work should be redefined to become a means to self-realization and not merely a block of time to be traded in the labor market. Modern competitive industrial society encourages firms to replace workers with machines and wastes the creative talents of hundreds of millions of unemployed people. This problem will explode into a permanent crisis as the world's population doubles in the next fifty years.

A first step to extricate ourselves from this problem will be to change our thinking to distinguish work from employment. We presently reward only the employed and look down upon the unemployed as less than fully human. Our faulty thinking fails to recognize that nearly everyone works even if they do not have a job. Persons doing their own work, or non-paid contributors to family and society, should be valued as much as those highly paid. Self-esteem should not be linked to employment but should derive more from skill, artistry, effort, and integrity.

RECONSIDERATION OF MODERN SOCIETY'S FOCUS ON ECONOMICS

Economic growth is a means and not an end, it cannot be our top priority, whereas a viable ecosystem must be society's top priority. Current rates of economic growth are impossible to sustain. Modern political leaders constantly proclaim economic growth as their top priority even though societies that do so are bound to fail. Our current misplaced emphasis on growth must give way to a recognition that there are limits to human population growth, and to economic growth, otherwise society will lose more highly treasured values such as the continued good functioning of global biogeochemical systems, the viability of ecosystems, the continued availability of vital resources, and the health of all creatures.

We must forthrightly recognize that there are limits to Earth's resources and to the ability of life systems to absorb pollutants; those limits will necessarily restrict population growth and economic activity. A sustainable society would recognize that basic fact and would emphasize making quality products to be loved and conserved for many years. Products would be designed to be safely and easily recycled to other uses when their original use is finished. People would learn to love beauty and simplicity. Packaging would be kept to a minimum and would be designed to be reused or recycled.

A sustainable society would support simple lifestyles by diminishing the role of advertising in communication and entertainment. Modern society fails to recognize that advertising which urges everyone to buy, consume, and throw away will so injure ecosystems that it will lead to that society's painful demise.

A sustainable society would utilize both *planning* and *markets* as basic information systems that supplement each other. Both are needed to guide economic activity and public policy. Modern society fails to recognize the fundamental inability of markets to anticipate the long-term future and to adequately assign social value to public goods such as clean air and parks. Modern society puts too much faith in markets; it even abdicates responsible moral choice to markets by allowing them to demand closing or moving factories, to make harmful and wasteful goods, to freely release pollutants, to insist on public subsidies, to insist on favorable laws and regulations.

A sustainable society would recognize that *public goods* (those that are available to everyone, such as schools, highways, parks, national defense, environmental protection, etc.) are just as important for quality of life as private goods. It also would recognize that markets, by themselves, are incapable of providing public goods; therefore it would expect government and other public agencies to provide public goods and to assess justly taxes to pay for them.

In contrast, many leaders in modern society mistakenly assert that only personal goods can bring quality in living and neglect public goods in order to reduce taxes. My country, the USA, vigorously promotes businesses, and a market economy oriented to the production of personal goods, to the point that Americans now live in a society in which privileged people have personal affluence while we all experience public squalor. Many millions of Americans cannot succeed in that system and are unable to earn enough income for a decent life. Their anger and frustration lead to unprecedented levels of violent brutality. We cannot find quality in living that way.

SCIENCE AND TECHNOLOGY IN THE SERVICE OF SOCIETY

Science and technology are not value-free; they make values; they change values; they are guided by values; and they profoundly influence everything about modern life. Yet, leaders in science, business, and government continually proclaim that science and technology are value-free and should be promoted as positive steps toward progress and the good life. The public is told that it is not proper for society to control science and technology. This abdication of public responsibility gives the ability to direct those forces, and to collect their benefits, over to those who can pay for specialized talents and equipment (especially business and government); therefore, science and technology primarily serve the values of the established order. Those who control science and technology can use them to dominate all other creatures – they can literally destroy any or all life.

A sustainable society would encourage further development of science and technology for the good they can do, but it would anticipate their potential for evil and would learn to develop social controls of those powerful forces. In contrast, modern society eagerly promotes their development without foresight as to consequences or recognition of the need for controls.

Powerful new technologies can induce sweeping changes in economic patterns, lifestyles, governance, and social values. They are even more powerful than legislation for inducing permanent change; we can repeal legislation but we do not know how to repeal a powerful new technology. Therefore, a sustainable society would not allow deployment of new technologies without careful forethought regarding the long-term impact of a proposed technology. It would learn how to design and enforce social controls of the deployment and use of technologies.

SOCIAL LEARNING AS THE DYNAMIC OF SOCIAL CHANGE

Social learning is different from the learning of individuals. When a society learns, the individuals within it also learn; but individuals often learn without the society learning. Even though a society cannot be said to have a mind, societies, as social entities, can be said to know or believe something. Social learning is embodied in societal memory, conventional terms of discourse, social norms, laws, institutional patterns, institutional memories, shared perceptions, and so forth.

Societies have always learned despite their inherent tendency to preserve the status quo; but we can make swift social learning a conscious societal policy. A society desiring to be sustainable would do this not only to deal with pressing problems but also to help that society to realize its vision of a good society. No single individual, not even a government, has the power to order a society to change. Meaningful and permanent social change occurs when nearly everyone learns the necessity and wisdom of accepting the change. Therefore, a society hoping to survive and thrive would emphasize swift social learning as its best strategy for evolving sustainable modes of behavior that also lead to quality in living.

In contrast, modern industrial society, driven by the desire for power and wealth, uses the market to guide its destiny. Markets cannot look ahead to deal with problems until they become powerful immediate threats. A society that hopes to become sustainable must use enhanced foresighted learning to anticipate problems and avoid crisis policy making.

We cannot make a society sustainable without changing the way we think. A sustainable society must cultivate ecological thinking which is different from the thoughtways in modern society. Amazingly, most people in modern society do not know the fundamental laws of nature such as the first and second laws of thermodynamics. For example, environmentalists derive four key maxims for thinking from the first law of thermodynamics which says that *matter and energy can neither be created nor destroyed, they can only be transformed*: (1) everything must go somewhere; (2) everything is connected to everything else; (3) we can never do merely one thing; and (4) we must continually ask, '*and then what?*' These maxims are routinely violated in contemporary thinking and discourse. Every schoolchild should learn them, yet almost none of them are given this instruction. A sustainable society would reaffirm the belief, once held in primitive societies, that a knowledge of nature's workings is basic to being educated. It would act on that belief by requiring environmental education of all students as it now requires every student to study history.

Ecological thinking recognizes that the geosphere and biosphere are systems and that proper understanding of the way the world works requires people to learn how to *think systemically, holistically, integratively, and in a futures mode*. Everything is connected to everything else; we must learn to anticipate second-, third-, and fourth-order consequences for any contemplated major societal action.

Modern society, in contrast, emphasizes simple cause-and-effect 'mechanistic thinking', which fails to alert people that most actions have unanticipated consequences. It encourages narrow expertise and short-term planning, while simultaneously discouraging holistic, systemic, and futures thinking. A sustainable society would correct that distortion and accord esteem to those who practice foresighted ecological thinking.

A society desiring to be sustainable would redesign government to maximize its ability to learn. It would use the governmental learning process to promote social learning. In Chapter 14 of *Envisioning a Sustainable Society* (Albany, New York: SUNY Press, 1989), I describe a learning system for government that would encourage inputs from citizens to enhance its learning ability. This learning system would add a new branch to government designed to give it a much needed foresight capability that I call 'a Council for Long Range Societal Guidance'. This learning system not only would help government to learn by enlisting the learning of the entire society but the government learning process would also help the society to learn.

In contrast, modern society takes a short-range perspective and mistakenly assumes that the future will be like the past. It insists that planners and decision makers must be immediately 'practical', which generally means that economic needs take precedence over all other values. It ridicules people who peer into the future and make plans to forestall future problems; it calls them 'impractical dreamers'. Yet, as we well know, modern society is constantly scrambling to deal with crisis after crisis that it did not anticipate.

The era when governors needed only to command and citizens meekly obeyed has passed. A learning sustainable society would affirm the inherent value of persons by requiring that governors listen to citizens. A sustainable society not only would keep itself open for public participation but also would cultivate mutual learning between officials and citizens as the central task of governance. The most successful governance occurs when citizens and officials mutually understand their problems and acknowledge the appropriate solutions.

A sustainable society would recognize that we are part of global biogeochemical systems; and that our destiny is tied to the continued good functioning of those systems. Our health and welfare are vitally affected by how people, firms, and governments in other lands behave. Therefore, it would strive diligently to build an effective planetary politics. It would encourage its citizens to join transnational social movements and political parties because they can make effective common cause with movements and parties in other countries and work together to preserve the viability of global biogeochemical systems. It would nurture social learning all around the planet, because the cooperation of all is needed to preserve the good functioning of planetary life systems. This necessity to work together may one day lead to the formation of a world society with a world government.

LEARNING OUR WAY TO A SUSTAINABLE SOCIETY

Learning our way to a new society not only is the preferred way, it is the only way – in my judgment, there is no shortcut. No individual has the power and the trust of the people to order new ways of thinking, new ways of perceiving, new architecture for institutions, new laws, new norms, new ways of making and doing things. We get those new ways of thinking and doing only by learning – it must be the learning of the entire society.

Fundamental relearning cannot occur, however, until people become aware of the need for change. So long as contemporary society is working reasonably well, and its leaders keep reaffirming that society is on the right track, the mass of people will not listen to a message urging change. For that reason, life systems on our planet probably must get worse before they can get better. Nature will turn out to be our most powerful teacher. We probably will not be able to listen until biospheric systems no longer work the way they used to and people are shocked into realizing how much their lives depended on the continued good functioning of those systems.

After a severe shock to wake us up, in times of great systemic turbulence, social learning can be extraordinarily swift. Regretfully, injuries to life systems may already be very great by that time. Life probably will not cease, but many will die and others will be gravely injured. Why can't we learn at less cost?

Even if I know they will be difficult to achieve, here are some specific recommendations about next steps to be taken to bring about a sustainable society. If we could wave a magic wand to obtain the cooperation of people and their governments, the following actions would be effective:

- Change the way we think as swiftly as possible. We need to clarify our values and adopt new priorities. In the process we should define our responsibilities so that people see what their part of the overall task is as well as the necessity to do their share. All of us must learn to think systemically, holistically, integratively, and in a futures mode. Renewed reflection on the true meaning of quality of living should be part of this relearning effort.
- Control and gradually eliminate weapons of mass destruction.
- Stop population growth as quickly as possible. With heroic efforts, population rise might be leveled off at 8 or 9 billion.
- Reduce material consumption in the more developed countries and use that reserve capacity to help the less developed countries meet their subsistence needs.
- Cut back as much as possible on use of fossil energy: develop and adopt more energy efficient technology; cut out energy waste wherever found; stop using fossil energy simply for thrills, fun, ease, or comfort; convert to use of solar energy.
- Aggressively reduce economic throughput so as to preserve more resources for future generations and to reduce discharge of wastes into the biosphere. Failure to do so will seriously reduce the carrying capacity of life systems.
- Find ways to share employment so we don't need to make unneeded goods just to provide jobs for people. Work should be redefined to become a means of self-realization, not merely a pawn in economic competition.
- Emphasize making quality products that can last lifetimes – beautiful things to be cherished and preserved. Products should be designed to be easily repaired and for safe eventual disposal. They should be marketed with as little packaging as possible.
- Diligently reuse, restore, and recycle materials that we now throw away. Carefully dispose of the remainder of wastes.
- Eliminate use of chlorofluorocarbons (CFCs) to allow the stratospheric ozone layer to restore itself. Recapture CFCs from current uses and destroy them (break them down into original constituents).
- Stop the release of toxic environmental chemicals into the environment.
- Protect and enhance biodiversity; revitalize ecosystems that have been injured by human actions; husband nature and resources so that future generations and other creatures can enjoy a life of decent quality.
- Plant billions more trees.
- Phase out energy-and-chemical-intensive agriculture so as to develop methods of tillage that are sustainable.

- Restore degraded ecosystems to flourishing health wherever possible.
- Develop an ethic that constantly alerts people that their actions should impact earth systems as lightly as possible.
- Affirm love (caring for others) as a primary value; it should be extended not only to those near and dear, but to future generations, other species, and people in other lands.
- Diminish rewards for power, competitiveness, and domination over others. A sustainable society emphasizes partnership rather than domination, cooperation more than competition, justice more than power.
- Develop a procedure for careful review and forethought regarding the long-term impact of a proposed technology. Bad consequences of new technology are easier to avoid or manage if they can be anticipated from the start.
- Redesign government to maximize its ability to learn; then use the government learning process to promote social learning. Develop a new governmental institution to better anticipate the future consequences of proposed policies, laws, and technologies.
- Societal learning of environmental thinking should become a national project. Require that every child receive environmental education (it is just as basic as history); institute environmental education programs for adults; make a special effort to educate media employees about environmental concepts and thinking.
- Don't merely work for a living but work for something that is truly important.
- Keep a sense of humor; sing, dance, affirm love; be joyous in your oneness with the earth.

Our common journey promises to be challenging and exciting, even though difficult. It will be much easier, and more likely to be successful, if we face it optimistically with a deep understanding of the pace and character of social transformation. We humans are special. Not because of our reason – other species can reason – rather it is our ability to recall the past and foresee the future. We are the only creatures that can imagine our extinction. That special gift of understanding places a unique moral responsibility on humans. Once we have contemplated the future, every decision that could affect that future becomes a moral decision. Even the decision not to act, or to decide not to decide, becomes a moral judgment. We humans, given the ability to anticipate the consequences of our actions, will become the conscious mind of the biocommunity, a global mind, that will guide and hasten societal transformation. Those who understand what is happening to our world are not free to shrink from this responsibility.

Chapter 11

Reconstructing our myths and mindsets for the new millennium

John C. Hinchcliff

Very soon we will embrace the new millennium. There is nothing particularly significant about the year AD 2000, other than being a symbolic marker of another era. However, it could represent a strategic beacon if only we could reconstruct our current myths, transform our mindsets and create a hopeful vision to be more confident that there is a better future for us in the next millennium.

I do not propose in this chapter to iterate a lengthy litany of woes but rather give some thought to ways of achieving a metanoia, that fundamental mindset alteration enabling us to break through the rampant pessimism of this age.

To know where we want to go, we need to know *which* myths shape our existence now, *which* alternative ideals and values we need for the metanoia of our myth structure, *whether* we *can* make an impact and, finally, the all-important *how* we can make the change. We are not discussing facts or a knowledge about the future. We are dealing with ideals, and values, conscious creations of our intuitive and intellectual activity, with which we seek to create our new society's new mythology.

According to the *Random House Dictionary* a myth is 'an unproved collective belief that is accepted uncritically and is used to justify a social institution'.

We can never prove a value or a myth. But we need myths. If we do not have a mythic point of view we cannot really orient ourselves to existence. Collingwood, a philosopher of history, said 'unless the historian has a point of view he can see nothing at all'. The philosopher Karl Popper argues that all knowledge requires a point of view: 'and the naive attempt to avoid it can only lead to self deception and to the uncritical application of an unconscious point of view'. Points of view or myths order our perceptions, govern our attitudes and guide our actions. They are especially important in our situation of 'information overload'. With the many million citations in our bibliographic databases, and with thousands of

With little sensitivity we dismiss myths of other lands as being super-stitious fetishes. But it is worth looking at our own mythic catalogue. In our experience they include the following:

The 'technical fix' that technical expertise can solve any problem.

Instant information is the most valuable information.

More information is necessarily good information.

Might makes right.

'Invention is the mother of necessity', or whatever can be done must be done.

Personal wants are elastic and so economic growth is essential to satisfy them.

Humans are primarily pleasure seekers.

Self-seeking behaviour will lead to social good through the operation of the invisible hand.

It is more difficult to change human nature than to develop technical solu-tions to solve social problems.

Knowledge is power.

There is nothing we cannot know.

Technology and science are neutral, value free and objective.

Western civilization is supreme.

Success depends upon being competitive.

Order, control, structure, logic, and reason are the key management values.

Freedom of the press exists in a democratic society.

These are not all our myths or our values, by any means. But by focusing on these particular myths we see our propensity to develop a society that is internationalized according to Western values, geared to Promethean attempts to add more and more complex technical solutions, with fragmen-tary specialist analyses aimed at solving fundamentally human problems, infatuated with bite-sized information presented as constant entertainment, obsessed with the will to power, to control, to regulate, while advocating also the right to do our own thing and to succeed in the revolution of rising expectations by a competitive self-seeking for growth. It follows that being competitive, efficient, focused, accountable, conforming, prescriptive, and managed, are the most sought after values.

Some of our myths are eroding. Various lead indicators suggest they are not appropriate for us to take into the third millennium. The alter-native story has been told often, but it has yet to be fully accepted, the reconstructed myths yet to be embraced. But they exist deep within our wisdom literature, and within various alternative cultures and mindsets. But first let us look at one or two of our eroding myths. There are many reasons for the erosion of these myths. There is no one essential trans-forming factor.

The sanctity of Western civilization with its self-infatuated tunnel-visioned mindset is being ushered into history by the ascendancy of the Asian nations, and in New Zealand challenged by the recovery of Maori mana and culture.

Clear thinking has allowed us to recognize that science and technology are value laden rather than pure and objective. Logical empiricism was destroyed by its own logic because its essential theory, being metaphysical, was thereby unacceptable by its own terms.

The central importance of growth is being challenged. Few now believe that Mother Nature with her limited resources, depleting ozone and polluted rivers can tolerate many more decades of insults from our boundless enthusiasm to develop.

The high value placed on competitive success shows that this myth still has idol status in our tribe. All too many argue that we can only become more productive when we can trade our way into the profit margins by enhanced competitive skills. Our future, it is alleged, depends on nurturing future generations of competitively successful entrepreneurial citizens. Political leaders welcome competition among educational providers.

Examining the significance and the value of competition is another subject for a dissertation. Suffice it to say that higher order values such as respect for other people, respect for the harmonies of Nature, respect for the whole before the part make it difficult to be impressed with this myth. A success oriented society is where people are encouraged to maximize their efforts in order to compete with others for a prize, better salary, status, etc. This means achievement is possible only in opposition to someone else and only when someone else loses out. Thus, collegiality and cooperation are rejected in favour of individualism and competition.

Those of us who accept the alternative myth based on cooperation have a great deal to do in demonstrating that organizations can benefit when people are motivated to work because of the values of community well-being, the personal sense of achievement and professional pride. Rigour, self-discipline, determination to do well, commitment to excellence, all can correlate with such a value. But such is our current mythology and our endorsement of competition that we have a long way to go.

In New Zealand education today, we are almost done to death with accountability – the myth of control. Auditors galore, reports to central authority by the filing cabinet full, annual reports, performance objectives, profiles, Qualification Authorities, Standards Bodies, and, I expect, a dose of TQM or ISO 9000 may be thrown in for good measure. If we are unlucky there is the Serious Fraud Squad. Thus, we are in danger of being buried in an obsessive and expensive infatuation with accountability that can strangle us into conservative decision making or, at worst, into non-performance. Accountability is a valuable essential obverse of empowerment. But when enshrined as a virtue in and of itself then it distorts and distracts.

Not surprisingly, administrators who are appointed to administer fear that misadventures through lack of control will be perceived to evolve from weak leadership. Corporate plans require administrators to meet targets set by a board, so the CEO's employment requires that the strategic imperatives of the institution are met. Control is regarded then as an essential ingredient of careful management so a tight administration is sought. But in a complex and turbulent society with so many aspirations for participative management and with such question marks over the status quo, such authoritarian control can be counter-productive.

Total quality management (TQM) seems like totalitarianism revisited, controlling us to do the 'right' thing as long as we record everything in our filing cabinets. We must 'get it right the first time' and 'eliminate defects' rather than take the risk of reaching out beyond the rigidly secure. Uniformity, conformity and predictability are proclaimed rather than creativity, innovation or personal vitality. In 1982 Deming, the architect of TQM, declared that quality refers to a low-cost, market appropriate, predictable, uniform and dependable product or service.

At the end of the second millennium, the reverence for quantification leaves me echoing the sentiments of T.S. Eliot 'Where is the wisdom we have lost in knowledge?' And adding 'Where is the vitality and innovation we have lost in accountability?'

The implications of this mindset for education are obvious. Education becomes a controlling, prescriptive and authoritarian process where students' minds are filled with knowledge by 'recipe book' teachers. The reaction against this is widespread.

Even more difficult to crack will be the myth that endorses the quest for power through reason, logic, systemic order. This is, and almost always has been, the key factor in Western civilization. Hence TQM is now a major idol of the tribe.

However, the management paradigms emerging in contemporary society are showing signs of demanding the wisdom of alternative myths. In the 1970s the social and economic environment was reasonably stable. We planned ahead by developing carefully defined structures and systems. And we believed the future could be structured by 'long range planning'. But in the 1980s changes in the environment rendered 'long range planning' less believable. So we turned to 'strategic planning', 'management by objectives' and 'zero based budgeting'. We sought goals enabling us to cope with the incrementally changing nature of things.

However, now we are in a highly complex, uncertain and almost turbulent era. In the shifting sands of political, social, technological and environmental uncertainty, we struggle to make decisions about the future with any degree of confidence. A kind of 'planning opportunism' seems to be most appropriate. This means seeking to exploit opportunities as they arise, while building synergistic coalitions even with alleged competitors.

This also means seeking a philosophical justification for saying that diversity, innovation, empowerment, creativity, quality and enterprise should become the guiding values of a progressive institution rather than tightly controlled and controlling structures.

To justify this assumption we might begin by exploring the differentiation between the Apollonian and Dionysian mindsets from classical antiquity. The Apollonian model, after the God Apollo, has always been attractive to the Western mind. It is a philosophical mind based on order, control, structure, logic and reason. Gaps are not left to enable mistakes to happen. Weaknesses are not permitted. There is no respect for subjectivity, inwardness, mystery, paradox or perplexity. Tight logical systems are crucial. There must always be a QED. The Dionysian approach of the Greek dramatists is substantially different. Dionysus was the god of passion, energy, vitality, and creativity. This means encouraging, empowering, stimulating, inspiring, enthusing.

Obviously, there are problems with both viewpoints. The result of radical Apollonianism is stultification and the bureaucratic deadhand. The result of radical Dionysian creativity is anarchy. What is needed then is some way to hold both elements in a healthy integrating tension. This tension will always be uneasy but it is this exciting creative tension which helps us cope with the ironies, mysteries, perplexities and paradoxes that defy the attempt to fashion a logical system of existence.

In this century the challenge to the Apollonian has been stated clearly by European existentialism which confronted neo-Hegelianism and analytic philosophy, and also by the chaos theory of the mathematicians and the quantum theory of the physicists. All have confronted the old Cartesian and Newtonian views of existence which presented reality as objective, inert, and separate from the Mind which speculates about, uncovers, examines, analyses, catalogues and defines the truth about bedrock reality. This old reality is an observable unity with determined patterns which are predictable according to the laws of cause and effect. Because Nature is thus defined and regarded as machine-like, it has been possible to build machines such as spaceships and there have been countless beneficial and lasting consequences of the old scientific paradigm.

The research of physicists such as Planck, Einstein, Bohr and Heisenberg found that the presuppositions of classical physics such as predictability, causality, determinism, were not ultimate as presupposed by Newtonians. For example, Einstein focused on energy as primary rather than observability, and Heisenberg's principle of indeterminacy reconstructed our attitude to reality. No longer could we continue to assume we could measure or order accurately everything.

Reality, according to quantum mechanics, comprises interactions and interconnections. Energy, activity and process are harnessed by agents in an organism. Fritjof Capra sees reality as a 'complicated web of relations between the various parts of a unified whole', and as 'a ceaseless flow of energy manifesting itself as the exchange of particles, a dynamic interplay in which the particles are created and destroyed without end in a continuous variation of energy patterns' (Capra 1975: 225).

Just as for the Greek dramatist and the European existentialist who proclaimed that 'truth is subjectivity', the new physicist sees the observer as a participant creating reality. We do not experience an essential bedrock of reality but rather we involve ourselves in it and with it. Heisenberg claimed that nature is partly dependent on our observations and our questioning. The existentialist wrote that we learn about existence as we exist our existence, as we decide and choose and thereby create our experience. So Capra (1975) says: 'The whole universe is thus engaged in endless motion and activity, in a continual cosmic dance of energy.' Truth is created by us, by Capra's 'improvisational dance of energy', by our creative engagement.

Perhaps the paradigm shift in favour of this new myth will be assisted by the statisticians' chaos theory. It tells us again that there are some phenomena that can be and should be organized, controlled and predicted. But there is much in existence that is beyond the reach of classical physics. Certainly space missions can be launched successfully because there are scientific laws. But there are no scientific laws to explain the turbulence in tap water or the shape of the snowflake. Predicting the weather has been attempted by sophisticated computer modelling but minute alterations dramatically alter weather patterns. In Auckland, at least, weather prediction is seldom accurate.

Interestingly, it has been the advent of super-sophisticated computers that throw up their complex calculations far beyond the rational capacity of scientists that has led to the development of the Chaos Theory. With mathematical insights and with a strange new language game of 'fractals and bifurcations, intermittencies and periodicities, folded-towel diffeomorphisms and smooth noodle maps' (Gleick 1988: 4–5), the Chaos theorists explore the relationship between order and chaos, structure and randomness. In other words, by ignoring the total infatuation with order, specialization and reductionism, and by exploring and accepting the vast richness of structural complexity, we can see that chaos *is* an essential aspect of reality and that we participate in and affect this complexity.

The wisdom of Chaos Theory has helped researchers analyse the human heartbeat, the orbits of planets, urban dynamics, marketplace behaviour and so on. So from science no less, we recognize that we do not have a clockwork universe where everything can be controlled, reduced and organized. Life is complex, dynamic, mysterious and beyond any narrow organizational theory. Again, this is not to deny the necessity for discipline and rigour in standards. Nor does it challenge the validity of scientific and technological developments. But it is *not* all there is. This is a 'science of process rather than state, of becoming rather than being' (Gleick 1988: 6). Joseph Ford, a physicist at the Georgia Institute of Technology, once proclaimed that in the new mindset, 'Dynamics freed at last from the shackles of order and predictability. . . . Systems liberated to randomly explore their every dynamical possibility. . . . Exciting variety, richness of choice, a cornucopice of opportunity'. Such a paradigm shift brings scientists together with scholars and professionals from other disciplines rather than separating them. By sharing their discrete complex perspectives, a new synergy can be embraced.

A physicist wrote: 'Relativity eliminated the Newtonian illusion of absolute space and time, quantum theory eliminated the Newtonian dream of a controllable measurement process; and chaos eliminates the Laplacian fantasy of deterministic predictability' (Gleick 1988: 6).

Similarly, the existentialist approach embracing such different writers as Kierkegaard, Sartre, Buber, Marcel, and Camus, turned the rationalists' 'I think therefore I am' into 'I am therefore I think'. From within the confusion and complexity of personal involvements and partial perspectives we must do our thinking and, wherever possible, in cooperation with others. There are no certainties and no props. We must take *our* intuitive 'leap of faith' and embrace our mindsets and myths and thereby create our reality in a never-ending process.

Of course, by embracing free will, in admitting the reality of chaos, and in releasing control or refusing total control, there is significant risk. There is the risk that new data will collapse our cherished presuppositions, that relationships will go haywire, that our friends, family members, or colleagues will do something we do not want. Looseness of control is traditionally anathema to managerialism where the control of power is all important.

But if we want vitality, or individual creativity, or openness to meet the challenges of our future, we must allow people to disagree, we must welcome different perspectives, we must allow for the vitality of new initiatives and new ideas. We must accept and value difference. We do not want an institution where the employees are all so well 'informed' that their views necessarily coincide with the views of the CEO, and where the will to enablement is buried by the next dictum.

Implicit in this is our attitude to the nature of our institution. If it is regarded as an *organism* then it will be regarded as dependent on autonomous synergistic relationships among essentially unpredictable, vital nerve endings of creation. If it is regarded as an artefact then all parts can be driven like a machine and total control is regarded as appropriate.

With the emphases by existentialists, quantum physicists and chaos mathematicians on interconnections, process, the holistic, organism, dynamism, interdependence and interrelationships, the old rationalist and classical philosophical dualisms of mind and body, space and time, objectivity and subjectivity, theory and practice, and force and matter can be overcome. As Capra says, in his 'continual cosmic dance of energy' we find that 'the unification of concepts which had hitherto seemed opposite and irreconcilable turns out to be one of the most startling features of this new reality' (1975: 149). Traditional ideological enclaves can be brought together. Liberal–conservative, radical–reactionary, left–right, wet–dry are no longer sensible. We seek an integrating structure that affirms dynamic values rather than divisive pigeonholing categories.

Karl Jaspers stated the new way in these words: 'The fall from absolutes, which are after all illusionary, becomes the ability to soar; what seemed an abyss becomes space for freedom; apparent nothingness is transferred into that from which authentic being speaks to us' (1951: 38).

Most assuredly we still have a paradigm standoff between the two great ontological myths. Some are still wedded to the Apollonian, Newtonian myth and some embracing the Dionysian, Existentialist, Quantum and Chaos Theory model. Tragedy can occur when the two myths conflict.

The former myth approaches complex issues in an analytical, linear manner separating things out, measuring things according to the reign of technical accountability, attempting to quantify the qualitative from the abstraction of a donnish bureaucratic ivory tower, preferring efficiency to complexity. Fragmentation, specialization of knowledge and alienation of people is the by-product. The latter myth with its holistic, dynamic, process approach calls us to be open to the opportunities of experience and education. But there cannot be a sacrosanct theory of reality. This theory in itself is another myth susceptible to change.

As an inseparable participant in a dynamic process of partial perceptives we need humility to be a learner whether teacher or student, to see the value of subjectivity as well as objectivity, intuition as well as reason, praxis as well as theoria, the process as well as the product, synthesis as well as analysis, the interdisciplinary as well as the disciplinary, integration as well as dissensus, reconstruction as well as review in discrete sections, ends as well as means, ethics as well as facts, and creativity as well as organizational control.

This integrating myth encourages us to build the synthesis, to see things in a multi-modal way where in a system everything relates to everything else, where problems are contextualized, visions are accepted as partial but nonetheless as absolutely crucial, and where fads that may work short term must relate to the demands of the whole. Instead of the Newtonian scientist methodically examining the smallest part, perhaps incrementally moving to construct a portion of the whole, the systemic thinker begins within the context of the whole and explores the relationships between parts within the whole.

Thus, in education, we should prefer the vision of the university where everything is related and where there are meaningful connections and synergistic thinking as opposed to a multiversity where everything is separated out, reduced, decontextualized. In our families and in our societies, and in our global community, this mindset suggests we should look first to the well-being of the whole and then to the discrete parts.

This alternative mindset, stressing as it does interrelationship and interconnectedness, suggests a restatement of the myth implicit in all great wisdom literature: respect for people, as in the Christian pronouncement to love your neighbour as yourself, as in Confucianism do not do to others that which you would not do unto you, or as in Hinduism do not do to others which done to thee would cause thee pain. As we celebrate our existence as part of the 'cosmic dance of energy' we seek to participate in the ontological quest of finding out who we are within the dynamic reciprocity of our human-all-too-human beingness. So today 'anyone's problems anywhere are everyone's problems everywhere'. This is the insight of existentialists such as Martin Buber and Gabriel Marcel who stressed the crucial importance of the intrinsically personal I–Thou primal relationship.

As is now so self-evident, we need a new ecology, a new way of caring for our natural home, Mother Nature. We have in the name of competitive progress, self-satisfying materialism, and with the aid of Apollonian science viewed Nature as inert, impassive, endless, and waged a cowboy warfare against Her. Our affluence has become the effluence of our environmental destruction. All too often our technical solution has provided only another problem, leaving us in the crisis of our crises.

According to the alternative mindset we are encouraged to see ourselves as participants within a living integrated Nature rather than some separable exploiters of a useful environment. The harmonies of Nature are interdependent, synergistic and 'the whole is greater than the sum of its parts'. It is a complex whole not understood by the specialist who must 'know more and more about less and less' until 'he knows everything about nothing'.

So we need to re-establish a second old myth: respect for the harmonies of nature.

Professionals who hide away from the contextual and the systemic, for example in the 'closed shop' of their professional cocoon, lose any sense of responsibility for the whole. Thus architect Albert Speer could build beautiful buildings for Hitler, thus developers take the quick fix of Western capital and modern industrial technology to a third world land with different climate, demographics, geography, and philosophy and wonder why their generous aid programme ends in disaster. Thus, Professor Calder described the Hiroshima bomb as 'the greatest sin of all time for not only did the scientists not know what they were doing, but they knew they did not know'.

Thus, another old myth is restated – respect for the whole context.

The alternative paradigm, especially with the contribution of the Existentialists, emphasizes the myth of individual responsibility. The message that I am what I choose to be leaves no room to hide behind a determinism or fatalism or escapism. It leaves no scope for saying we cannot make a difference.

So philosophically, we are free to reject determinisms whether shaped by theological predestination, scientific utopianism, the Greek fates, genetics, or behaviourism. We need not see ourselves as being on a roller-coaster on a dark night predetermined to follow the track laid out in front of us. The message of this alternative world-view is one of liberation for action. We have the right, indeed the obligation in the nature of things to intercede, to interconnect, to interrelate with the myths and structures of our institutions and societies. We are empowered according to this holistic vision to be dynamic, responsive, proactive, and interventionist within the process of becoming.

Again we reconstruct and reaffirm another old myth – respect for personal autonomous decision making.

This sense of agency responsibility is reaffirmed by the belief of Lewis Mumford that the trend is not destiny. Metanoias do happen. New myths have caused historical mindset changes and altered history. Jesus Christ, Buddha, Mohammed, Copernicus, Newton, Freud, Darwin, Marx, Gandhi and Te Whiti of Parihaka, have purposively altered the mythological status quo of societies, impacting significantly on the lives and actions of so many. Those involved in causing Auschwitz, Hiroshima, the building and collapsing of the Berlin Wall, the Industrial Revolution, air travel, etc. have contributed to historical shiftings of mindsets.

Our engines, machines, annual reports, buildings are not just things or objects, but projects. They project our purposes, our values, our intentions, our mindsets. As Max Planck wrote in the *New Scientist*: 'no science can wholly be disentangled from the personality and values of the scientist'. Thus, a radical emphasis on personal responsibility in choosing our myths is essential to us if we expect to move into the next century with any degree of confidence.

So despite the proclamations of some social scientists, another old and respected myth is embraced – respect for personal responsibility.

Another value to include in the alternative pantheon of integrative ethical principles is respect for the community. The concepts of 'public good' and of 'public servant' are almost old-fashioned these days, with the concern being on the individual self rather than the long-term future of the community. In emphasizing the good community we reject the structure of society whereby people exist to pursue their own pleasure and competitive self-interest, where control becomes more important than empowerment, and where negotiation relies on advocacy within the we–they arena. Because of the pre-eminence of the individualist emphasis, we are in the New ICE age (standing for Intensely Competitive Era). Our ecological and community concerns have difficulty breathing in such a society. We need the good community where people are respected as people, where respect and trust shape communications, and negotiation implies mutual dialogue for the greatest good.

I must emphasize that our alternative paradigm allows for and encourages the integration of order within the process. It accepts that the Apollonian does have a place within the vitality of the Dionysian, unlike the restrictive Apollonian myth which cannot abide the Dionysian. And lest I be regarded as a 'soft fuzzy trendy lefty', I wholeheartedly affirm the need to value the intellectual rigour associated with European learning, the disciplined and focused effort of the Asians, careful and responsible research, and responsible management. Furthermore, I believe that before one can be genuinely interdisciplinary it is important to gain some significant mastery in at least one field of learning. So the methods of careful stewardship, rigour, the disciplined and focused effort, and research can all be embraced while valuing the integrative myths of the alternative mindset.

A young woman entered a shop asking for forty yards of cloth for her wedding night gown. Why on earth forty yards? Because she said, we are academics more interested in the search than the discovery. Rather than leave this as an academic exercise I attempt to be prescriptive. My list of suggested actions emerging from what I have said, include the following:

1 Educators, especially, have a significant opportunity and responsibility to transmit to the citizens of tomorrow a vision of a better world – especially to the extent that H. G. Wells is correct when he said that 'history is a race between education and catastrophe'. A comprehensive or global vision will tie together the organizational structure, the personal commitment and the political purpose.

2 Act in such a way that the future is not fixed, that trend is not destiny, that in the ceaseless flow a willed agency can be interventionist, creative and reconstruct a different direction.

3 Accept that no single change is sufficient. It is the responsibility of each one of us to respect the contributions of others and make a difference in our unique area of responsibility. Our individual contributions may be minor, unspectacular and even boring. They will be incremental and depressingly inadequate to us, but in the process of transformation they may be 'straws that break the camel's back'. Individually they are crucial.

4 Recognize that most people prefer a state of equilibrium, that 'old ideas do not die out, only old people with old ideas die out' and the way ahead will be difficult. Because we must break away from past

dogma, state the alternative and the antithesis for the dialectic, and grind our way ahead to attain a higher synthesis, there will be unrest, frustration, dissonance, dissensus ... a hard slog all the way. And, as someone said, 'dogs don't bark at parked cars'.

5 Prepare to fail and make mistakes. Allow others to do likewise. Our perspectives are partial and readily challenged and the best of us will be wrong. Lord Rutherford wrote after splitting the atom that there was no way the process could be used for harm.

6 Realize there are no easy solutions. Remember the danger of the reductionist black and white fallacy that in the complexity of reality the interconnections make simple answers very difficult, and the minor details of each operation can cause considerable perplexity. But on the other hand it is sometimes an incredibly simple factor that makes all the difference. Sometimes a simple idea will be presented in the most complicated way possible.

7 Accept, with John of Salisbury in the thirteenth century, that 'we are but dwarfs on the shoulders of giants'. The institution we seek to change has its own ethos and authenticity. We can but gradually and steadily 'chip away at the edges', as Michelangelo explained how he sculpted David. A Rambo with a jackhammer let loose in an institution can hinder the best cause, however appropriate it may be.

8 Recognize that each situation, each process is different. Plagiarism seldom works.

9 Invite as many colleagues as possible to consider in dialogue the various changes proposed. Each should share their concerns, their knowledge and their wisdom and thus be empowered and enabled to become an essential part of the process.

10 Prioritize our myths and emphasize them in speeches, staff meetings, papers so they are understood and become accepted. Our myths are the key indicators and generally they are noticed by others.

11 Encourage people to 'blow the whistle' on some idea, procedure, process, or machine that is not in the best interests of society. This fine art of 'conscientious dissidence' is not easy because it might involve personal sacrifice, pain and expensive lawsuits. But as Koestler once said, we are guilty of treason in the eyes of history if we do not denounce what deserves to be denounced. There can be no progress if there is no challenge. This critical thinking is not negative thinking but essential autonomous thinking.

12 Stimulate the moral imagination of our students, encouraging them to consider other visions empathetically and to respond in disciplined and sensitive ways to ambiguities and complexities of the moral challenges they encounter. Impress upon them the moral duty to be intellectually rigorous as well as creative and imaginative in their intuitions. Inspire them with a love of learning within 'the cosmic dance of energy'.

13 Emphasize the essential humanism wherever the technocratic occurs; be clear about our relationship with the computer – who owns it, who controls it, how does it control us?

14 Conduct an ethics audit in terms of a developed and deliberately selected hierarchy of values such as respect for people, respect for nature, respect for the whole, respect for the future.

15 Network with key movers and shakers and build a dedicated community of socially responsible futurists.

16 Teach or take a course in Future Studies.

CONCLUSION

The Jeremiahs of today have the advantage of scientific research and computer printouts but instead of being persecuted by Judaean monarchs the warnings of our prophets gather dust in our bookshelves. It is easy to despair and be pessimistic about the problems of the age because we seem both incapable of heeding the prophets and capable of too little too late. We must be hopeful and positive and see the crises as challenges for *us* to *act*. Hope is only realistic when we are involved doing something. The pessimist and cynic drop out. The person with hope endeavours to transform the situation while part of the situation.

REFERENCES

Capra, Fritjof (1975) *The Tao of Physics: An Exploration of the Parallels between Modern Physics and Eastern Mysticism*, London: Fontana.

Deming W. E. (1982) *Quality, Productivity and Competitive Position.*

Gleick, James (1988) *Chaos: Making a New Science*, London: Cardinal.

Jaspers, Karl (1951) *The Way to Wisdom: An Introduction to Philosophy*, New Haven: Yale University Press.

Chapter 12

Social innovation and citizens' movements

Hazel Henderson

Citizens' movements and people's associations of all kinds cover the whole range of human concerns – from service clubs, churches, self-help and spiritual groups to chambers of commerce and professional associations of teachers, doctors, farmers, scientists, musicians, and artists. All share some concern for human society that crosses national borders. The rise of such organizations as one of the most striking phenomena of the twentieth century is described by Elise Boulding as 'a major shift in the nature of the international system.'[1] Other futurists who study citizens' organizations and social movements as precursors of social trends include Magda McHale, Johan Galtung, Eleanora Masini, Ziauddin Sardar, Robert Theobald, Riane Eisler, Anthony Judge, David Loye, the late Barbara Ward and Robert Jungk, as well as this author. Criminal and terrorist groups, urban gangs, mafia-type syndicates, drug cartels, and other violent religious and ethnic extremist groups have also proliferated. Their negative potential in the post-Cold War period is studied more by military, intelligence, and law enforcement strategists than by futurists. A notable exception is the insightful *War and Anti-War* (1993) by Alvin and Heidi Toffler. My own inquiry examines the more positive potential of groups, movements, and associations for social innovation and their attempts at evolving human ethics and societies.

The United Nations (UN) recognizes these proliferating non-state actors only as 'non-governmental organizations' (NGOs) or international non-governmental organizations (INGOs). Furthermore, in UN terminology, giant trans-national corporations (TNCs) are also subsumed as NGOs or 'non-state actors.' Clearly, TNCs should be excluded from these definitions, as well as their national and international trade associations such as the US Council for International Business and the International Chamber of Commerce. However, associations of small, locally-owned businesses which are represented by such charitable service groups as Rotary Clubs and Rotary International do qualify as NGOs and INGOs. In 1909 there were 176 NGOs in the world.[2] In the 1985–86 *Yearbook of International Organizations*, published by the Union of International

Organizations (UIO), 18,000 NGOs are listed of which about 1 percent are federations of other NGOs, 8.5 percent are 'universal,' 17 percent are intercontinental, and 74 percent are regional (i.e. European, Latin American, Asian).[3] The *1994–95 Yearbook of International Organizations* lists a total of 36,486 international organizations in a proliferating number of categories beyond the conventional forms listed above. Anthony J. N. Judge, Assistant Secretary-General of the UIO, emphasizes the ambiguity of the concept of 'civil society,' the need to review national legislation relevant to associations and collective civil action, and also noted that the European Union in 1994 outlined a plan 'to assist cooperatives, mutual societies, associations, and foundations.'

These networks of NGOs often are freer to act and respond to humanitarian concerns than nation states. Often they serve as precursors to new national and international government structures. For example Amnesty International has prodded governments all over the world toward more protection of human rights. The intellectual styles of such NGOs tend toward envisioning preferred futures and scenarios and engaging in organizing civic activities as well as advocacy and 'action research' (to use Kurt Lewin's term). Thus, they invoke the *possible* by mapping social potentials, rather than employing the 'objective' stance of those futurists who identify trends or create scenarios driven by scientific and technological innovation. Since most technological innovation emerges from institutions that are culturally dominant, whether corporations or government-sponsored, often military research bodies, citizens' organizations and their preferred futures often are at variance with more technologically oriented forecasters. Instead, they focus on social impacts of new technologies and social scenarios that are normative (implying changing values) and are often utopian. However, citizens' organizations usually reframe terms such as 'utopian,' 'idealistic,' 'naive,' etc. as actually more *practical* for human societies they see as in crises than more incremental or marginal changes.[4]

Of course, in many cases, citizens' organizations and movements can be destructive and retrogressive or led by demagogues. They often arise out of social pressures due to increasing migration or those experienced in the reunification of Germany; the painful economic transitions appearing in Russia and Eastern Europe or during failures of macroeconomic management which produce unemployment or exacerbate poverty, as in many Latin American countries; or the failure of governments in Somalia, Cambodia, Rwanda, and the former Yugoslavia. Other movements have arisen in reaction to industrial 'modernization,' whether Christian fundamentalists' movement to ban abortion in the USA or other fundamentalist religious movements, particularly in the Islamic world which protest Western, technocratic, secular domination of their cultural traditions. Indeed, the world-wide movements of ethnic and indigenous peoples – Brazil's Yanomami, Scandinavia's Sami or 'Lapp' peoples, Native Americans in Canada and the USA, Basques and Catalans in Spain, as well as the ethnic tribalism which has emerged in Eastern Europe and the former Soviet Union – present the greatest future challenges to nation states and to the globalization of industrialism which most of these nations still espouse.[5]

As I have described elsewhere,[6] most nations' sovereignty has been eroding for over a decade due to forces now globalizing technology, finance, information, labor markets, arms trading, pollution, and culture. At the same time, nations are crumbling from within, often due to their inability to deliver on their promises of 'progress' and 'economic growth' to their people, or because significant minority populations do not want their identities to be homogenized into the mass-consumption and production conformity required by industrialism. Recently, Western academics have reacted with alarm. For example, Samuel Huntington, whose 'Clash of Civilizations'[7] was based on an earlier study by Moroccan futurist Mahdi Elmanjdra[8] and Paul Kennedy and Robert Kaplan's writings in *Atlantic Monthly* (1994) see anarchy and chaos in the proliferation of non-state actors and movements. Their views of this coming 'chaos' are rarely framed within the context of the general crisis of global industrialism which is upon us, as its globalizing forces over the past decade continue to sweep away the borders between nations. Today's trillions of dollars' worth of currencies sloshing around the planet each day now clearly overwhelm the macro-economic mechanisms: monetary and fiscal levers by which countries have managed themselves. Thus futurists will find it imperative to study social movements and citizens' groups even more carefully as old structures and nations devolve.[9]

The Cold War era (1945–91) called forth much additional blossoming of NGOs focusing on peace, human rights, nuclear test bans, nonproliferation, disarmament, development, globalizing educational curricula, student exchange programs, as well as humanitarian relief – offering major new kinds of expertise to governments. By the 1960s, emerging planetary issues spawned massive citizens' movements for protecting the earth's biosphere from degradation, pollution, desertification, species extinction, and resource depletion. They also addressed unchecked human population growth, the widening poverty gap between North and South, and extending human rights and fuller political and economic participation to the world's women.

The UN became a natural venue for these new national and transnational concerns. Citizens' organizations emerged such as the National Organization for Women, Friends of the Earth, Greenpeace, and Zero Population Growth in the USA. They joined older NGOs, such as Planned Parenthood and the Swiss-based International Union for the Conservation of Nature, to push these new issues onto the agendas of their national governments. Such pressure on member states, from NGOs in both the North and South, resulted in a series of *ad hoc* UN conferences, notably on Environment (1972), Population (1973), Food (1974), Women (1975), Habitat (1978), and New and Renewable Sources of Energy (1981). The more recent Earth Summit (1992), as well as conferences on Human Rights (1993) and Population and Development (1994) will be discussed later. The most comprehensive source on global issues is the 1994 edition of *The Encyclopaedia of World Problems and Human Potential*, a brain-child of Anthony Judge of the Union of International Associations.

At these UN conferences it successively became more recognized that the agenda had been shaped by NGOs, new citizens' organizations, and broader social movements bringing pressure on member states and governments. In such early conferences as that on Environment, held in Stockholm, Sweden in 1972, these citizens' organizations were grudgingly recognized with their own parallel environmental forum held a half-hour bus ride away from the press and the main conference in the city's center. While often ill-informed government delegates droned on in the main conference (the US delegation was headed by former child movie star, Shirley Temple Black) the people's Environmental Forum hosted brilliant debates by many of the world's leading intellectuals from North and South, including representatives from indigenous peoples from all over the world. The air was charged with excitement as NGOs hammered out their own declarations of principles and drafted treaties and protocols for protecting the Earth; changing the course of economic development toward new values, ecological sustainability and poverty reduction; recognizing the key role of women as the world's primary food producers, educators of children, and protectors of the environment.

Indeed, many of the policies and social innovations proposed by NGOs at the Stockholm Environmental Forum – from environmental auditing of corporations, socially responsible investing, and 'green' taxes to subsidizing research and development in renewable-resource and energy efficiency technologies – are now government policies in scores of countries. Government and corporate elites often remain ignorant of such viable policy alternatives, insulated within top-down hierarchies from such inconvenient information. They and their institutions are creatures of the existing order, conventional thinking and past investments in earlier technologies. At all levels, from local to global, citizens' organizations arise around the *social and environmental costs* of existing policies and industrial technologies. Such status quo institutions hire most of the scientists and engineers (and futurists!), as well as subsidizing universities and academic research. This leaves 'early warning' feedback to a minority of dissident academics and independent researchers in under-funded, interdisciplinary programs addressing broad concerns over the direction of science, technology, environment, and society. Thus, citizens' organizations form around social and environmental impacts overlooked by the dominant culture – from air and water pollution, toxic chemicals, nuclear wastes, and distorted energy intensive development policies (such as those promoted by World Bank economists) to coercive family planning programs and male-dominated foreign assistance which reinforces social, economic, and gender inequalities.[10] Although such groups often organize around problem-identification, they quickly move to more positive and prescriptive agendas – often forced to innovate because existing institutions cannot respond to their proposals. For example, the US-based Council on Economic Priorities pioneered social evaluations of corporate performance because Wall Street security-analysis firms did not understand this need.[11]

During the Cold War era, opportunities for NGOs to link up with citizens in the former USSR and Soviet bloc nations were severely limited by lack of communication channels. In addition, the coopting of such popular expression and the distorting of citizens' movements agendas by government control, intervention, or by preemptive funding (such as that of the official Peace Committee in the former USSR) inhibited contacts due to suspicions of interference. Thus, a main avenue for debate, cross-pollination of ideas, and social innovation of both capitalistic and socialist models of industrialism and economic 'progress' was foreclosed by this rigid Cold War ideological climate in both superpowers and their global spheres of influence. For example, in Latin America the well-motivated 'liberation theology' of thousands of Catholic priests and nuns and their charitable organizations became caught in the Cold War cross-fire and was often unfairly labeled 'Marxist' for espousing goals of social justice, land reform, and other poverty-alleviation efforts.

Similarly, in the US, during this same period, the creativity of citizens' organizations addressing the worsening social and environmental impacts of traditional, free-market industrialism were often stifled by Cold War labels such as 'leftist,' 'liberal,' 'socialist,' or even 'Marxist.' In other cases, citizens' groups were neutralized by US foundations, which exercise a deeply conservative influence on such groups because accepting grants imposes limits on lobbying and activist approaches, reducing their mandates to 'education.' Another Cold War perversion in the US included the formation of corporate and industry 'front groups' which adopt names implying they are citizen-based and fighting for individual freedom and property rights, when their function is actually that of lobbying against legislation to mandate corporate compliance with environmental or social goals. For example, the US auto industry fought the Corporate Automobile Fuel Efficiency (CAFE) standards for higher-mileage cars in the 1991 Clean Air Act under the banner of a group of supposedly citizens' coalitions, using expensive lobbying, public relations, advertising, and direct mail which overwhelmed genuine citizen groups' budgets. Thus, it is now ever more necessary to investigate all citizens' organizations,

NGOs, and INGOs to determine their sources of funding and political or corporate backers.[12]

The Cold War era, which froze the UN into impotence through the superpowers' constant use of their veto in the Security Council, also froze the vital debate about industrialism and alternative approaches to human and social development. Consequently, today we see the people of the states of the former Soviet Union and Eastern Europe still struggling to recover from the failures of Stalinist-style, centrally planned socialism by adopting helter-skelter nineteenth-century capitalism. Knowledge of Western capitalistic countries was sparse and gleaned from government propaganda rather than via citizens' groups' exchanges of information, visits, and experiences as well as other civilian and academic channels. Thus, too many policy makers and citizens in these former Soviet bloc countries have unrealistic views, gleaned from outdated textbooks, about how 'free' markets and 'perfect' competition are supposed to work. Many academics I have met in these countries initially believed that capitalistic economies, like that in the United States, functioned almost without regulation. They were surprised to learn that there are many thousands of regulations – city, state, and federal – that circumscribe all economic activities in the US and that *all* the world's economies are, in fact, *mixtures of markets and regulations*, and that different cultural norms and ethical standards and citizens' lobbies additionally constrain free markets according to differing 'cultural DNA codes.'[13] Indeed, the 1994 Nobel economics awards were all given to game theorists who study rules of interaction in human societies. Even economists are now acknowledging that rules and regulations are as fundamental as markets.

We may expect an enormous burst of creativity and social problem-solving as old Cold War labels and ideological constraints become increasingly irrelevant. NGOs and their proposals are now more often judged more pragmatically on their merits. Today, citizens' organizations are interpreted within the context of emerging global debates about redefining what is meant by development, and about perfecting democracy itself along the spectrum from elitism to populism. Today's concerns are about how to make both governments and global corporations more accountable to citizens, consumers, workers, investors, and the unrepresented, i.e. children, indigenous peoples, future generations, other species, as well as the environment. In addition, if more states break up, as sovereignty continues to erode emerging NGOs, INGOs, ethnic minorities and indigenous peoples' activities and goals will assume a much greater significance as trend setters for the future.[14] For example, such preparatory documents as the draft Declaration and Program of Action for the World Summit for Social Development held in 1995 contain no fewer than fifteen references to 'participation,' 'consultation,' and 'partnerships' between governments and the civil society.

Social innovations pioneered by citizens' movements are still widely resisted by the dominant culture and media as 'impractical,' or frivolously portrayed, unlike those innovations in technology, production, and marketing in the private sector which are usually hailed as progress. This contrast is stark but understandable, since private sector innovations arise in businesses for competitive and profit motives highly approved in all Western and industrializing cultures. Such business sector innovation is routinely 'hyped' in advertising and marketing and also supported by government subsidies (including contracting of weapons research and procurement to high-tech corporations) and by grants to universities, research labs, and think tanks. However, Western and other industrial societies provide few resources to researchers or organizations to identify the *social and environmental costs* of such private sector technological and social innovations. For example, the inappropriate computerization and automation of US-based corporations has only recently been estimated at a colossal $3 trillion dollars. Most of this huge investment which added imperceptibly to productivity involved 'paving old cowpaths' (i.e. setting in concrete old organization charts). These costs must now be written off and replaced with more costly 'second-generation' computerization.[15] The social and environmental costs of inappropriate industrialization and automation from jobless economic growth and widening poverty gaps to unsustainable resource-consumption were the focus of the World Summit on Social Development organized by the United Nations in Copenhagen (1995).

Research into the costs and adverse impacts of market and industrial policy-driven innovation still lags – often by decades. This phenomenon led in 1974 to the launching of the US Congress Office of Technology Assessment (OTA), after several years of academic and political debate and grass roots lobbying efforts. As a member of its Advisory Council from 1974 to 1980, I can attest to the broad opposition it encountered from both political parties, from government agencies (for example, the Department of Defense), and from much of the business sector. The argument most often used was that OTA was unnecessary, since markets could quite well determine the course of technological innovation for the benefit of consumers without costly government regulation or interference. This argument derives from outdated economic textbook models of perfect competition which ignore structural aspects of mature economies.[16] OTA survived by developing links to the most highly-respected academic institutions; by contracting out to such organizations and consulting firms a portion of its research; and by appointing impeccable advisory panels representing the full spectrum of expert knowledge to steer each study; and also due to its bipartisan, Technology Assessment Board composed of Congress members. While OTA overcame the early opposition through a track record of high-quality, unbiased, and innovative research and spawned similar institutions in many countries – in 1995 it came under severe attack from Republicans, as has multi-lateral aid and the UN itself. While foreign aid was cut, OTA was closed.

In the case of OTA, its functions were anticipated and performed for over a decade by citizens' groups, including many concerned professionals, which organized to research technological impacts on society and alternative, more benign ways of meeting human needs. Ralph Nader's Washington-based Public Citizen and its campus spin-offs, the Public Interest Research Groups, are examples of such prototype technology assessment research, as are the US-based Scientists' Institute for Public Information, the Union of Concerned Scientists, and Physicians for Social Responsibility (now worldwide). Although such groups are woefully underfunded, they and many others have prodded governments and their in-house, scientific bureaucracies to develop their own technology assessment capabilities. They also urged government agencies to utilize their highly creative, alternative problem-definition methods and the analyses of other private groups, such as the US-based Rocky Mountain Institute (which pioneered demand-side management of electric utilities and energy-efficient technologies now being adopted worldwide).[17] Much of the new ferment, as noted earlier, is about industrialism itself, its ideology and goals, and the consumerist, mass-culture it produces, which often violates other norms and cultures as it violates the Earth.

Such citizens' organizations are often a priceless social resource offering new paradigms to societies stuck in old ways or trapped, as Western industrial societies are, in wasteful consumption and production habits and obsolete technologies that are proving unsustainable. The reason that independent citizens' organizations often provide so many innovative programs and concepts, and furnish whole new paradigms for problem-definition, is their ability to tap and organize information laterally. They can network across borders, as well as corporate and government boundaries, enabling rapid syntheses of overlooked and new information into new approaches and paradigms.[18] They can question conventional wisdom and relentlessly point out cases where the 'emperor has no clothes,' and how information quality can be assessed (see Figure 12.1). The coalescing of INGOs with indigenous peoples, which began in the 1960s, brought forth new agendas based on ancient wisdom and spiritual traditions about how to live sustainably on Earth, which industrial societies have largely forgotten.[19]

Another information function NGOs and INGOs perform is to serve as nodes and 'magnets' attracting previously censored information, as well as that from 'whistle blowers' in business and government. For this reason, all competent citizens' organizations establish good relationships with mass media and investigative journalists, who rely on them for such bootlegged research (even if the citizens' group is not usually credited publicly or its

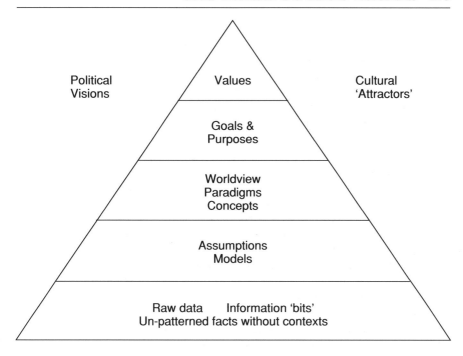

Figure 12.1 Information quality scale (i.e. meaning of information as relevant to human purposes and various 'cultural DNA codes')
Source: Hazel Henderson in *Politics of the Solar Age: Alternatives to Economics* (1981)

general programs are labeled 'too far out'). For example, citizens' organizations such as the Kenya-based Greenbelt Movement and India's Chipko Movement, as well as countless other environmental groups were busy planting trees long before scientists studying climate change began advocating the need for reforestation and support for these programs, while mass media ridiculed them as 'tree huggers.' This uneasy, symbiotic relationship between citizens' organizations and media can lead to many policy and ethical dilemmas. For example, some citizens' organizations can 'run ahead' of their research or sensationalize their data to attract media attention in their search for badly needed funds. In the environmental movement since Earth Day, 1990, when businesses adopted 'green' marketing policies, some citizens' organizations made alliances with companies, even endorsing their products in apparent *quid pro quos* for funding, often thereby losing credibility.[20]

Citizens' organizations, to stay true to their highest function as social innovators, must resist constant temptations to join the dominant culture. If they do decide to join the mainstream, they should give up their favorable tax exemptions and compete as market-driven enterprises. Non-profit, tax-exempt citizens' organizations often *create* new 'markets' over a period of years by offering attractive new values and life styles, such as the now multibillion-dollar new markets for 'green' products and technologies. As these fledgling markets become viable through news stories and mass-media-driven public acceptance, such NGO innovators can often gradually shift from donated funds and grants to 'packaging' their leading innovations (often books and research reports) and move to greater reliance on earned income. Indeed, some can become fully self-supporting. Others, however, choose to move to more cutting-edge concerns, breaking new ground and remaining innovative while wearing their unpopularity as a badge of honor.

As this process unfolds, it illustrates the dysfunctionality of rigid ideo-logical categories (also left over from the Cold War) that divide Western industrial societies, particularly the US, into 'public' and 'private' sectors. Public sector organizations are expected to be socially concerned, coop-erative, and less than efficient, while private sector organizations are encouraged to be greedy, competitive, self-interested, and even rapacious. Happily, this wall is also coming down, as the voluntary 'civil society' is being widely recognized as a 'third sector' or 'independent sector' comprising all kinds of innovative citizens' organizations – NGOs, INGOs, and PVOs (private voluntary organizations).[21] In addition, many hybrid, public–private organizations now address needs too large for any one company: for example, COMSAT and INTELSAT in telecommunications and SEMATECH, a consortium of computer-chip makers, share R&D costs, thus allowing them to compete globally. Even US anti-trust laws which enforced the ideology of competition are now recognizing that competition and cooperation are equally valuable strategies – just as the people of the former USSR have recognized the limits of enforced coop-eration and the bureaucratic welfare state. Indeed, competition and co-operation are the key strategies of all species, along with creativity, the most rare and evolutionary strategy. In human societies and their 'cultural DNA codes,' *replication* is basic (as it is in the coding of all DNA), while *innovation,* i.e. mutation, is a much rarer phenomenon.[22] Too much innovation can destabilize a society, and, as students of complex systems know, the trick is to find and study the regime operating at the edge of chaos. Roger Lewin in *Complexity: Life at the Edge of Chaos* reports how the US-based Sante Fe Institute has shifted its attention from its earlier interest in global financial markets and economies to studying cultures, and its Board Chairman, Murray Gell-Mann, has adopted my concept of 'cultural DNA' as a conceptual tool in researching complex adaptive systems, chaos, complexity, and the emergent properties of such systems.[23]

Nowhere have citizens' organizations played a larger role than in the world's 'informal economies' (actually, statistical anomalies spawned by the narrow paradigms of macro-economics and its highly aggregated statistical tools: Gross National Product (GNP) and Gross Domestic Product (GDP), averaged rates of saving, investment, unemployment, interest rates, trade balances, etc.). I have described elsewhere[24] the extent of such informal economies which, even in industrial societies, represent the approximately half of all production that is unpaid and, therefore, not accounted for in macro-economic statistics. In most countries of the southern hemisphere, such informal sectors are much larger than their official, cash-based GNP/GDP-measured sectors – often comprising three-quarters of all production. The voluntary associations of citizens, villages, tribes, cooperatives, and families of these informal sectors represent traditional, self-reliant forms of production, consumption, savings, and investments only recently recognized by Western, market-trained economists or their socialist counterparts, at $16 trillion in 1995.

Prototypical of the people's organizations operating in these areas are Sri Lanka's Sarvodya Shramadana movement, which pioneered a viable form of development based on Buddhist principles in over 8,000 villages;[25] the Philippines' Green Forum coalition, which has produced its own plan for the future of the Philippine economy;[26] and the Self-Employed Women's Association (SEWA) of India, which funds small enterprises. When such movements succeed they are often persecuted by governments, as in the case of Sarvodya. Indeed, micro-lending programs – such as SEWA; Women's World Banking (in forty-eight countries); the Grameen Bank of Bangladesh; ACCION, which lends to Latin and Central-American micro-enterprises; as well as the US-based First Nations Financial Project, lending to native American community-development groups – are all providing a new paradigm of sustainable development. The new development form is a 'trickle-up' model – the mirror opposite of the elitist, technocratic 'trickle-down' model promoted by traditional economic development theorists, whether trained at Harvard or MIT, the London School of Economics or Moscow State University. All these models proved to be over-centralizing, resource-wasting, often poverty-exacerbating, and ecologically unsustainable. These failed development models are finally leading to today's global debate about what we mean by 'development'; whether it has anything much to do with GNP/GDP-measured economic growth and how to make such processes sustainable for future generations.[27] Today's accelerating globalization of financial markets forces the rethinking of development, debt, and indicators of progress – but also sovereignty itself, as well as how best to restructure the Bretton Woods institutions and the UN for the next fifty years.[28]

An unprecedented outpouring of interest in these paradigm-shifting debates and their pioneering organizations in the world's independent sectors occurred at the United Nations Conference on Environment and Development, the Earth Summit held in Rio de Janeiro, Brazil in June 1992.[29] The Rio Conference boosted the growth of these citizens' organizations by providing a global forum for some 13,000 such groups and reinforced their networking activities, which were encouraged by Secretary-General Maurice Strong and his Danish-born wife, Hanne Strong, herself an organizer of the citizens' Earth Restoration Corps. Many of the citizens' organizations attending Rio's Global Forum were already sophisticated and linked on computer-conferencing systems, such as Peace-Net and Eco-Net. A similar outpouring of civil society participation was evident at the UN Conference on Population and Development in Cairo, Egypt (1994). As at the Earth Summit, the creative mixture of media and civil society groups focused world-wide attention on the issues and pushed the official delegates and the Action Plan beyond boundaries previously set by patriarchal leaders. Formerly 'radical' notions entered the mainstream, including the idea that the most effective 'contraceptive' is the economic and political empowerment of women and that the best investment society can make in its development is to invest in its people and particularly the education of girls.

Today, electronically linked citizens' groups are becoming a truly global independent sector, a third way for global problem-solving and in Boulding's phrase, 'a global civic culture.'[30] Dr Howard H. Frederick, of the International Association for Mass Communications Research, described the burgeoning of communications-based citizens' organizations, NGOs, and INGOs in *Edges*, a Toronto-based publication of the Institute for Cultural Affairs, itself a global INGO (see Figure 12.2).[31] Frederick points out the global reality that at present such communication technologies are dominated by global corporations, financial markets, and global banking electronic funds transfer systems (EFTS), as well as giant information wire services, such as Reuters and the Associated Press. We still live in the world of the info-rich and the info-poor. For example, 95 percent of all computers are in the industrial countries of the North, while 75 percent of the world's people, living in the South, only manage 30 percent of the world's newspapers. While the USA and the Commonwealth of Independent States (CIS), with only 15 percent of the world's population, use more than 50 percent of the world's geostationary orbits with their communications satellites, the South uses less than 10 percent of these orbits.[32]

THE FUTURE OF THE PLANET'S INDEPENDENT SECTOR

The further growth of independent, civil sectors world wide will be driven by the increasing loss of sovereignty and competence of nation states. States are splitting up into proliferating smaller nations, including Slovenia, the Baltic states, Moldova, the Czech Republic, and Slovakia. Breakaway movements continue to proliferate, from Canada's Parti

Quebeçois, and the enclaves on Russia's Caucasian and southern borders to Norway's rejection of membership in the European Union. Failed states include Cambodia, Somalia, Rwanda and others teetering in Africa. Many futurists, including this author, expect a large increase in new nations seeking seats in the UN. As mentioned earlier, globalization forces now eroding national sovereignty are extremely powerful and so far unchecked by countervailing institutions.[33] These forces will continue to operate until international treaties, protocols, and new global governance structures emerge to control them. Currently, national politicians and trade negotiators still believe that the global economy, trade, and financial anarchy can be tamed by 'leveling the global playing field' via the General Agreement on Tariffs and Trade (GATT) and its new form as the World Trade Organization (WTO), while they lay off bets by forming new regional trade blocs. Yet the North American Free Trade Agreement (NAFTA), for example, is already running into resistance from labor and social movements, such as Chiapas uprising in Mexico. In Canada and the US, unions still unite with environmentalists over the social and environmental costs already visible in the 'maquiladora' plants along the US–Mexican border, which are not yet accounted for by economists or trade negotiators. However, nostalgic cries such as those of both Ralph Nader and isolationists, warning of 'loss of sovereignty' through the WTO and NAFTA trade do not acknowledge the reality: sovereignty was lost a decade ago when the world's capital markets began deregulating. Such financial flows, over 90 percent of which represent speculation, dwarf actual trade.

Even the European Union (EU), with its past successful unification of twelve Western countries and its 1994 inclusion of Austria, Sweden, and Finland is still in turmoil. Citizens' organizations in Denmark, representing small businesses in renewable energy, 'green' technologies, organic and small farmers, environmentalists, and social welfare groups, all saw the 1992 Maastricht Treaty and the move toward a single European currency as little more than making Denmark safe for global banks and corporations. Like the Norwegians who opted not to join the EU at all, the Danes saw few safeguards for Denmark's distinctive culture, social programs, and its environment. Elites, which continue to see their independent sectors as rabble-rousers, know-nothings, or NIMBYs (not-in-my-back-yarders), will miss the point. If citizens' viewpoints are not taken seriously by politicians and media and channeled positively, their only recourse will be to continue simply *resisting* by hitting the donkey on the head to get its attention. Today, there is much new soul searching by 'Eurocrats' in Brussels about how to democratize, to implement the principle of subsidiarity and share power with the elected European Parliament.

All this augurs the need to restructure first at the *global* level. A new 'Bretton Woods,' this time fairer to all the UN member nations, is needed

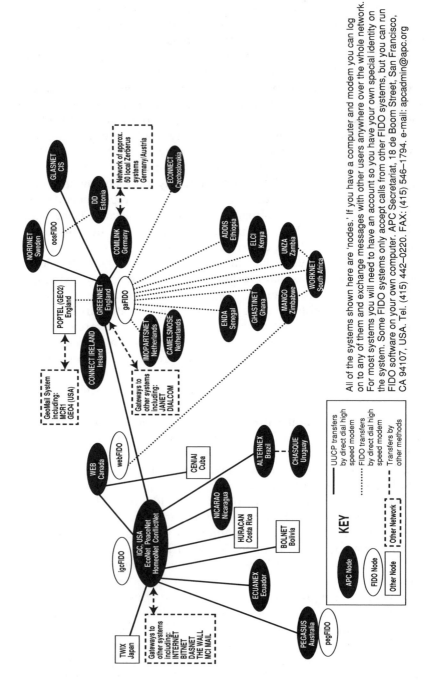

All of the systems shown here are 'nodes.' If you have a computer and modem you can log on to any of them and exchange messages with other users anywhere over the whole network. For most systems you will need to have an account so you have your own special identity on the system. Some FIDO systems only accept calls from other FIDO systems, but you can run FIDO software on your own computer. APC Secretariat, 18 de Boom Street, San Francisco, CA 94107, USA. Tel: (415) 442-0220. FAX: (415) 546-1794. e-mail: apcadmin@apc.org

The following abbreviated international messages were downloaded from Toronto's Web bulletin board service. They include title, sender's e-mail address, electronic conference name and date.

Zen Jokes
IGC:BSTAUFFER   gen.humor
Apr 22, 1992
Two examples of Zen humor told to me by a wise old six-year-old. What do a pig and a fish have in common? They both have gills except the pig. What is the difference in a duck? One of his legs is the same.

Campaign Against Herbicides
IGC:PANNA   ax:amlatina
Jan 17, 1992
The Colombian government wants to begin a major marijuana eradication program involving the aerial spraying of 2,4–D and Roundup (glyphosate.) Ms. Amparo Cardenas has requested well-documented, thoughtful letters to Colombian officials, from individuals and organizations in the United States, emphasizing the hazards of spraying herbicides to human health, wildlife and ecosystems.

Host requested for Ukrainians
IGC:BAIKAL   cdi.sovsis
Mar 22, 1992
Ukraine group, club, business, social or other organization requested to host twelve Ukrainians arriving SFO some time in April. These visitors are a group of new entrepreneurs arriving as members of a business association. If you wish to extend a welcoming hand please email Allan Affeldt at peacenet:om

Petrozavodsk/Karelia
GLAS!PETROZ   en.ussr
Apr 30, 1992
The city of Petrozavodsk, USSR together with the Republican Union of scientific and engineering organizations is going to conduct an auction-fair of ecologically clean materials, technologies goods and products from October 20–23, 1992. Applications for advertising are gladly accepted.

Post-referendum statement
GN:WACC   reg.safrica
Mar 23, 1992
Post-Referendum Statement by the Rev. Dr. Frank Chikane. We are relieved that the majority of voters in Tuesday's referendum chose to vote 'yes' to the

continuation of the process of reform in this country. It is now clear that the majority of South Africans are against apartheid. The March 17 whites-only referendum must be the nation's last racialistic vote.

Women: Equal Responsibility & Benefits
AX:CAFONSO   ax:fondad
Mar 9, 1992
The IDB has adopted a new plan of action for promoting the role of women in economic development. . . . Credit programs will be analyzed to determine if their regulations directly or indirectly exclude women. Do loan applications, for example, require a husband's signature or collateral that only men typically can provide?

Bantering Winds
AX:GHOLLAND   io.yacht
Mar 4, 1992
We have lived on a yacht for 13 years and we are now at Thursday Island, waiting out the wet to go west. The above address will always find us. Looking forward to hearing from you.

Figure 12.2 Map of Association for Progressive Communications (APC) nodes and connected systems, January 1992
Source: Ilona Staples, *Edges*, Vol. 5, no.1, July–Sept., 1992, Journal of the Institute for Cultural Affairs, Toronto, Canada

to address global currency speculation, banking abuses, and to bring some rules to the global financial 'casino.' Here again, social innovation and new proposals are coming from groups outside of governmental and corporate sectors. Environmentalists joined forces with groups calling for sustainable human development, such as the Malaysian-based Third World Network and other humanitarian aid organizations, in convening the conference at American University (Washington, DC) on Rethinking Bretton Woods in 1994.[34] Already, the US public approves, by large majorities, of many such new global regulatory proposals, as well as regulation of cross-border pollution.[35] The independent Global Commission to Fund the United Nations has extended the debate about innovative ways to expand financing of sustainable development, restructuring the UN, and new ways of managing and taxing the global commons. Other efforts to reform the UN include new studies and recommendations by scholars Erskine Childers and Brian Urquhart,[36] and Secretary-General Boutros Boutros-Ghali's *An Agenda for Peace* (1992).[37] Many INGOs, including the World Federalist Association and the Commission on Global Governance, call for a world summit on 'Global Governance.' The UN Commission on Sustainable Development is a disappointment so far in maintaining progress toward implementing *Agenda 21*. The newly formed INGO, the Costa Rica-based Earth Council, is an ongoing forum for debates about the direction of human development. The Earth Council, which grew out of the Rio Earth Summit, may well become a better watchdog for implementing *Agenda 21*, with its *Earth Report*, launched in 1995.

Only when the UN is reshaped, together with other needed global structures, can a more limited but effective form of sovereignty be exercised by nations – often in new partnerships with both the private and civil sectors. The UN is well positioned for today's Information Age and can build on its strengths as the world preeminent networker, broker, convenor, and setter of norms and standards. An example of innovative public/private partnerships is the United Nations Security Insurance Agency (UNSIA), modeled on INTELSAT, which would offer contractual peace-keeping 'insurance policies,' risk-assessed and written by the insurance agency for fees – which, in turn, would fund professional, trained standing UN peace-keeping forces. This social innovation is now an official UN document.[38] The UN has already modified its concept of sovereignty to embrace global changes and to address the new humanitarian concerns in world public opinion, which no longer sanction dictators who oppress their own people.[39] Regional trade blocs serve as interim alliances, whether NAFTA, MERCOSUR, the America's Freetrade Area agreed at a Miami Summit, 1994, the Asia Pacific Economic Council, and other blocs proposed by south-east Asian countries. However, they cannot function in the global playing field without a reshaped WTO which must expand its traditional economics approaches to include social and environmental costs reflected in true pricing and correcting the workings of capital markets which also 'externalize' such costs. The world has become too complex for the old global and national institutions, due to the proliferation of actors. Global corporations, global satellite-based communications, media companies, electronic securities, and currency trading, as well as the world's information highways constitute a new 'electronic commons.' This global complexity is growing daily. The citizens' organizations of the global independent sector will continue to proliferate in *response* to this private-sector, corporate, technological globalization. Many will hold the seeds of new concepts and social forms vital to innovate the new contracts, agreements, and institutions to manage the global commons.

The issues are about nothing less than the direction of human social evolution on this small, ecologically compromised planet. The debate about 'sustainable development' which I have described elsewhere[40] has become a metaphor for this complex cluster of issues. But at its core, it is a debate about values and which cultural, social, technological, and behavioral repertoires embedded in the various cultural DNA codes of the world's people actually contain the 'programs' which may serve as the seeds for human survivability. In *Creating Alternative Futures* (1978), I proposed an international data bank to store and access such cultural DNA codes and value-systems, since they drive all societies, their economic systems, laws, and technological 'furniture.' These cultural DNA codes need to be unpacked and researched to determine how well they 'fit' each society to survive within its ecosystem niche. Value-systems are a *resource*, just as surely as coal, oil, and biodiversity.[41]

Survivability should be the overall criterion of success, i.e. those cultural DNA codes that proved to be sustainable over the longest term within their ecological contexts – by providing for material needs, developmental opportunities for their people, while offering satisfying meanings, purposes, roles, and coherent metaphysical and philosophical 'stories.' I speculated that core values would probably be identifiable, including: reverence for life and the natural world, love, honesty, and sharing, i.e. the same core beliefs encoded in all the world's great religious and spiritual traditions. For example, one can interpret the Golden Rule, the Hindu concept of 'karma' and many other expressions of human *responsibility* (as well as rights) as precise statements describing dynamic, non-linear systems. Systems theorists will also recognize the biblical concept of 'Judgment Day' as a system coming up to real time – where there are no information lags and all accounts must be settled.[42] The global independent sector is today's last repository of such 'common wisdom' encoded in myth, spiritual traditions, folklore, art, dance, and ritual, as Jean Houston has shown in her many books.[43]

Lastly, the future of democracy, now on the march all over the world, will also be most advanced and perfected by pressures from the global and national independent sectors. As I pointed out in the *Columbia Journalism Review* in Spring, 1968, citizens' movements for democracy had already identified access to mass media as their major tool. In the late 1980s we saw the independence movements in Eastern Europe, the Philippines, and elsewhere capturing, not parliament buildings, but TV and radio stations. In the US, Ross Perot bypassed the political parties and their nominating processes in the 1992 Presidential campaign, by going on CNN's *Larry King Live* call-in talk show and airing his own TV 'infomercials.' Twenty percent of the US electorate resonated to his call for electronic town meetings, opinion surveys to ask the American people (i.e. 'the customers') what policies they wanted for health care, education, to reduce the budget deficit, and curb the fiscal irresponsibility and corruption in Washington. In 'Perfecting the Tools of Democracy'[44] I reiterated the need for retooling of democracies, including the US and its eighteenth-century machinery of participation, also referring to other earlier work in anticipatory democratic design by Alvin and Heidi Toffler, Theodore Becker, Christa Slayton, Clement Bezold, and David Loye. Access must be opened to political decision making beyond voting every few years – now no longer adequate for precise feedback on multiple issues.[45] Similarly, new indicators of overall quality of life beyond GNP/GDP indexes are needed to give more precise feedback on citizens' goals as well as to hold politicians accountable (Figure 12.3).[46]

All these issues of perfecting democratic processes, in systems theory terms, concern the need for *feedback* that all complex systems require. As Warren Bennis and Philip Slater pointed out in the 1960s, complex human organizations, whether corporations or countries, *require* democratization of their decision-making, that democracy is *inevitable*.[47] The human species has never existed on this planet in such unprecedented numbers and our experience for millennia has been that of managing ourselves in tribes and villages. The history of the twentieth century can be viewed as a series of ghastly experiments at managing larger and larger numbers in cities, states, mega-states, and dealing with the cruel legacy of nineteenth-century colonial organizations. Most of these tragic experiments cost millions of lives from Hitler's Third Reich, Mussolini's and Franco's Fascism in Italy and Spain, Lenin's and Stalin's USSR, to Mao Zedong's China. The Cold War aftermath of World War II subtly changed the nature of these experiments in organizing human affairs toward the idea of industrial 'progress' and technocratic visions of material plenty espoused by economic theories from left to right, since Karl Marx and Adam Smith were in fundamental agreement about such goals and differed only on means to achieve them.

Re-formulated GNP to Correct Errors and Provide More Information:

- PURCHASING POWER PARITY (PPP) corrects for currency fluctuations
- INCOME DISTRIBUTION is the poverty gap widening or narrowing?
- COMMUNITY BASED ACCOUNTING to complement current enterprise-basis
- INFORMAL, HOUSEHOLD SECTOR PRODUCTION measures all hours worked (paid and unpaid)
- DEDUCT SOCIAL AND ENVIRONMENTAL COSTS a 'net' accounting avoids double counting
- ACCOUNT FOR DEPLETION OF NON-RENEWABLE RESOURCES analogous to a capital consumption deflator
- ENERGY INPUT/GDP RATIO measures energy efficiency, recycling
- MILITARY/CIVILIAN BUDGET RATIO measures effectiveness of governments
- CAPITAL ASSET ACCOUNT FOR BUILT INFRASTRUCTURE AND PUBLIC RESOURCES (Many economists agreed this is needed. Some include environment as a resource.)

Complementary Indicators of Progress toward Society's Goals:

- POPULATION birth rates, crowding, age distribution
- EDUCATION literacy levels, school dropout and repetition rates
- HEALTH infant mortality, low birth weight, weight/height/age
- NUTRITION e.g., calories per day, protein/carbohydrates ratio, etc.
- BASIC SERVICES e.g., access to clean water, etc.
- SHELTER housing availability/quality, homelessness, etc.
- PUBLIC SAFETY crime
- CHILD DEVELOPMENT World Health Organization, UNESCO, etc.
- POLITICAL PARTICIPATION AND DEMOCRATIC PROCESS e.g., Amnesty International data, money-influence in elections, electoral participation rates
- STATUS OF MINORITY AND ETHNIC POPULATIONS AND WOMEN e.g., human rights data
- AIR AND WATER QUALITY AND ENVIRONMENTAL POLLUTION LEVELS air pollution in urban areas
- ENVIRONMENTAL RESOURCE DEPLETION hectares of land, forests lost annually
- BIODIVERSITY AND SPECIES LOSS e.g., Canada's environmental indicators
- CULTURE, RECREATIONAL RESOURCES e.g., Jacksonville, Florida

Figure 12.3 Country futures indicators: beyond money-denominated, per capita averaged growth of GNP

Source: Hazel Henderson, *Paradigms in Progress* (1991, 1995), Berrett-Koehler Publishing, San Francisco

As unstable mega-states and nations break up, humans must deal with unmanageable, but still growing mega-cities: such as Tokyo, Mexico City, São Paolo, and Los Angeles – the focus of the UN Habitat II Conference in Istanbul (1995). At the same time, we humans keep experimenting with trade blocs such as the EU, NAFTA, MERCOSUR and others mentioned earlier. It behoves futurists to study history and how earlier human attempts to organize growing populations repeatedly derailed, for example, Joseph Tainter's accounts of *The Collapse of Complex Societies.*[48] What we have learned is that hierarchies collapse and leaders topple because of lack of feedback from the governed, i.e. they lack the requisite complexity and receive too little valid, reality-tested information. I have described elsewhere this phenomenon of the Entropy State,[49] where the growing organization reaches a stage where more effort is spent in coordination than in useful, productive output and the society bogs down in transaction-costs. The operational metaphors are: 'only the *system* can manage the system,' and its corollary 'only the system can model the system.' The *Economist* described this phenomenon in the growth of government bureaucracy and the numbers of lawyers in similar terms.[50] A key issue is how to flatten or replace old structures by substituting lateral, networked, real-time information flows to allow all parts of a complex system to coordinate, align their knowledge of changing environments and their activities toward flexible, adaptive responses.

Research into complexity and chaos in living and non-living systems is providing metaphors and clues. For example, Tainter, an archaeologist, has identified precursors to the onset of collapse of earlier human civilizations. He notes, for example, a flurry of collective activity often involving construction, just prior to the collapse, as if the society was trying to counter rising stress, as in the fall of the Roman Empire and the Mayan civilization.[51] Such rising stress may correlate with the onset of the Entropy State, where *de*-structuring and *re*-structuring are needed – not more construction on the existing structural base. Elsewhere, I compared this de-structuring of societies approaching evolutionary 'cul-de-sacs' to the phenomenon of 'paedomorphosis' in species, where a maladapted adult form is 'discarded' over time, and that species, instead, takes a new path by evolving further from its younger, more flexible larval stage.[52] Analogies exist between our unsustainable, over-structured, capital- and resource-intensive industrialism and its centralized control, 'trickle-down' models of replication and the new, still misunderstood, grass roots, village models of 'trickle-up' development – founded on people-intensive livelihoods using renewable resources and the lateral information flows and networking of citizens' movements and organizations.

Clearly, the much vaunted paths to 'progress' via industrialization and GNP/GDP-measured economic growth went into reverse in the 1980s which was wistfully named by the UN as the Third Development Decade.

Mature industrialized societies already energy and resource 'junkies' are also becoming technological innovation and capital-investment 'junkies' as they try to 'hype' traditional economic growth with construction projects and tax incentives for further investment in plant and equipment. Industrialism is about labor saving and its outdated economic formulas lead to overuse of resources and underusing human talent – leading to the world-wide phenomenon of jobless economic growth, as I have described elsewhere.[53] Europe's Industrial Revolution was over the past 300 years a unique historical event – not replicable for many reasons. We see today's tragedies of desertification, deforestation, polluted water and air, destruction of species, and of viable indigenous cultures, as well as widespread famine in Africa and social collapses such as that of Somalia. One inescapable factor is now clear – the 6,000-year rise of cities, states, and nations has been necessitated by the enormous increases of human populations from their beginnings in Africa to dominate almost every ecosystem on the planet. These forms of human civilization have been male-dominated and steered exclusively by patriarchal religious belief systems, in contrast to earlier matrilineal societies based on partnership between men and women and reverence for nature.[54] This patriarchal 'spin' became exacerbated through deviation-amplification processes (as in chaos models) and eventually led to wider, even more competitive territorial expansion and the human population explosion. Obviously women must be in control of their fertility for human populations to remain stable and within ecosystem carrying-capacity. Today, while there is wide acknowledgement that the empowerment of women and reproductive choice is the best contraceptive, we find that two-thirds of the world's women remain in male-dominated societies and *increasing* percentages of these women are still forced into involuntary childbearing.[55] The world's leadership and power structures are still overwhelmingly dominated by men, with the UN itself as perhaps the worst example. It is no surprise, therefore, that the global independent sectors were pioneered by women, and women, often volunteers, are overrepresented in its ranks, as well as in the world's informal economies.[56]

Alternative information processing of formerly discounted, overlooked or suppressed data is the currency and *modus operandi*, as well as the social gift of citizens' organizations. As Walter Weisskopf pointed out, all civilizations involve different sets of *expressions* and *repressions* of the full range of human ways of being and behaving.[57] Social revolutions always involve a 'return of the repressed' onto the social scene. Gregory Bateson described complex adaptive systems such as human societies, as in a constant, overall trade-off between adaptation and adaptability.[58] If the society's store of adaptability has been depleted by too much successful adaptation to past conditions, then the society is too rigidly committed to these old structures to evolve. This 'nothing fails like success' problem is stated by cultural anthropologists as the Law of the Retarding Lead, i.e. those societies less adapted to old environments will often spurt ahead as conditions change.

Today, all these dramas are being played out on a global stage, and the global independent sectors are still pointing to evolutionary paths for human societies: learning to live within nature's tolerances; designing in much more feedback by perfecting democratic feedback (i.e. votes) and market feedback (i.e. using fuller-cost prices which includes both social and environmental impacts); more feedback from citizens' organizations and independent sectors; as well as better decoding of feedback from natural systems (e.g. acid rain, ozone depletion, and the buildup of carbon dioxide in the atmosphere), and new quality-of-life indicators to correct GNP/GDP. Only more comprehensive models can allow for better chances of success in future governance. Citizens' organizations have propagated (often to the discomfort of scientists) new theories such as the Gaia hypothesis, which sees the entire planet as a complex adaptive system with its living biosphere controlling atmospheric and other variables. Paradigms *are* changing and becoming more comprehensive and inter-disciplinary.[59] Materialistic science and reductionist, dualistic Cartesian models are finally yielding to more systemic views driven by the need to address planetary-scale change processes.

Citizens' organizations have emerged world wide as major actors, for example in leading the search for global ethics and healthy, survival-enhancing cultural DNA codes. They have staged 'citizens' summits' on vital issues wherever leaders have dragged their heels, such as 'The Other Economic Summit,' (TOES) in which I have been involved, which dogged the G-7 nations' annual summit meetings since 1984 with alternative approaches. TOES released communiqués on the need for 'trickle-up' forms of sustainable development, highlighting that the world's women, whose work has been uncounted by economists in GNP/GDP, produce over half of the world's food, manage 70 percent of its small businesses but receive only 10 percent of the world's wages and own 1 percent of the world's property. Citizen diplomacy activities helped end the Cold War and are, at last, welcomed at the UN – rather than merely tolerated. Secretary-General Boutros Boutros-Ghali in 1994 called for non-governmental organizations to mobilize *states*, as well as public opinion – to promote peace, adding:

> the United Nations was considered to be a forum for sovereign states alone. Within the space of a few short years, this attitude had changed. Non-governmental organizations are now considered full participants in international life . . . largely due to the quick succession of historical events. . . . Today, we are well aware that the international community must address a human community that is profoundly transnational. The

movement of wealth, people, capital, and ideas is as important today as control of territory was yesterday.[60]

Today, formerly scorned citizens' groups are now asked to mobilize nations themselves, promote peace, and help support United Nations activities in many new ways. Citizens' organizations are not only urged to become more involved with peace-keeping, peace-making, and sustainable development, but also with watchdogging reduction of arms sales, disarmament, and conversion to civilian economies. The new watchword to global business and government leaders in the perilous decade of the 1990s is 'Lead, Follow, or Get out of the Way.' The militancy of citizens' organizations is related to the evolutionary urgency they sense. Many groups believe, along with INGO-research groups such as Worldwatch Institute (on whose board I serve), that humans now have only a few decades to avert social and ecological disaster. In the long run and the planetary context, all our individual self-interests are *identical.* Human responsibility and global ethics have simply become pragmatic.

NOTES

1 Elise Boulding. *Building a Global Civic Culture.* New York, USA: Columbia University Press, 1988 (p.36).
2 Ibid., p. 35.
3 The Union of International Organizations and its Secretary-General, Anthony Judge, also produce *The Comprehensive Encyclopedia of World Problems and Solutions* (Rue Washington, 40, 1050 Brussels, Belgium. Fax: 32–2–649–3269). Other information sources on NGOs and INGOs include *World Directory of Environmental Organizations*, compiled by Thaddeus Tryzna and Roberta Childers, 4th edn. California Institute of Public Affairs (PO Box 189040, Sacramento, California 95818 USA), 1992; The International Council of Voluntary Organizations (C.P. 216, 1211 Geneva 21, Switzerland. Fax: 41–22–738–9904); The Independent Sector (1828 L Street, N.W. Suite 1200, Washington, DC 20036 USA. Fax: 202–416–0580).
4 Hazel Henderson. *Creating Alternative Futures.* New York, USA: G.P. Putnam, 1978. (Available from the author: Fax: 904–826–1381.)
5 Ibid. Ch. 21 (pp. 351–370).
6 Hazel Henderson. *Paradigms in Progress.* Berrett-Koehler Publishing, San Francisco, 1995, 1–800–929–2929; (Ch. 1: 'Riding the Tiger of Change,' pp. 23–44).
7 Samuel Huntington, 'The Clash of Civilizations,' *Foreign Affairs,* Vol. 72, no. 3 (Summer, 1993).
8 Mahdi Elmanjdra, *Première Terre Civilisationnelle.* Les Editions Toubkal: Casablanca, Morocco, 1992.
9 Ibid. (Ch. 3: 'From Economism to Earth Ethics and System Theory,' pp. 71–110.)
10 Hazel Henderson. *The Politics of the Solar Age.* New York, USA: Doubleday, 1981. Apex Press, P.O. Box 337, Croton-on-Hudson, New York 10520, 1–800–316–2739; (Ch. 9: 'Workers and Environmentalists: the Common Cause,' pp. 245–282).
11 Council on Economic Priorities' Reports on Corporate Performance are available from 30 Irving Place, New York 10003, USA.

12 See for example, Michael S. Greve and Fred L. Smith, Jr., eds. *Environmental Politics: Public Costs, Private Rewards.* New York, USA: Praeger, 1992.

13 Henderson. *Politics of the Solar Age* (Ch. 8: '300 Years of Snake Oil,' pp. 184–241).

14 See for example, World Commission on Environment and Development, *Our Common Future.* New York and London: Oxford University Press, 1987.

15 Don Tapscott and Art Caston. *Paradigm Shift.* New York, USA: McGraw Hill, 1992 (p. 231 and p. 332).

16 Reports of the US Office of Technology Assessment are available from Washington, DC 20515 or from the US Government Printing Office.

17 Rocky Mountain Institute Reports are available from 1739 Snowmass Creek Road, Snowmass, Colorado 81654 USA.

18 See for example, Jessica Lipnack and Jeffrey Stamps, *Networking.* New York, USA: Doubleday, 1982. And updates from the Networking Institute (505 Waltham Street, West Newton, Massachusetts 02166 USA. Fax: 617–965–2341).

19 See for example, *The Elmwood Quarterly,* Vol. 8, no. 3 (Center for Ecoliteracy, 2522 San Pablo Avenue, Berkeley, California 94702 USA. Fax: 510–845–1439).

20 See for example, Mark Dowie's 'American Environmentalism' in *World Policy Journal.* New York: Winter, 1991–92 (pp. 67–92).

21 Henderson. *Paradigms in Progress* (Ch. 7: 'Greening the Economy and Recycling Economics,' pp. 193–229).

22 Henderson. *Politics of the Solar Age* (Chs 10, 11, 12, pp. 283–354).

23 Roger Lewin. *Complexity: Life at the Edge of Chaos.* New York, USA: Macmillan, 1992 (p. 15).

24 Henderson. *Paradigms in Progress* (Ch. 4: 'Beyond GNP,' pp. 111–129).

25 J. Perera, C. Marasinghe, and L. Jayasekera. *A People's Movement under Siege.* Sarvodya, 41 Lumbini Mawatha, Ratmalana, Sri Lanka, 1992.

26 White Paper on the Philippine Economy, 1992 (Green Forum, Liberty Building, Pasay Rd., Makati, Metro, Manila, Philippines).

27 See for example, South Commission, *Challenge to the South.* New York and London: Oxford University Press, 1990.

28 Jo Marie Griesgraber, ed., *Rethinking Bretton Woods.* Center of Concern: Washington, DC, 1994.

29 Proceedings, *Agenda 21: the Rio Declaration* from Room S-845, United Nations, New York, 10017 USA. Fax: 212–963–4556.

30 Boulding, *Building a Global Civic Culture.*

31 *Edges,* Vol. 5, no. 1. Institute for Cultural Affairs (577 Kingston Road, Toronto, M4E 1R3 Canada. Fax: 416–691–2491).

32 See for example, *Globalizing Networks.* Linda Harasim and Jan Walls, eds. Also 'Electronic Democracy' by Howard Frederick. Oxford University Press, Oxford, 1993.

33 Henderson. *Paradigms in Progress* (Ch. 8: 'Toward a New World Order,' pp. 231–258).

34 See Griesgraber, *Rethinking Bretton Woods.*

35 Americans Talk Issues Foundation. Survey no. 17: 'Perceptions of Globalization.' Alan F. Kay and Hazel Henderson with Greenberg-Lake, Inc., and Market Strategies (Americans Talk Issues Foundation, 10 Carrera St., St. Augustine, Florida 32084. Fax: 904–826–4194), 1992.

36 E. Childers and B. Urquhart. *Toward a More Effective United Nations.* Dag Hsammarskjold Foundation, Uppsala, Sweden, 1992 or from the Ford Foundation (320 E. 42nd Street, New York, NY 10017 USA).

37 United Nations, 1992 (p. 6).

38 Alan F. Kay and Hazel Henderson. Policy Document: 'United Nations Security Insurance Agency' (UNSIA). Available upon request. Write to: Global Commission to Fund the UN, 1511 K St, NW, Washington DC 20005 or, P.O. Box 5190. St. Augustine, Florida 32085 USA.

39 Boutros Boutros-Ghali, *An Agenda for Peace*. New York: United Nations, 1992 (p. 6).

40 Henderson. *Politics of the Solar Age* (Ch. 13: 'Thinking Globally Acting Locally,' pp. 355–405).

41 Henderson. *Creating Alternative Futures* (pp. 287–295).

42 Ibid. (p. 403).

43 Jean Houston. *The Possible Human*. Los Angeles: Tarcher, 1982. And *Life Force*. New York: Quest Books, 1992.

44 *New Perspective Quarterly*. Los Angeles, California: October, 1992.

45 The Americans Talk Issues Foundation, Washington, DC. Promotes use of non-partisan scientific surveys of US citizens on all major policy issues (Dr Diane Sherwood, 1511 K St, NW, Washington, DC 20005 USA).

46 Henderson. *Paradigms in Progress* (Ch. 6: 'The Indicators Crisis,' pp. 147–190).

47 Warren G. Bennis and Philip E. Slater. 'Democracy is Inevitable,' *Harvard Business Review*. Boston, Massachusetts USA (April, 1964).

48 Joseph Tainter. *The Collapse of Complex Societies*. Cambridge: Cambridge University Press, 1988.

49 *Planning Review*. New York (May, 1974).

50 'The Papers that Ate America,' *The Economist* (October 10, 1992, p. 21).

51 In Lewin. *Complexity*.

52 *Futures Research Quarterly*. Vol. 2, no. 1 Washington, DC, USA. (Spring, 1986).

53 Hazel Henderson, 'Changing Faces of Work in a Global Society: Implications for Human and Career Development.' The 4th Lowell Hellewick/Personnel Decisions, Inc. Lecture. University of Minnesota (April 13, 1994).

54 Riane Eisler. *The Chalice and the Blade*. New York: Harper & Row, 1987.

55 Jodi L. Jacobson. *Worldwatch Paper #110*. Washington, DC, USA (September, 1992).

56 Elise Boulding. *Women in the Twentieth Century World*. New York, USA: Sage, 1977 (p. 167).

57 Walter Weisskopf. *Alienation and Economics*. New York: E.P. Dutton, 1971.

58 Gregory Bateson. *Steps to an Ecology of Mind*. New York: Ballantine, 1973.

59 See for example, Ervin Laszlo, *The New Evolutionary Paradigm*. New York: Gordon and Breach Science Publishers, 1991.

60 United Nations Department of Public Information. S.G./S.M. 5416, September 19, 1994.

Index